Thy Kingdom Come

Studies in Daniel and Revelation

By
ROUSAS JOHN RUSHDOONY

THOBURN PRESS
FAIRFAX, VIRGINIA
1978

Library of Congress Catalog Card No. 70-139853
Printed in the United States of America

TABLE OF CONTENTS

Part One

Daniel

DANIEL 1: THE OFFENSE OF DANIEL

The Book of Daniel, which begins very innocently with a chapter involving the diet of four young men, is nonetheless one of the most explosive books in all human history in that it assumes at every point a philosophy of history which is anathema to autonomous man. Not only is this concept of history assumed as an article of faith, but it is asserted as in very deed manifested in the minute details of history by a sovereign God whose eternal decree does in fact mark the sparrow's fall and numbers the very hairs of man's head (Matt. 10:29, 30). To assert such a faith *in retrospect* is one thing, to assert it in prospect, another. In Daniel, it is asserted in prospect and verified by the courses of men and empire, if Daniel is to be taken at face value.

But it is commonly asserted that Daniel is in essence forgery, and to be dated, not from the sixth century B.C., from the days of the Chaldean Empire and the Medo-Persian power, but from the Maccabean period, 168-165 B.C. The ostensible *basis* of such assertions is textual criticism; the *premise* is a philosophy of history radically at odds with Daniel. In terms of this premise, Daniel is a thoroughly impossible and offensive book; it cannot possibly be true, for its veracity would require a reversal of every accepted world-view and philosophy of history of modern man. It is accordingly a crass and crude work on such an assumption, too blatant in its supernaturalism to be in any sense acceptable.

The offense of Daniel, however, is the offense of all Scripture, for here are concentrated basic elements of biblical faith in sharp and compelling terms that admit of no "poetic" reading but require, with harsh urgency, a submission intolerable to autonomous man. These points of offense can be briefly summarized as four, each in itself entailing beliefs of wide circumference.

First of all, Daniel is an offense because it manifests in unavoidable terms the biblical concept of God—God the Lord, the sovereign, uncreated, ontological Lord Jehovah, He who is, and beside whom there is none else. This God is to be sharply distinguished from the god of the critics, who are not atheists in that they affirm faith in a god, but believe in a god who is essentially value, or else himself only a being among beings, a senior citizen of the universe. The god of value is the epitome of the good, the true, and the beautiful, the essence of all virtues which man prizes. This god of value finds expression in and through man, so that, in terms of the familiar homiletical phrase, "God has no hands but mine to use." This, in terms of Daniel, is a blasphemous concept, for God the Lord is self-sufficient and completely independent of His creation, in no wise needing His creatures in order to act or to manifest himself. In terms of this concept of God as value, and its corollary, "God has no hands but mine to use," neither creation nor redemption can be explained in biblical terms. Biblical history, the plagues of Egypt, the crossing of the Red Sea, the miracles of Daniel, the virgin birth, and the resurrection, all these and more, if retained, are emptied of biblical meaning and subordinated to a new kind of history in which man's consciousness and existence are paramount, and God's activities hidden and shadowed. The limited god of being is again markedly different from the God of Scripture. Because he is merely one aspect of the universe, however superior an aspect, he cannot control that of which he himself is a product. His power is thus limited, hidden, and vague, and his "revelation" no less uncertain. *Only a self-sufficient, sovereign and omnipotent God can give a full and sufficient revelation of himself.* In man, potentiality and actuality are never one, and, accordingly, man can never fully reveal himself, both because he can neither know himself perfectly, nor control absolutely his present and future actualities. *But, because the sovereign God of Scripture has no unconscious element in himself, is self-sufficient and omnipotent, and because, knowing himself perfectly, He can know all His present and future activities fully and perfectly, His revelation is inevitably full and sufficient and inescapably so.* He is incomprehensible and inexhaustible but never hidden or unconscious in any respect. Because God is never hidden to Himself, His revelation is inevitably open and free from the prospect of hidden and future surprises. It follows inevitably, therefore, that if the God of Daniel be the true God, that His revelation be both infallible and perspicuous, and Daniel has with equal inevitability been a testing-ground and battlefield of that faith. *If revelation is hidden in the Bible, then God is also hidden in the universe.* If newer revelations of new aspects of truth or of new truths are possible, it is because a changing and partially unconscious God is incapable of a complete revelation. The infallible and inerrant Scripture is the only possible word from an omnipotent and sovereign God, and the doctrine of the infallible word is the inevitable corollary of the doctrine of God the omnipotent. The nature of Daniel forces this association upon us, and hence the importance of this book for its broader implications as well as for its own immediate contents.

This doctrine of God is offensive to man since man, by his anthropocentricity, would reverse God's role and usurp His throne. In terms of this, man would become knowable, and God unknowable; man would stand forth revealed, and God would become hidden. But Scriptures asserts the contrary: "A man's heart deviseth his way: but the LORD directeth his steps" (Prov. 16:9); "Man's goings are of the LORD; how can a man then understand his own way?" (Prov. 20:24). If the sovereign decree is God's and not man's, then it follows that a man cannot understand his own way. First, the ultimate determination is not his, and he at best is only partially aware of his own nature. Second, lacking both the fulness of epistemological self-consciousness and historical maturation, he is not yet completely himself. Third, this means that not only is much of his life as yet unconscious but, more than that, as yet unborn into the unconscious because as yet future even to that degree of appearance. Accordingly, such psychologies, psychiatries, and theologies as follow the ancient siren song, "Know thyself," seek a manifest impossibility. What measure of self-knowledge a man can have he can have only in terms of the interpretation God places upon him as a creature, rebellious or redeemed. Since the primary causality of his life rests in God, no true interpretation or comprehension of his life is possible apart from God. God, on the other hand, being omniscient and omnipotent, is knowable, having no hidden nature and no subconscious strains, but He is not exhaustively knowable to man, for to know God exhaustively would require a mind equal to God's; but He can be and is known truly and consistently through His self-revelation. Our knowledge of God is analogical of divine knowledge. Although man's knowledge of God cannot, because of his creaturehood, be exhaustive or comprehensive, it is, by virtue of his creation in God's image, true knowledge, while exhaustive and comprehensive knowledge is found only in God. God is completely knowable to Himself, because, as Van Til has stated it, "God's Being is coterminous with his self-consciousness."[1] God's being and his self-knowledge are identical, whereas for man, no such identity of being and analytical knowing exists, nor can it exist, since all his knowledge is synthetic and depends on reference to something other than himself. The substitution therefore of psychology for theology and the psychology of religion for the philosophy of religion, is an indication of the radical reversal of the roles of God and man. It involves a search for an impossible and non-existent wisdom in terms of an autonomy of man which is mythological and irrational. The God of Daniel is the sovereign Lord who shatters man's illusions of autonomy and humbles his claims to knowledge. Dreams therefore have an important part in Daniel; man is tormented by the ghost of the future and the unknown, and made mindful, against his wishes, of the temerity of his rebellion and the insanity of his claims.

Second, Daniel is offensive because it sets forth predictive prophecy in its plainest form, unpoetic, blunt, and unmistakable. Written on its claim in the sixth century B.C. by Daniel, it charts the course of empire for centuries ahead, sets forth the coming of Christ and the establishment of the church, and does all this with a specific and

[1] Cornelius Van Til: *The Defense of the Faith.* Philadelphia: Presbyterian and Reformed, 1955, p. 52.

singular confidence that this is not only a revelation from God but the manifestation of God's normal and continuing government of men and of nations. And this is a stumbling block. Men and nations want to believe in their autonomy, their independence of God; they prefer to see themselves as masters of their own destinies, as the movers and shapers—creators, not creatures. But, against all this, Daniel affirms emphatically that God is the only independent agency in history, both the creator and governor of time and eternity. God, who determines all things, and in whom we live and move and have our being, determines our every today and tomorrow and knows and determines history because He knows and determines Himself. Even as God has no unexplored potentialities in Himself, no subconscious whatsoever, knowing Himself and governing Himself absolutely, so history, His creation, has no unexplored potentialities within it and no unconscious elements that can develop apart from God's eternal decree. The nations are as nothing in His sight, and men, nations, and empires He moves to His ends, not theirs. He uses all history, is never used by it, bends it, molds it, shapes it in terms of His eternal purpose, and none can stay His hand. But men seek a god they can use, not a God who uses them, and hence the offensiveness of Daniel. So very specific predictive prophecies make inescapable the subordination of time to the eternal decree.

Third, Daniel is offensive because of its miracles, miracles whose nature predicates certain things concerning God and history. Common to antiquity was the faith that the truth of a religion was apparent in the success it brought to man. This ancient pragmatism saw religion as instrumental to man. The truth of a religion depended on its results. If the gods of Egypt gave success to Egypt, they were to that extent true. If Babylon gained precedence, then its gods acquired precedence also. Daniel 1:2 indicates that Nebuchadnezzar, in taking the temple vessels from Jerusalem to the house of his god, thereby expressed the preëminence of his faith and the necessary subservience of Judah's faith to his own. Basic to this practice is a man-centered orientation: God is to be judged in terms of His usability, what He can do for man, and the extent to which He prospers him, a faith as common in the church as in the world, unfortunately. This pragmatism and anthropocentricity rests again on the premise of man's autonomy. If man is for himself the final truth, and his existence the basic premise of his faith, then God and religion can have no independent character or truth but can be only relational in meaning; they are not substantive but adjectival, and hence, as with modernism, a changing faith is a necessity in terms of the changing conditions and needs of man. The rigidity of biblical faith becomes proof of a false rationalism and evidence of irreligion, and biblical faith becomes despised, scorned, and persecuted. The miracles of Daniel are an affront to man-centered and pragmatic religion, and rightly so, for these miracles are a declaration of war against all such faith and a reduction of it to absurdity even as it lords itself over godly man. These miracles also transcend the faith of the church and reveal the sovereignty of God in His salvation, His power towards the powerless, and His contempt of the mighty of this world.

Then, fourth, Daniel is offensive because it assumes and asserts the total providence and government of God, that God governs, rules, and overrules in every event of history to the minutest detail. Men prefer the anarchy of chance, which permits them to be gods of their little corner of chaos, to the sovereignty of God and His total predestination of all things. A God who can place us, weeping, by the waters of Babylon, or young and alone, a prisoner under training in Nebuchadnezzar's palace, is a God who obviously governs and uses man and is never governed or used of him. This is not what man has sought in religion, to which he has turned for power, healing, good fortune, in short, for a general liability insurance policy. God, in return for certain kindnesses from man, should be thereby placed in debt to man and subjected to emergency call on notice. But Daniel and his friends, however exalted in the empire, are still the instruments of Nebuchadnezzar, or man, and behind and beyond that, of God. Such a God indeed constitutes a poor insurance to a man in search of his own exaltation, but He constitutes the only security and joy for a man who knows himself to be a creature.

Four such men, very young men, were chosen by Babylon from the newly conquered Judea and taken to the king's palace for a three-year training course, studying languages, astronomy, astrology, mathematics, natural history, agriculture, architecture, and political science. The ancient dream of one world characterized Babel, Assyria, and Chaldea, and nations were broken, populations shuffled to break down national ties, and young men of conquered countries trained to high office to help hold the loyalties of their people and give a cosmopolitan and international character to the empire. The diversity of leadership and the shifting of populations would lead to a "melting pot" society whereby the unified world concept would take root.

Accordingly, while in a sense prisoners, they lived in luxury, eating a portion of the king's meat. According to I Kings 4:22, 23, Solomon's provisions for one day amounted to 30 measures of fine flour (a measure being equal to 75 gallons), 3 score measures of meal, 10 fat oxen, 20 oxen out of the pasture, 100 sheep, and much wild game, such as harts, roebucks, fallow deer, and fatted fowl. We can certainly assume that Nebuchadnezzar's provisions were likewise luxury abounding. Certainly such luxury was calculated to weaken old loyalties, already severed by time and distance, and to foster a new allegiance. In terms of all this opulence, Jehovah and Judah could become both remote and primitive.

"But Daniel purposed in his heart that he would not defile himself with the portion of the king's meat, nor with the wine which he drank: therefore he requested of the prince of the eunuchs that he might not defile himself" (1:8). Daniel was clearly the leader of these four unblemished youths (clearly therefore not themselves eunuchs although others of royal blood were made eunuchs [Isa. 39:7]), young men possibly at best in their early 'teens at the time of their deportation. No asceticism was involved in this request, but two clear-cut principles. First, eating was then a sacrament of communion with not only men but their gods. In such a difficult situation, the kind of accommodation permitted to Naaman in the house of Rimmon (II Kings 5:18, 19) was hardly possible to four young men who, if they did not begin on principle, could not continue therein. The stand was made diplomatically, with every intention of furthering their service to Nebuchadnezzar by means of their higher loyalty to God. Second, if they could make no stand in simple matters, how could their faith stand the testing of heavy responsibilities later? Biblical holiness is never in terms of an abstract principle, or in terms of withdrawal from this world, but in terms of meeting the problems and struggles of this life victoriously. Accordingly, their purpose was preparation in terms of very real necessities and struggles. No biblical saint ever sought holiness in and of itself; it was a product of his faith and an aspect of his strength. His purpose was not holiness per se but the glory of God, and his own enjoyment of life under God, thus never a flight from the world, but a preparation for problems and responsibilities in the world.

The "pulse" requested in place of the king's meat and wine was vegetables and grain, things not normally offered in sacrifice or consecrated at the Babylonian altars prior to regular use. Until such time as they could be masters of their own table, they preferred the restricted diet, by no means normal to Hebrews, and were prospered by God therein.

When the time of examination arrived, the king found them "ten times better than all the magicians and astrologers that were in his realm . . . in all matters of wisdom of understanding" (1:20, mg.).

Judah was broken, Jerusalem despoiled, and her most excellent youth made servants of Babylon's might. But that same word which requires faithfulness and obedience of servants (Col. 3:22-25), makes clear also that, having been bought with a price by Christ (I Cor. 6:20), they can never become servants of men in the abject sense, but, in their obedience, must deliberately do it "as to the Lord, and not unto men" (Col. 3:23). Such service is possible only if the God served is He by whose decree kings reign, the sparrow falls, and masters exercise authority. In terms of His sovereign will, He shall be served, willingly or unwillingly, by every creature, so that men of faith can serve a Nebuchadnezzar in the confidence that God's shall be the glory. In this faith and in this confidence, these four young men of Judah moved.

The issues thus are clearly brought into focus. Babylon, echoing the ancient dream of Babel of a one-world, a paradise without God, a cosmic unity on a principle other than the Creator, had in Nebuchadnezzar a brilliant and proud agent of that faith, a man dedicated to that unity and order which statesmen have sought since Cain built the city of Enoch (Gen. 4:17). Thorkild Jacobsen has described the early Mesopotamian concept:

> The fact that the Mesopotamian universe was conceived of as a state—that the gods who owned and ruled the various city-states were bound together in a higher unity, the assembly of the gods, which possessed executive organs for exerting outward pressure as well as for enforcing law and order internally—had far-reaching consequences for Mesopotamian history and for the ways in which historical events were viewed and interpreted. It vastly strengthened tendencies toward political unification of the country by sanctioning even the most violent means used toward that end. For any conqueror, if he was successful, was recognized as the agent of Enlil. It also provided—even at times when national unity was at a low ebb and the many city-states were, for all practical purposes, independent units—a background on which international law could work.[2]

This background gave a principle of continuity and of common ground to human relations, a substructure common to all men everywhere. As will appear, much more was involved in the concept of continuity, a principle of unity which made possible not only political but religious unity without disruption to the components, but also made all men constituents of a common divinity if they but successfully exercised themselves. Against all this, the faith of Daniel and his friends was an alien and disruptive force, *a violent rupture of human society.* Such a God as Daniel's Lord, Adonai, was too jealous a Creator, too exclusive a Covenant-Husband, and too alien and discontinuous with the universe of man to be other than an offensive intruder to Babylonian man. The issue was thus clearly visible.

The concept of continuity meant growth and development in God as well as in man, whereas the God of Daniel is discontinuous with His creation and is beyond growth, being himself the omniscient and omnipotent creator of all things and of all growth. Because God is absolute in His being, His word and work inevitably share in

[2] H. and H. A. Frankfort, John A. Wilson, Thorkild Jacobsen: *Before Philosophy, The Intellectual Adventure of Ancient Man.* Penguin Books, 1949, p. 210.

that absolute self-consciousness which makes all hiddenness impossible. Thus, the infallibility of His word and the predestination of all things are necessary consequences of His being, nor can any one aspect of His being and revelation be limited without limitation imposed on another. A hidden word means elements of hiddenness in God; a limited decree again re-introduces the hidden into God's being. Against all these sunderings, the Book of Daniel is a bulwark, and, to its critics, an unalterable offense ·

DANIEL 2: THE TERROR OF DREAMS

While there are no unconscious activities and hidden potentialities in God, man is largely governed by them, and dreams are a persistent reminder of that fact. Dreams are a constant resuscitation of a dead and impotent past:

> Sleep, kinsman thou to death and trance
> And madness thou hast forged at last
> A night-long Present of the Past.[1]

By this reminder of man's frailty and lack of absolute freedom and determination, they speak thus also of death, trance, and madness to proud man. Even the joy a man experiences in dreams is illusory, as one of John Ray's proverbs asserted: "After a dream of a wedding comes a corpse." The unreality of man's power as revealed in dreams casts shadows on the reality of his waking self-government, so that, from the ancient Chinese to Bret Harte, the question concerning waking also arises: "Do I sleep? do I dream? . . . Are things what they seem?" Prospere, in Shakespeare's *The Tempest,* expressed a cynicism concerning life by reference to its similarity to dreams because of its insubstantiality:

> We are such stuff
> As dreams are made on, and our little life
> Is rounded with a sleep.

Indeed, wherever man aspires to be as God, and to assert an absolute freedom, dreams are a terror in that they are a reminder of creaturehood, culpability, and condemnation. The terror of dreams, therefore, is the terror of mortality and guilt, and the desperation of mutability.

Nebuchadnezzar, both consciously and unconsciously, had come face to face with this terror. Prior to sleeping, he had been deeply

[1] Tennyson: *In Memoriam,* Canto 71.

concerned about the future (2:29). His great empire, built on the principle of continuity and the dream of one world, might some day meet that radical discontinuity of death and destruction which had overwhelmed previous towers of Babel. Such grievous facts have often led men, from the ancients to Nietzsche and the present, to a cyclic view of history, to the meaningless horror of eternal recurrence. Sleeping after such unhappy meditations, Nebuchadnezzar had been subjected to a dream from God in answer to his urgent concern about "what should come to pass hereafter" (2:29), but his response had been terror (2:1).

His waking response had been a hatred of the impotence of the religious and scientific practitioners of his day and a desire to expose their futility. Having known the terrors of the unseen, and knowing vividly how man in his proudest knowledge only skated on the thin ice of the seen, his urge was to mass destruction. It was comparable to the resentment of the sick for the healthy, of the dying for the living. Having seen the reduction of all his life's work to nothing in essence, he savagely sought the reduction of all man's wisdom to the same death and chaos. His demand that his wise men interpret the dream without knowledge of it was not based on forgetfulness of the dream but a deliberate concealment of it. The older English wording, "The thing is gone from me" (2:2, AV), has been rendered by Leupold as, "The matter has been fully determined by me." The deliberate concealment is re-stated:

> They answered a second time and said: "Let the king tell his servants the dream, and we shall make known the interpretation." The king answered and said: "Now I know with absolute certainty that ye would gain time. Just because ye see that the matter is fully determined by me, that, if ye do not make the dream known, one law applies to you, and ye have been agreed among yourselves upon lying and corrupt words, to speak them in my presence, until things change; therefore tell me the dream, and I shall perceive that ye can show the interpretation."[2]

These learned men, faced with a decree of death, were both con-

---

[2] H. C. Leupold: *Exposition of Daniel*. Columbus, Ohio: Wartburg, 1949, p. 90, trans. of 2:7-9.

sciously and unconsciously evasive. Their conscious evasion was an attempt to stall for time until the king's mood changed, and thereby save their lives. Their unconscious evasion was an unwillingness to face the implication of the terror of dreams. The dream could be told without any knowledge of details: all man's hopes for autonomy, his rejection of God's eternal decree, his insistence on the hiddenness of God, and the knowability of man, were reduced to nothingness and terror by any dream. Man's unconscious witnesses in dreams to his burden of guilt concerning the past, his impotence in the present, and his ignorance and dread of the future. When latter-day wise men, starting with Freud, began, however mistakenly, to turn to dreams and the unconscious with a more systematic searching, it was the beginning of man's epistemological self-consciousness, and Freudianism has been as often rejected for this reason as for its errors. Man forgets his dreams and forgets the significance of dreams in order to escape epistemological self-consciousness. His attempt to reckon with the fact of his unconscious being has been oblique: dreams, and the ostensible government by stars and planets (i.e., astrology, man's recognition of outside control) are parts of a continuum, so that man's unconsciousness is shared with a cosmos whose determinism is also shared by man, so that a common divinity and essence and a common struggle characterizes the whole of being. The fact of creaturehood is thus obviated and avoided. Dreams and stars are also used to evade responsibility, so that man, in his ambivalence, asserts, on the one hand, total autonomy and responsibility as a god, and, on the other, denies his manhood and all responsibility in the name of total conditioning and chance.

Nebuchadnezzar, impelled by a desire to expose the pretentiousness of man's autonomous knowledge, forced the issue on terms requiring a surrender by man, or an acknowledgement of the omnipotence of terror and death. Having known futility, he would tolerate no hope and no knowledge. Having smelled death, he hated life. The decree of execution was passed, and left to Arioch to carry out. The decree included all members of the royal college, including those not immediately consulted, such as Daniel and his friends, who were ignorant of its cause (2:13ff.). It was in essence a decree against

knowledge and an assault on all learning as futility. If Nebuchadnezzar was doomed to mutability and meaninglessness, and Babylon
also, then least of all must its philosophers and wise men be permitted the luxury of self-deception.

It is important to understand this mood, because it is increasingly
the temper of modern man. Warner, in *The Urge to Mass Destruction,* has described this sense of impotence and defeat, and its lust
to destroy, as an impulse *"to organize the mass self-destruction,"* t~
"seek *a mass grave for all"* and to find "victory through defeat" and
total destruction.[3] Nihilism and the blood-bath are the defeated
man's revenge on life and his means of triumph, and this in a measure
Nebuchadnezzar felt, as do all ungodly men, potentially or actually, in
varying degrees. A man who has no reason for living has a reason for
hating life, and a man without hope resents all hope as an ugly disease.
It will not do merely to condemn this cynicism: it must be answered.

Daniel and his friends, sentenced to death without any offense,
immediately besought God in prayer, and Daniel received his answer
in a night vision. The significance was immediately grasped by
Daniel: "Blessed be the name of God for ever and ever: for wisdom
and might are his: And he changeth the times and the seasons: He
removeth kings and setteth up kings: he giveth wisdom to the wise,
and knowledge to them that know understanding: He revealeth the
deep and secret things: he knoweth what is in the darkness, and the
light dwelleth with him" (2:20-22). Young's comment here is
especially to the point:

> . . . the course of history lies in the hands of God. These critical
> periods which occur in the realm of time as such, are determined
> by God. . . . It is not in heaven alone that we are to seek for
> evidences of God's power, but also on earth where this power is
> daily manifested in God's control over all things. . . . God has
> sovereign determination of all political changes. "In this expres-
> sion," says Montgomery, "lies a challenge to the fatalism of the
> Babylonian astral religion, a feature which in its influence long
> survived in the Graeco-Roman world."[4]

[3] Samuel J. Warner: *The Urge to Mass Destruction.* New York: Greene and
Stratton, 1957, pp. 152, 99.
[4] Edward J. Young: *The Prophecy of Daniel.* Grand Rapids, Mich.: Eerdmans, 1949, p. 67.

Here is a clear-cut assertion of the eternal decree: darkness does exist, and the realm of creation is heavy with the weight of potentiality and the unconscious, but wisdom and light dwell with God, who is in totality entirely omniscient and self-conscious and hence inevitably acting purposefully and in terms of an eternal decree. All mutability is in terms of this goal, and the changes and seasons of time are accordingly never futile but purposive. Moreover, present time is not merely manure for future time but in itself is revelatory of God and His eternal decree, which is always made manifest to the wise and understanding, those who are the Lord's and whose lives are governed by His word. The cynicism of Nebuchadnezzar is thus without excuse as an end in itself, although a necessary step in his disillusionment with the constructs of autonomous man's philosophy. Daniel's prayer of thanksgiving (2:23) is his rejoicing in God's sovereign grace; no merit on Daniel's part is the ground of this revelation, but rather the free and predestinating grace of God.

Daniel, brought before Nebuchadnezzar, emphasized the impotence of man as against the eternal decree (2:27), placing all the power and glory with God, who alone is the source of all determination, interpretation, and power. Daniel denied any merit in himself: God used him as an instrument to bring epistemological self-consciousness to Nebuchadnezzar (2:28f.), so that he might see and know himself in relationship to God.

Nebuchadnezzar's dream, Daniel stated, was of a great and awe-inspiring image whose (1) head was of fine gold, (2) his breast and his arms of silver, (3) his belly and his sides of brass, and (4) his legs of iron, his feet part iron and part clay, clearly a picture of deterioration. A stone, "cut out without hands" and in no man's hand, "smote the image upon his feet," destroying it so radically that its fragments were like "the chaff of the summer threshing-floors: and the wind carried them away, and no place was found for them: and the stone that smote the image became a great mountain, and filled the whole earth" (2:31-35).

Daniel then gave the interpretation thereof:

1) There is a sovereign decree, emanating from a sovereign God,

by whose ordination alone Nebuchadnezzar reigns. Nothing can be understood apart from this presupposition.

2) The head of gold is Nebuchadnezzar and his empire, representing in especially powerful form the dream of empire and cosmos by autonomous man.

3) A second empire shall follow, embodying the same dream, but of lesser capacity. Subsequently, this power is seen by Daniel as the Medo-Persian Empire.

4) The third, of brass, then follows, later revealed to be the Macedonian Empire of Alexander the Great, and the states established by his successors.

5) The fourth power then takes over, identified later as Rome, and represents the culmination of antiquity's dream of empire as the reconstitution of man's dream of paradise apart from God. Its parts, however, have no cohesiveness, and, like iron and clay, will not mix.

6) In the days of this fourth empire, a Fifth Monarchy, supernatural in origin, shall destroy the ancient dream and replace it with a true empire which shall conquer the earth and "shall stand forever" (2:36-45).

Nebuchadnezzar, faced with the terror of dreams, of government and conquest by the cosmic unconscious, the revolt and over-lordship of the universal hiddenness and sleep as it overwhelms man's brief awakening, was now given an answer other than chance or fatalism as the key to history. The issue, ultimately, is between chance and the eternal decree, but men have seen it as also involving another and an illogical alternative. The alternatives thus become:

1) The reign and ultimacy of chance. Predication and meaning become impossible, as do law, knowledge, science, and life itself. No culture has ever faced the implications of the ultimacy of chance without collapse.

2) Blind and materialistic determinism or fatalism. The fortuitous concourse of atoms has somehow and illogically led to a blind and insentient law which is irrelevant to consciousness, lacking in all meaning, and leading only to the misery of eternal recurrence. Oriental philosophies and Nietzsche have alike found this

the ground of despair and of world and life negation; however, they may have, as in Nietzsche's case, struggled against it. The Babylonian astral religion held to a form of fatalism, and Nebuchadnezzar was under its malign influence.

3) The eternal decree or total predestination, The contingency of second causes is established, and responsibility, meaning, and direction given to history and to man's life under God. Apart from the eternal decree, no meaning is possible, and only brute factuality, beyond interpretation, reigns.[5]

This rescue of history brought joy to Nebuchadnezzar and promotion to Daniel and his three friends (2:46-49). More than that, it led to Nebuchadnezzar's worship of Daniel as the representative of the "God of gods" and "Lord of kings," the God whose eternal decree undergirds all creation (2:47).

Nebuchadnezzar, however, had failed to understand the full import of the vision. It was *a rescue of history,* but in terms of what, and to what end?

Common to the imperial goals of antiquity is the motive of the world savior and the return to paradise. The secularization of historical studies has led to the castration of history and the excision of all religious goals in favor of a projection of purely politico-economic or other modern objectives on to the empires of antiquity. Ethelbert Stauffer's *Christ and the Caesars* is an important statement to the contrary of the Roman messianic dream.

The goal was a magnificent one, sought with power, passion, and intensity: *paradise regained.* From Cain's city Enoch to the Tower of Babel, and on through imperial Rome and the present, man has sought to efface the burden of human guilt and misery, unite mankind into one world, and restore paradise to man. The depreciation of the past as primitive has led to the obscuring of the amazing approximations of order, unlimited wealth, peace, and prosperity in some ancient empires, all envisioned conditions of paradise, but these and more were approximations only, never the reality.

The Fifth Monarchy succeeds where all its false messianic predecessors failed, so that any Christian concept of history which is

[5] Van Til: *op. cit.*

defeatist or other-worldly stands under the condemnation of Daniel. The world is not merely a vale of soul-making, nor does it culminate in the sorry historical triumph of Anti-Christ as amillennial and pre-millennial interpretations would have it. The Fifth Monarchy succeeds not only in destroying its rivals but in accomplishing what they on false premises sought to do. The empires then, the modernists today, and the states of this age, are all in this one respect wiser than the church, in that they do not deny meaning or triumph to history, but seek it earnestly, if on false premises and in terms of autonomous man.

There is, however, a difference between the goal of these four empires and the biblical purpose. *It is not an earthly paradise in itself which is the goal of history as Scripture depicts it, but rather the restoration of communion with God, of which an earthly paradise, as depicted by Isaiah and Revelation, is a by-product.* Man is keenly aware of the loss of paradise, but not conscious of the broken communion with God. This communion and its new world order Isaiah depicted as the consequence of the atonement. Moreover, it is not a return to Eden, not the re-creation of the Garden, but paradise in terms of community with God and man, in the New Jerusalem. The romanticism of isolation and self-exaltation is replaced with communion in community. This requires a long process of historical maturation, beginning with the call of Abraham, who in vision saw that city and rejoiced (Heb. 11:8-16; John 8:56), and culminating with Christ's coming again, the eschatological end of history, when the process is culminated. Then the tares will be fully tares, and the wheat fully wheat. Epistemological self-consciousness, man's knowledge of himself as a creature, and his analogical knowledge of God, will effect the full restoration of godly man, even as the full implications of the fall overwhelm the covenant-breaker or the reprobate. The implications of history having been developed, time shall be no more.

The four empires are depicted as one man, fallen and pseudo-messianic man. This image is met wherever man and the state assume the messianic control of history, wherever Hamlet's cry is echoed: "Time is out of joint, O cursed spite, that ever I was born to set it right." Noble-sounding though this cry may be, it is the essence of pride and madness. None of us is called to set the world or our time aright but rather to meet our responsibilities under God. The responsibility and work at hand is ours; the issue is in the hands of God. History gives us the perpetual crisis and defeat of that presumption, from Babel to the U. S. Point Four Program and beyond. No man or state can play Atlas without incurring judgment, for we are called to be men, not God, and to attempt more is not nobility but insane presumption. Given Hamlet's delusion that he was the god of judgment and restoration, his tragedy was inevitable, and his life a blasting of good and evil alike in terms of a more radical evil than the murder he condemned. Nebuchadnezzar's image is fallen man in all his pride attempting to issue his own eternal decree and seize the reins of history for himself. This dream is thus a condemnation of men and states as wedded to this hope.

It is also an offense to the Jews, and gives an important clue to the neglect of Daniel in antiquity and subsequently. Daniel makes clear that God by-passed His chosen people in favor of four great monarchies, which were to work out the implications of ancient history, and then called forth a Fifth Monarchy which is by no means identified with Israel. The God who raised Assyria, "the rod of mine anger," Nebuchadnezzar, into whose hands the whole earth was given and to whom God spoke as He once spoke to the kings of Israel and Judah, and the God who called Cyrus His anointed, was clearly not the exclusive God of Israel, nor one who limited His eternal purposes to His chosen people. The priority of the eternal decree over the historical call of Israel is too manifest, too openly present, and presumed beyond the necessity of statement. This priority of the eternal decree over history and its status as the ground of all history, i.e., Israel and the church, was an offense to Israel, as it is today an offense to the church. But the priority of the eternal decree is over all time, over Israel and Babylon alike, and the presumption of the outward Israel and church is no less an offense than the pride of Babel and of Rome. Autonomous man has always feet of clay.

Thus, God the omnipotent reigns, not a God on the sidelines who merely awards prizes to the determiners of history, but God the Lord, who ordains all things and by whose will alone kings reign, empires fall, and in terms of whose will alone history has purpose, meaning, and direction. And history is God's process whereby the unconscious in creation is brought to consciousness, the implicit made explicit, and the maturation of tares and wheat effected, until the vision of Joel be fulfilled:

> In with the sickle!
> the harvest is ripe!
> Come, tread the winepress, tread it,
> it is full;
> the troughs are overflowing
> with their wickedness (Joel 3:13, Moffat's trans.).

"And it shall come to pass in that day, that the mountains shall drop down new wine, and the hills shall flow with milk, and all the rivers of Judah shall flow with waters, and a fountain shall come forth of the house of the LORD, and shall water the valley of Shittum" (Joel 3:18).

DANIEL 3: THE CONTINUATION OF GOD

Men can accept logical conclusions without making logical deductions from them, and Nebuchadnezzar could accept the rescue of history by the eternal decree of God without drawing biblical inferences therefrom. For him, the context of the dream and the rescue of history was the revived Babylonian concept of continuity. To this triumphant if erroneous conclusion he gave witness by the erection on the plain of Dura "an image made of gold, whose height was threescore cubits, and the breadth thereof six cubits" (3:1). This image was unquestionably an echo and an embodiment of his dream, setting forth not only the glory of Babylon, but his own majesty, glory, and dominion as the great head of gold. According to the dream, as Nebuchadnezzar saw it, the great Fifth Monarchy would be preceded by four great empires, of which he was the head, and to whom God had given "kingdom, power, and strength, and glory" (2:37). For God to give glory to a man meant one thing to men of antiquity, outside the Hebraic faith—to share His divinity and kingdom with the man. It meant for them participation in the life and kingdom of God, and made them and their order a continuation of God and a manifest incarnation of Him. Thus, Nebuchadnezzar could move in the confidence, based on his interpretation of Daniel's words in terms of the semantics of continuity, that God had given him certain things:

1) Although the great kingdom was of the future, Nebuchadnezzar's present kingdom was its forerunner.

2) In terms of all the forerunners, Nebuchadnezzar had preëminence and was their "head of gold."

3) God had handed over the world to Nebuchadnezzar, His vicegerent, and made him God's power and presence to that age.

4) History therefore was in Nebuchadnezzar's hands and derived its meaning from him.

5) As God's power and will for that age, Nebuchadnezzar could
not be resisted without resisting God.

A hard, harsh element of truth undergirds these presuppositions,
however faulty they may be. While the glory God gives to man as
man is creaturely glory, never Himself sharing His glory with man,
yet the fact remained that God gave the world into Nebuchadnezzar's
hands. It is equally certain in the twentieth century that God has
at various times handed power and dominion to such men as Hitler,
Mussolini, Chamberlain, Stalin, Daladier, deGaulle, Roosevelt, Mao,
Kennedy, Nasser, Nehru, and others, while leaving His saints helpless and apparently impotent in the face of these ordained powers.
Not without reason, as they contemplated these things, the saints in
Babylon gave voice to their grief:

> By the rivers of Babylon, there we sat down,
> yea, we wept, when we remembered Zion.
> We hanged our harps upon the willows in the
> midst thereof.
> For there they that carried us away captive
> required of us a song; and they that wasted us
> required of us mirth, saying, Sing us one of the
> Songs of Zion.
> How shall we sing the Lord's song in a strange
> land? (Ps. 137:1-4).

This, unhappily, is constantly our calling now, to sing the Lord's
song in a strange land, in a world handed over to the sons of
Babylon.

In the midst of all this comes the summons, "Fall down and worship the golden image that Nebuchadnezzar the king hath set up"
(3:5). The penalty for failure to worship was the "fiery furnace,"
a manner of execution common to the Assyrians and the Chaldeans,
and prevailing in Persia through 1662. In that year, in Isfahan,
during a great famine, the furnaces were fired for a month in threat
to any grain merchant found guilty of defrauding the poor or violating
the government controls on prices.

Daniel was possibly absent at this time, or too strong for his
refusal to comply to be attacked. Daniel's power was attacked in

the persons of his three friends and associates, arrested on the accusa-
tions of "certain Chaldeans" (3:8), resentful of this Jewish preëminence in Babylonian affairs.

The answer of Nebuchadnezzar was "rage and fury" at this inso-
lence, at this refusal to accept the inevitable testimony of their own
channel of revelation from the supernatural order of things. Nevertheless, according to his light, that monarch was fair-minded to these
three rebels, giving them another opportunity to make their obeisance
and return to their homes and positions. How could they dare, he
asked, refuse him, for "*who is that God that shall deliver you out
of my hands?*" (3:15). Here is the essence of the emperor's faith.
In terms of the concept of continuity, Nebuchadnezzar was the continuity of God and the incarnation of His power or glory. To resist
him was to resist God, not in the Pauline sense, but as the continuity
in terms of which man alone could prosper, and, apart from whom
no mediation could properly exist. The priestly role of the Chaldean
king, as the great mediator, had been reënforced by the dream, and,
as long as Nebuchadnezzar held sway, he was the hand, head, power,
and mind of God for his day. To by-pass him in worship was to
despise both God and God's incarnate glory; other and peripheral
worship of lesser powers was permissible only when Nebuchadnezzar's image and his glory were first acknowledged. Polytheism was
thus permissible and a part of the policy of religious toleration,
provided the religion of state was given its due; to all other gods, the
left-overs only belonged. The humanism of modern man, his claim
to autonomy, and the religions of statism are all equally tolerant of
other faiths and polytheistic, provided their claim be first acknowledged, and the triune God be doled out only the left-overs of man's
allegiance. These man-centered orders, closing in on man's being
and seizing him by the throat, declare in effect, "Who is that God
that shall deliver you out of my hands?" Which God indeed will
rescue His people from this polytheistic world, from the powers of
statism, scientism, and anthropocentric creeds? The god of Nebuchadnezzar was a very present power, manifest through the natural
processes of history and in and through the social order. While
inevitably a growing and changing god, as is the god of existentialist

theologians, he was still the ever-present power and glory and beyond resistance. He could be transcended but not resisted, and hence his worship was to be required.

The answer of these three rebels against the polytheism of continuity was clear-cut: "Our God whom we serve is able to deliver us." He need not do so, nor did they have such an assurance as to the divine response to their stand. Irrespective of the consequences, "be it known unto thee, O king, that we will not serve thy gods, nor worship the golden image which thou hast set up" (3:17, 18). Notice the challenge to Nebuchadnezzar's faith. These three men unquestionably hoped and prayed for deliverance, but they felt it imperative to make clear the transcendental and unbounded nature of God, and His radical discontinuity with His creation and His saints. They denied the continuity of God either with Nebuchadnezzar or themselves: God was under no obligation to deliver them, and it was precisely this unbound God whom they worshiped and none other. So "futile" a faith no doubt seemed a radical perversity and treason to Nebuchadnezzar and made these men, as it did the Christians of Rome, anarchists of the worst order, enemies to all law and order. The Christians of the Roman Empire prayed for the emperor and obediently gave him his due; the philosophers and writers worshiped at the imperial shrine and then cynically mocked what they worshiped. It was nevertheless the Christians who were persecuted, in that their religion of discontinuity was radically subversive of the entire philosophy of the empire. So it was with Daniel's friends.

As a result of this resistance, the three men were thrown into the furnace, a furnace fired to so great a heat that it killed the men charged with hurling them into the fire (3:22). The three "fell down bound into the midst of the burning fiery furnace" (3:23). They were immediately thereafter seen walking about in the fire, unhurt and unbound, with a fourth man present, who, according to Nebuchadnezzar, "is like the Son of God" (3:25). That monarch then called out the three witnesses of faith, "servants of the most high God" (3:26), for only that preëminence of association could have preserved them, he was certain. They came forth unhurt, without a hair singed, nor with even the smell of fire upon them (3:27).

Nebuchadnezzar, made more aware of the transcendence of God, but yet without losing his Chaldean orientation, immediately praised God and recognized His exclusivism with regard to worship (3:28). More important, he recognized an element of discontinuity: God had, by His sovereign and overruling act, "changed the king's word" (3:28). History was thus not a single process: God had a people whose integrity and exclusivism of worship could not be challenged without danger. Therefore, a royal decree forbad any misrepresentation concerning that God on penalty of death and total dissolution of their family, "because there is no other God that can deliver after this sort" (3:29). The three men were promoted and favored "in the province of Babylon" (3:30). The power of God as manifest in His saints was thus linked closely with the power of God as believed manifest in throne and empire.

The decision, from the world's point of view, was fatal to Nebuchadnezzar, and the world prefers to doubt the historicity of the entire incident and thereby escape its challenge. If true, the incident reveals a widening crack in man's wall and his defenses. History is not in man's hands, and the government is not upon man's shoulders. The eternal decree became, not an insurance policy to Nebuchadnezzar, but a decree of abdication, had he but known it. With such a God, no compromise is possible, and man's dreams are set aside as rebellion and futility: "Why do the heathen rage, and the people imagine a vain thing?" All their counsel against the Lord and His anointed, all their hopes of escape from the bonds and cords of His decree, are mocked by God: "He that sitteth in the heavens shall laugh: the Lord shall have them in derision." God declares to His Son, concerning the world powers: "Thou shalt break them with a rod of iron; thou shalt dash them in pieces like a potter's vessel." Therefore, "Serve the Lord with fear, rejoice with trembling. Kiss the Son, lest he be angry, and ye perish from the way" (Ps. 2:1, 4, 9, 11, 12).

The true perspective, thus, was not a broad picture of the world's continuity as process with God, with a discontinuity and immediacy apparent in certain great saints, but a total discontinuity and a radical and exclusive government of all creation by God the Creator. Far from being part of the process of being, God the uncreated being was the creator and governor of the entire course of created being and Himself beyond change, process, growth, or decay. Such a God leaves no recourse but surrender to His terms and worship, or else death.

But compromise, now as then, is man's vain hope and way. Church, state, and school claim to be an incarnation of God and of His anointed, a continuation of the incarnation and a true priesthood. The use of holy garments in the church, the use of clerical robes by jurists and by schoolmen (caps and gowns), are witnesses to this concept of priesthood and mediation as the visible wisdom, power, and glory of God. But, according to Scripture, Jesus Christ *alone* is the incarnation of God, and *alone* the Messiah, and in and *only* in Him, as members of His body, do believers have a priesthood, a priesthood held in common by all believers by virtue of their membership in Christ and not held in terms of any priority of office or sanctification. In terms of this, a similar insistence on the concept and declaration of continuity in these and all other areas of man's self-exaltation must be resisted in the name and power of God.

DANIEL 4: THE RITUAL CENTER OF THE EARTH

The Tower of Babel was an affirmation of the concept of continuity and an attempt, through societal and state unification and a program of self-righteousness, to reach up to heaven, to strengthen the continuity with heavenly powers by participation in the work of world redemption. It is not the "evil" of "sins of the flesh" which characterized the Tower of Babel and the continuing city of Babylon, the great "mother of harlots" (Rev. 17:5), but its status as a rival righteousness and a rival concept of unity and redemption.

By their architecture, the Babylonian ziggurats, ladders to heaven, affirmed the concept of continuity. In all such tower faiths, stone by stone, step by step, story by story, degree by degree, man reaches up to heaven and makes the kingdom of man the goal and reality of history.

The "Centre Concept" was closely related to this dream. The square and cube, ancient symbols of perfection, of completeness, and full communion, became vital symbols of the true City of Man, of Babylon the Great. Akhenaton built a city on a square plan, and, according to Herodotus, Babylon was also a square. The same concept was apparent also in some Greek thinkers.[1] *The Center, Throne, and Sanctuary* were related and basically the same concepts, in that the concept of continuity identified gods, state, and man and saw them as existing in one society celebrated in a ritual focus. Both Jerusalem and Gerizim were regarded by some Jews and some Samaritans in similar terms (John 4:20), so that the pagan concept of the ritual center was apparently to be found in Israel, not only in Jeremiah's day but in Christ's time also.[2] Against all this, the New Testament affirmed emphatically, as did the Old (Ps. 87, etc.), that the true center is not in man, nor in his kingdom or city, but in Christ and

---

[1] Plato, *Protag.* 344a, Aristotle, Rhetoric iii, II, 2.

[2] See V. Burch: *Anthropology and the Apocalypse.* London: Macmillan, 1939, p. 202.

His new Jerusalem, a city built foursquare, a perfect cube, with "the throne of God and of the Lamb" (Rev. 22:1) as the fountainhead of all things. By reserving the throne to "God and the Lamb," rather than to the Lamb as such, the ontological trinity is brought into central focus, and not God only as revealed and related to creation. As the Alpha and Omega, this Christ is also seen as beyond creation and discontinuous with it while incarnated without confusion of natures.

This concept of the true center had been set forth in the design of the tabernacle. The Holy of Holies was a cube. The Camp of Israel, the assembly and church of God, was a square, as Numbers 2 makes clear, with the tabernacle or throne of God in the center. This pattern, given by revelation on the mountain (Ex. 25:9, 40; Ezek. 43:10; Heb. 8:5; Num. 8:4), was designed both to affirm and set forth the true and transcendent center, throne, and sanctuary, and to attack all purely immanentistic conceptions thereof.

The Babylonian concept of continuity was clearly set forth in the form of investiture of Chaldean kings, which was in essence "taking the hand of the god," a ritual observed from time immemorial and observed also by the Assyrians at Nineveh, and by its conquerors, e.g., Sennacherib, Esarhaddon, Ashurbanipal, in Babylon. Cyrus, on conquering Babylon, became king in the eyes of the Babylonians only after "taking the hand of the god" at Esagila.[3] By this ritual, the empire, in the person of the king, assumed fellowship, on the basis of a common life, with the gods.

A further symbol set forth the nature of the continuity in animate form, the tree or "pole" as the ritual center of the earth. This sacred tree or column *supports* heaven and is the tree of life, and the bond between heaven and earth. Because a tree is a living thing, it is therefore a growing bond that this tree of life sets forth, a concept in marked hostility to the fenced tree of biblical revelation (Gen. 3:24). Again, the shepherd concept of kingship asserted the divine authority and power of the monarch, who, as guardian of his people, controlled their destiny, which was inseparable from their life as subjects of the state. Against all this, Jehovah, God the Father, and Jesus Christ, God the Son, are asserted to be the Good Shepherd

[3] G. R. Tabouis: *Nebuchadnezzar*. London: Routledge, 1931, p. 69.

(Ps. 23; John 10:11; I Pet. 2:25), and the Wisdom or Logos, Christ, is the true tree of life (Rev. 2:7; 22:2, 14; Prov. 3:18; 11:30; Ezek. 47:7, 12; Gen. 2:9; 3:22). For Nebuchadnezzar, however, it was natural and inevitable, in terms of the concept of continuity, to dream of himself as the tree of life for his generation.

But, however "natural" the conception was to Nebuchadnezzar as a Chaldean monarch, he was also a creature of God, and, in terms of that fact, the faith was "unnatural" and a sin. Cultural conditioning is real, but basic to man's every state is the fact of his creaturehood and his creation in the image of God. This prior and ultimate reality cannot be effaced by the conditions of history or the tyranny of man and his philosophies. Thus, in every age, men are without excuse in that they have wilfully exchanged the truth of God for a lie (Rom. 1:25) and submitted to the common and democratic lie in preference to the unpopular word of God.

In such circumstances, God frequently uses man's crutches to witness against him, confounding him by his very mainstays. According to Diodorus, the Chaldeans explained dreams as portents, interpreting them in terms of rules as hard and fixed as Freudian symbols, and we find them often recorded as important items of state.

Nebuchadnezzar's dream, as Daniel observed with distress, "be to them that hate thee," i.e., "is for" them, and will please them that hate thee (3:19).[4] Nebuchadnezzer saw himself as a "tree in the midst of the earth," i.e., the ritual center and the tree of life, "and the height thereof was great" (4:10). The tree was "meat for all" (4:12), support and sustenance for his generation, so that Nebuchadnezzar represented the principle of life for his time, the tree of God, in whom the power and presence of God was manifested. The dream, however, saw "a watcher and an holy one" (4:13) descend from heaven and pronounce a divine decree of hewing against the tree, with only a stump to be left as the source of new growth. A beast's heart would replace his human heart, i.e., he would be as an animal, till "seven times pass over him" (4:16), until the fulness of the decree be established. The declaration to Nebuchadnezzar was even more explicit: "This matter is by the decree of the watchers,

---

[4] Leupold, *Comm. ad loc.*

and the demand by the word of the holy ones: to the intent that the living may know that the most High ruleth in the kingdom of men, and giveth it to whomsoever he will, and setteth up over it the basest of men" (4:17).

This dream was seen by Nebuchadnezzar in its cultural context, but the absolute thrust was paramount. Daniel made clear also the source of the decree: not of "the watchers" but "of the most High" (4:24), a sentence of humbling unless Nebuchadnezzar "break off" his "sins by righteousness and . . . iniquities by showing mercy to the poor" (4:27).

There is no reason to doubt that, in the twelve months (4:29) before the sentence fell, Nebuchadnezzar tried to do that very thing. The only supposed portrait of him, a cameo now in the Berlin Museum, indicates an earnest and sensitive countenance. In terms of his Chaldean concepts, he sought to be that righteous king, had always sought to be, and now, more so than ever. The Grotefend inscription indicates his self-evaluation: "Nebuchadnezzar, the just king, the faithful shepherd, who directs mankind, who rules over the subjects of Bel, Shamash, and Marduk, the arbiter, the possessor of wisdom, who cares for life, the lofty one, the untiring one, the maintainer of Esagila and Ezida, the son of Nabopolasser, King of Babylon, am I." Nebuchadnezzar then wrote of his reverence for his creator, Marduk, the richness of his sacrifices, and the unification of "numerous peoples" under Babylon. "Under its enduring protection I gathered together all mankind in comfort, and stored up there great heaps of grain beyond reckoning."[5] Nebuchadnezzar saw himself as "the faithful shepherd," in the Winckler Inscription, "the legitimate shepherd,"[6] the divine king whose love of the god had begun at birth. He had succeeded in furthering the great kingdom of gods' and man's dreams by bringing numerous peoples into unity in a common empire, one dedicated to righteousness and peace. In the Borsippa Inscription, there is an earnest plea to the "eternal son, exalted messenger," Nabu:

---

[5] Robert Francis Harper: *Assyrian and Babylonian Literature*. Selected Translations. New York: Appleton, 1904, pp. 147-150.

[6] *Ibid.*, p. 143.

> Do thou proclaim the length of my days, do thou
>   write my offspring!
> In the presence of Marduk, the king of heaven
>   and earth,
> The father, my begetter, look with favor upon
>   my works,
> Command that I receive favour!
> May Nebuchadnezzar,
> The king, the restorer,
> Be ever established in thy mouth![7]

In another inscription, Nebuchadnezzar prayed

> Truly answer me
> In judgment and in dreams![8]

By his very dependence on Daniel, Nebuchadnezzar gave evidence
of the intensity of his desire to be righteous, but his conception of
this was entirely in Chaldean terms. The ladder-like structure of
the ziggurats, with each story recessed successively, gave from a
distance the appearance of a gigantic ladder reaching up towards
heaven, a fitting symbol of this religion of continuity and its belief
in the bond of heaven and earth. The humility of Nebuchadnezzar
was real, but it was not godly, being set in the context of one who
took the hand of the god for his people in awed humility and pride
at his function as center, throne, tree, shepherd, column, and glory.
In this concept, God was involved in the dialectic of history and not
beyond it, and the point of involvement was Nebuchadnezzar and
his empire.

Accordingly, Nebuchadnezzar, in terms of his faith, spoke hon-
estly and with some awed humility as well as pride, in affirming,
"Is not this the great Babylon, that I have built for the house of the
kingdom by the might of my power, and for the honour of my
majesty?" (4:30). This is not to be construed as merely vain-
glorious boasting, but rather as the happy and proud summarization
of a man who rejoices in his work and righteousness, affirming that
his order is indeed a fulfilment of the kingdom and the true ritual

---

[7] *Ibid.*, pp. 150-152.
[8] *Ibid.*, p. 156f.

center of the earth, the human focus of the divine glory. The statement is thus an affirmation of his satisfaction that the threat of the
dream has been stayed, that the dream, recorded no doubt in the
archives of state as other dreams were, had been stayed by the human
righteousness of the king and his order. It was the consummate expression of self-righteousness, the accentuation of that very faith
which God was challenging.

It is thus precisely at the moment that Nebuchadnezzar believed
the kingdom to be securely established that the sentence came: "The
kingdom is departed from thee" (4:31). Moreover, wherever man
seeks to be more than man, he becomes less than man. His every
attempt to be as God results in a reduction of his manhood and a
retreat into unreason and irresponsibility. In Nebuchadnezzar, the
ostensible tree of life, this metamorphosis manifested itself as what
has been termed both lycanthropy and, more properly, zoanthropy,
an ailment in which man, hating God and therefore himself also as
created in the image of God, tries to strike at God by trying to efface
every trace of his own humanity and the divine image in himself.
There is some evidence that Nebuchadnezzar was completely absent
from power for four years.[9]

The purpose of the humbling of Nebuchadnezzar had been that
he "know the most High ruleth in the kingdom of men, and giveth
it to whomsoever he will" (4:25). There is good reason to believe
that Nebuchadnezzar's experience culminated in his regeneration.
Although his proclamation is in part couched in polytheistic terms, it
is significant that such references appear in his description of his
thinking prior to his recovery. Certainly the document is remarkable
as compared to other documents of antiquity in its humility and
confession of sin. The statement asserts three things: (1) the
absolute sovereignty and discontinuity with man of God (4:34, 35,
37); (2) the entire proclamation is a declaration of repentance and
(3) is a confession of sin. Much less is asked of many a modern
"convert," clearly, and to hesitate with regard to Nebuchadnezzar's
integrity of faith seems unjustified. Moreover, even as Job's latter
end was blessed more than his former (Job 42:10-13), so Nebu-

[9] Tabouis, *op. cit.*, p. 341.

chadnezzar was strengthened in his kingdom "and excellent majesty was added" (4:36) to him.

The significance of Nebuchadnezzar's entire attitude has been overlooked but is of no small importance. Even granting to the dubious that the monarch never became a true worshiper, the fact still remains that his signal preference for Daniel and his associates, and for their faith, gave to the Hebrews a privileged position in that empire. This was sufficient to create an anti-Hebraic sentiment among jealous Chaldeans both then (3:8) and later (6:4), under Darius. The position of the Hebrews was thus one of security, privilege, and prosperity, so that their captivity became not a curse but a protection. They were under a king whose attitude towards God, even with a minimum interpretation, compared favorably with that of the kings of Judah, and if, as Young ably argues, his faith was now genuine, their situation was markedly better. Thus, even in the harshness of captivity, the grace, protection, and blessing of God was openly manifested.

DANIEL 5: THE BALANCES OF JUSTICE

The faith of Nebuchadnezzar was effective in his life but not in terms oᶠ Babylonian history. After that monarch's death, Babylon passed through a succession of weak hands until Nabonidus, son-in-law to Nebuchadnezzar, came to the throne. His son, Belshazzar Nebuchadnezzar's grandson, was made vicegerent to strengthen his position, and to give him independence in extending the empire. Nabonidus' campaign in Arabia led to the establishment of a new capital at Tema, on the highways of the ancient world, to control the trade routes leading to the Red Sea, the Indian Gulf, to Egypt, India, and to all the world of that day. Tema, half way between Damascus and Mecca, is still a main trade center of interior Arabia, but under Nabonidus reached its glory as "the real capital of the Neo-Babylonian empire, for the king lived there in a palace which equalled that of Babylon."[1] The value of Tema was conditional, however, on the continued power of Babylon itself, in that Nabonidus was on alien ground and able to make the imperial power further effective only insofar as the home base could support him. The reign of Nabonidus thus marked a further development of imperial power as well as its close.

The rise of the Medes and Persians, at first a cloud no bigger than a man's hand, developed into a major storm as these powers reached Babylon. The confidence of the Babylonians, however, was based on their ability to withstand, as they believed, a seventy-year siege, with the Medes and Persians likely to destroy themselves in time by their distance from home and the problems attendant upon

[1] Raymond Philip Dougherty: *Nabonidus and Belshazzar, A Study of the Closing Events of the Neo-Babylonian* Empire. New Haven: Yale, 1929, p. 146. Dougherty's study gives excellent evidence of the historical reliability of Daniel by confirming the existence and position of Belshazzar. See also Edwin Yamauchi: *Greece and Babylon*. Grand Rapids, Mich.: Baker Book House, 1967, pp. 70f., 89ff.

elongated supply lines. Accordingly, Belshazzar felt free to proceed with a religious festival.

At the great new year's festival, only the high priestly king, Nabonidus, could preside, but at other festivals, Belshazzar, as vicegerent, could officiate. The occasion was marked by no small drinking and banqueting, Belshazzar himself presiding at a dinner before a thousand of his lords (5:1). This extravagance of splendor and celebration was common to antiquity, as witness the 15,000 who later ate daily at the table of Persian monarchs, according to Athenaeus, and to which Esther 1:3-5 gives witness. But the religious motive was central, and basic to the exuberant observances. In affirmation of that religious motive, Belshazzar, a devout man, expressed the official Babylonian condemnation of the recorded dreams of Nebuchadnezzar as interpreted by the Hebrew, Daniel. The sacred vessels from the temple at Jerusalem were brought out so that "the king, and his princes, his wives, and his concubines" (5:3) might drink from them. This was an act of deliberate sacrilege, and also an affirmation of faith. Babylonian faith was (1) a belief in salvation by works, a faith which implies inevitably that, (2) since man saves himself, he controls his destiny, and the future is therefore in his hands. This latter deduction Belshazzar clearly made. His pretended ignorance of Daniel is corrected by Daniel himself: "Thou knewest all this" (5:22), i.e., the dreams and experience of Nebuchadnezzar, God's judgments, and the central role of Daniel in all this very well-known sequence of events. Belshazzar, confident of victory over the Medes and Persians, expressed by this sacrilege his defiance of Jehovah and his ability to use Him. He was not bound by the dreams or Daniel's prophetic interpretation thereof, but only by his own will and might. As a devout priest-king, giving evidence repeatedly of his faith,[2] this monarch asserted his independence of this discontinuous God who high-handedly refused man's hand or works, this God who acted in contempt of human glory. It can perhaps be said that in that hour Babylonian religion came into its clearest and sharpest focus in Belshazzar's

[2] *Ibid.,* pp. 87-92.

priestly act. As they drank from the temple vessels, "they praised the gods" (5:4).

"In that same hour," a man's hand appeared and wrote on the wall in an unknown script, filling all with terror, the priest-king in particular. His own counsellors were unable to decipher the script, in spite of every inducement. The queen-mother[3] urged the consideration of Daniel, perhaps speaking as though Daniel were unknown to Belshazzar in order to gloss over the shame of needing a man whose God and whose prophetic interpretations had only an hour before been openly despised and defied.

Belshazzar accordingly sent for Daniel, offering him third place in the kingdom (after Nabonidus and himself) for the interpretation of the writing. His comments to Daniel stated in part, "Art thou that Daniel, which art of the children of the captivity of Judah, whom the king my father [or, grandfather] brought out of Jewry?" (5:13). What the queen-mother had said concerning Daniel had reference to his eminence under Nebuchadnezzar, not to Daniel's origin. Belshazzar chose to pass over that fact, giving every evidence that he knew full well who Daniel was, and to reduce Daniel to silence as far as preaching to him was concerned. He said, in effect, to Daniel: "You are a Jew, brought here as a prisoner years ago. Any eminence you gained was borrowed, Babylonian eminence. Remember your place. What can your God offer me, or say to me, when He can do no more for His people?" The offer to make him "third ruler in the kingdom" (5:16) was an offer of restoration to an eminence Daniel once possessed under Nebuchadnezzar, and from which, perhaps for religious reasons, he had been since removed.

Daniel's answer was fearless and pointed: "Let thy gifts be to thyself, and give thy rewards [or, fee] to another; yet I will read the writing" (5:17). Daniel then reminded the monarch of the sovereignty of God, who "gave" to Nebuchadnezzar all that he possessed, and then "deposed him from his kingly throne" for a season because of his pride (5:18-20). Pride here is clearly an aspect of the religion of continuity and is premised thereon. Belshazzar, knowing all this, had deliberately proceeded on a course of contempt for God,

[3] Young: *Comm. ad loc.*

a contempt openly manifested in the use of the temple vessels, lifting himself up, i.e., setting himself up against and in independence of "the God in whose hands thy breath is, and whose are all thy ways" (5:21-23).

The writing on the wall was from this God, and its meaning was clear-cut and direct: MENE, MENE, TEKEL, UPHARSIN, or, as Young renders it, MENE, MENE, TEKEL UPERES.[4]

The image here is of the scales of Justice, that deity of antiquity who appears implicitly or explicitly in one religion after another, in Egypt, Babylon, Persia, Greece, China, and Rome. The scales of justice appear also in the Church of Rome, in St. Michael the arch-angel, one of whose duties in the life to come is asserted to be the weighing of the souls of the departed on the scales of justice. Pere La Chaise, Jesuit confessor of Louis XIV, urged the revocation of the Edict of Nantes as a means of tipping the scales of St. Michael favorably. In every works religion, wherever the concept of self-salvation has the slightest foothold, the concept of the scales appears. It is the epitome of self-righteousness and of independence of God, a concept of merit which gains for man an absolution from God and His claims.

Now, in conformity to his own creed, Belshazzar is weighed and condemned by the sovereign God. Let a man lower his moral law as low as he will, he will still violate and destroy it. Let him reduce righteousness to bare sincerity, and he will inevitably be a hypo-crite. Man cannot justify himself even in terms of any law he himself creates, because, being a covenant-breaker with God, he cannot avoid being a covenant-breaker with himself, a creature made in God's own image. Hence, his life is one of radical alienation from not only God and His word, but from himself, and from any law or order he himself creates.

MENE, MENE: "God has numbered thy kingdom, and finished it" (5:26).

TEKEL: "Thou are weighed in the balances, and art found wanting' (5:27).

---

[4] Young: *Comm. ad loc.*

PERES: "Thy kingdom is divided, and given to the Medes and Persians" (5:28). "In the word PERES (*divided*) there is an allusion to PARAS (the word which is translated *Persians*), which would seem to indicate that the Persians were the dominant power in the *dividing* or dissolving of Babylon."[5]

As a matter of religious and royal dignity, Belshazzar kept his word and exalted Daniel to third office in the empire (5:29). That same night, Babylon fell and Belshazzar was slain. Cyrus had diverted the waters of the Euphrates and entered the city, according to his claim, without encounter or battle. Darius the Mede, at the age of 62, became king of Babylon.

For the believer, the scales of justice are an impotent concept. Alive in Christ, he is free from the power of sin and death; living by grace, he is not under the sentence of the law. The cross of Christ is his charter of liberty. The radical alienation of man from God, man, and self is destroyed, and freedom becomes the order of his life, the freedom of the creature, freedom to be *a man under God* and vice-gerent over creation. But as long as man, whether in religion, politics, or any area of life, tries to play god, he cannot be man or enjoy the liberty, glory, and freedom of man the creature. He inevitably gravitates to a concept of *law as the ground of order,* as contrasted to the biblical ground of *life in Christ,* and *the law is always a sentence of death.* Every law he creates, however minimal, reveals him to be a covenant-breaker and law-hater, and his every scale, however falsified, registers him nonetheless a condemned man. The law of his life becomes therefore death, while the law of the believer is the life and nature of Christ and a glorious liberty. The law of death, as it works in man, cries out for judgment and the grave, and men invoke and create their own judgments, fashion their hells, and refuse to allow their cultures and histories to be other than a harvest of wrath and a sorry tale of self-punishment. Faced with the destinies they themselves invoke, the Belshazzars of history turn back to their drink and wait for death.

---

[5] Young: *Comm.,* p. 127.

DANIEL 6: KINGSHIP, JUSTICE AND MONOTHEISM

The experience, eminence, and integrity of Daniel were recognized by Darius the Mede, who made him first president over the 120 princes who governed his kingdom.[1] This occasioned no small jealousy. As Joseph Parker has observed, with reference to this passage, "All primacy has to be paid for." If that primacy is as faithful and righteous a one as Daniel's, it must be doubly paid for. The levelling demands of evil are for a democracy of being, a cosmic democracy in which all distinctions are nullified in favor of a commonality which blurs identity, responsibility, and meaning. Evil men seek to make all things evil; men who are failures demand a universal failure. And men unable or unwilling to rise above their low estate seek savagely to raze all eminence into a common democracy of mediocrity and defeat. Democracy is the great love of the failures and cowards of life, and involves a hatred of differences, because freedom is inseparable from differences, distinctions, discernment, and wise discrimination. But freedom is an enemy to those who hate responsibility, and accordingly must be destroyed as an aristocratic principle to make way for the "freedom" of total democracy, which is the end of all meanings, discriminations, and divisions, whether good or bad, in the name of this higher virtue, the mystical oneness and absorption into the mass of a fallen and corrupt humanity. "All primacy has to be paid for," either by total war against a hostile world, or by radical concession and submission to that world. Religiously and politically, Daniel refused to concede in any measure.

His one vulnerable point, his political enemies concluded, was his religious faith. Accordingly, Darius was persuaded to issue an interdict "that whosoever shall ask a petition of any God or man for thirty days, save of thee, O king, he shall be cast into the den of

[1] Concerning the identity of Darius, see John C. Whitcomb, Jr.: *Darius the Mede*. Philadelphia: Presbyterian and Reformed Publishing Co., 1959; see also Yamauchi, *op. cit.*, p. 89.

lions" (6:7). This decree, once issued, could not be reversed, "according to the law of the Medes and Persians, which altereth not" (6:8).

Several very important politico-religious beliefs come to focus here, all considerations of continuing relevancy and importance:

1) The priestly kingship of the monarch is here manifested, a particularly highly developed conception thereof. The priest-king was the mediator between God and man, the link between heaven and earth, a living Tower of Babel, and the point of continuity between the two worlds.

2) Accordingly, the good life was possible only in terms of that order manifested in and through that sacred link, apart from whom no true order existed. To ask a petition through the king as mediator, to pray in his name as Christians now pray "in Jesus' name," was thus to give witness to the cornerstone of society and the fundamental fact of life.

3) The fundemental law of all being was expressed in and through the mediator-king, that is, in his official interdicts or ex cathedra utterances. These laws indeed were in terms of concrete historical situations and were nonetheless fundamental law as related to history and hence unalterable.

4) The priest-king was thus the focal point of heaven and earth and the voice of law, and law incarnate, and yet in a very real sense *under law,* bound by his own utterances and helpless to reverse them, as both Daniel 6:14f. and Esther 1:19 and 8:8 testify.

To this position of the Medo-Persian monarchs, secular history gives no small confirmation. Diodorus Siculus reported the inability of Darius III to revoke his hasty death sentence on Charidemos. Quintus Curtius reported, "The Persians worshipped their kings among the gods."[2] Plutarch recorded a similar report in his *Themistocles,* quoting Artabanus to Themistocles, who sought audience with Xerxes:

O stranger, the laws of men are different, and one thing is honourable to one man, and to others another; but it is honourable

---

[2] See Young, Keil and Delitzsch, H. C. Leupold: *Comms. ad loc.*

for all to honour and observe their own laws. It is the habit of
the Greeks, we are told, to honour, above all things, liberty and
equality; but amongst our many excellent laws, we account this
the most excellent, to honour the king, and to worship him as the
image of the great preserver of the universe; if, then, you shall
consent to our laws, and fall down before the king and worship
him, you may both see him and speak to him; but if your mind be
otherwise, you must make use of others to intercede for you, for
it is not the national custom here for the king to give audience to
any one that doth not fall down before him.

Such a concept was by no means limited to the Persians; the
Greeks deified their city-states and saw the *polis* as itself the locale of
deity, so that their "democracy" was a democracy of gods. This
concept of true order and divine mediation is the inevitable concommitant of every social theory, including those that deny the
supernatural, or deny even the concept of truth in favor of relativity
or pragmatism. For democracy, the voice of the people is the voice
of God, *vox populi, vox dei;* for Marxism, the dictatorship of the
proletariat is history come to incarnate focus; and pragmatism, for
all its claims to anti-metaphysical thinking, is based on a series of
a priori assumptions concerning the nature and destiny of man which
are staggering acts of faith. There is no social theory without its
"voice of law," its great mediator and link between process and
reality, between time and eternity, between history and the end of
time order, between God and man. Churches, governments, schools,
and philosophies all proffer links, mediators, and voices of law, and,
whether they admit the reality of God or not, seek to temporalize
eternity and give meaning, purpose, and direction to time and history
thereby. Each will grant toleration to the other, provided its prior
claim to truth be recognized. Worship God, but first bow down to
the state as the true order of man. Religion, private experience, and
learning can be tolerated only as long as the primacy of the democratic order be admitted. Each philosophy, church, or political order
is insistent on this point: "I am the door. The true order is unattain-
able apart from me." Against all this Christ spoke as the one true
mediator, the bond of heaven and earth by His incarnation, but a
union without confusion of the two natures, so that God remains

God, and man remains man. In declaring himself to be the one and true door, Jesus declared that *all* who sought entrance into the kingdom, into the fulfilment of man and of history, by any other door than He were *thieves and robbers* who sought the death of man and the destruction of all order (John 10). God and man must be brought together if man and history are to be saved and fulfilled, but without confusion, for that temptation to confusion is the satanic temptation, "Ye shall be as God" (Gen. 3:5, RV). This confusion means the destruction of history and of man; it means the attempt to eternalize time and process, and to negate the fact of creation and the necessity of growth, development, and maturation. It means the end of time, and the end of the meaning of time. The cultural pyramid builders of every generation seek to arrest process and decay and to eternalize their real or dream orders, but vainly, for the confusion is an impossibility, and the attempt is confounded by God—ordained confusion (Gen 11:1-9). In Christ, the two orders, time and eternity, God and man, are brought together, incarnated but without confusion, so that history's redemption is made possible, man's salvation effected, and the integrity of time preserved. The Council of Chalcedon, in recognizing this fact, gave to Western history its basis of freedom, the freedom to function as process in time, and not all the medieval and modern attempts at arresting time have succeeded in negating that victory. Chalcedon (451) declared in part that this "one and the same Christ" is

> Son, Lord, Only-begotten, recognized IN TWO NATURES, WITHOUT CONFUSION, WITHOUT CHANGE, WITHOUT DIVISION, WITHOUT SEPARATION: the distinction of natures being in no way annulled by the union, but rather the characteristics of each nature being preserved and coming together to form one person and substance, not as parted or separated into two persons, but one and the same Son and Only-begotten God the Word, Lord Jesus Christ; even as the prophets from earliest times spoke of him, and our Lord Jesus Christ himself taught us, and the creed of the Fathers has handed down to us.

The devices whereby men have sought to achieve that false bond of heaven and earth are not only institutional but also experiential, as witness asceticism and mysticism. Thus Polycarp Sherwood,

O.S.B., S.T.D., in analyzing St. Maximus the Confessor, has written: "Deification is the ultimate fulfilling of human nature's capacity for God . . . deification and salvation are the same."[3]

Whether in experience, person, office, or institution, the goal is the bond of time and eternity, the representation or manifestation of "the image of the great preserver of the universe," so that man might escape from time, or that history be arrested by that manifested order.

Daniel, however, refused to be swayed into fear or compromise by the law of Darius. Indeed, his reaction to the decree, which he recognized as aimed at him, was prayer. "Now when Daniel knew that the writing was signed, he went into his house; and his windows being open in his chamber toward Jerusalem, he kneeled upon his knees three times a day, and prayed, and gave thanks before his God, as he did aforetime" (6:20). Not in Babylon was Daniel's mediator, but in ruined Jerusalem, in the temple typically, in that altar wherein Christ and His sacrifice had been ritually set forth. The impossibility of the temple of Jerusalem to be indeed the house of God, that is, to contain Him, Solomon had declared at its dedication, at which time also the temple's typical significance was hinted at in this indication that both Israelite and foreigner prayed "toward this place" (I Kings 8).[4]

Apparently the enemies of Daniel had at least one informer in his household to enable them to secure his arrest and conviction, because this private practice was conclusively proven in a public hearing before Darius, to the consternation of that monarch. Darius was now bound by his own law to sentence to death his most trusted associate and chief president. His grief and agony are unmistakable, and his position a tragic one. As the voice of law, he could not deny himself without ceasing to be that bond of heaven and earth. His office and power required, whatever vice he might indulge in, this one unswerving allegiance to law. Thus, Darius' *law* said *death* to Daniel, while

[3] Polycarp Sherwood, trans. with intro.: *St. Maximus the Confessor: The Ascetic Life, The Four Centuries on Charity*, Ancient Christian Writers, 21. London: Longmans, Green, 1955, p. 71

[4] See concerning this practice Robert Dick Wilson: *Studies in the Book of Daniel*, Second Series. New York: Revell, 1938, p. 241ff.

his *love* said *life*, and the two could not be united. In every non-biblical system of thought, this conflict appears in some form, the irreconcilable and unbridgeable conflict and gulf between law and love. Let law triumph, and its harshness turns it ultimately into a cold scheme of organized injustice. Let love triumph over law, and again injustice holds sway as antinomianism infects every bulwark of order. The tension between law and love is thus a continuing tension that works to the dissolution of one civilization after another and is today basic to much contemporary tension, as humanitarian impulses seek to over-ride the requirements of strict justice and the dictates of its law. The tension is by no means limited to the political order but is endemic to the family, society, school, and every other order.

Only in the biblical revelation is the tension between law and love resolved, with vast social and historical implications, in the person and work of Jesus Christ. By His perfect righteousness and His vicarious atonement, the strictest requirements of law and justice were fully met and fulfilled, and the statutes of God observed to every jot and tittle, and yet, at one and the same time, the love of God unto salvation manifested in and through Him. The cross thus is the symbol of the unity of law and love in Jesus Christ and of the full requirement and mutual integrity of both. The radical injustice of every order apart from Christ is overcome by this synthesis, and the historical realization of an order founded on this unity, as yet unrealized, is opened up. The attempts of men to create an equitable and livable order apart from the atonement have been doomed to radical collapse, as witness Julius Caesar's attempt to supplant the failing law with his graceless *clementia*.[5] Love or forgiveness which is unable to regenerate man becomes only a license to and subsidy of evil, and law itself is equally incapable of any creative role or regenerating function.

Darius, caught by this tension, could only cry out, "O Daniel, servant of the living God, is thy God . . . able?" (6:20). And Daniel, out of the depths of the lion's den, was able to declare that God had that night stopped the mouths of the lions and delivered

---

[5] See Ethelbert Stauffer: *Christ and the Caesars*. Philadelphia: Westminster, 1955, pp. 42-53.

him without any hurt. The overjoyed king restored Daniel to his position, and sentenced his adversaries, and their families (an injustice forbidden in Deut. 24:16, II Kings 14:6), to that same death they had planned for Daniel.

The decree of Darius (6:25-29), while commemorative in purpose, and self-commendatory with reference to this living God of Daniel, recognizes his omnipotence and sovereignty clearly and plainly. But, lacking as it is in a personal relationship to that God, and without any sense of man as sinner, it is not a confession of faith but an acknowledgment of power. This Darius could believe, and by honoring Daniel further and attaching him more closely to his throne, as did Cyrus (6:28), seek to strengthen his own throne as the living bond between heaven and earth. Polytheism was not necessarily overcome; indeed the multiplicity of man, his cultures and powers, was seen as the counterpart of the multiplicity of the supernatural order. The unification of the one order, that of man, under a great priest-king, meant also the coalescence of the supernatural order in and through that one and same divine-human link, the great priest-king. Accordingly, as the great empires of antiquity developed and expanded, they were characterized by a double note, first, a cultural synthesis and amalgamation, and, second, a religious syncretism, as the various gods and faiths were brought to focus in and through the ritual bond of heaven and earth. Monotheism was thus a development of empire, and an aspect of its concept of unity.

Monotheism is, historically and essentially, a close relative to polytheism and an aspect of the same basic philosophy. At first glance, this seems a radical contradiction, in that polytheism is, as the word indicates, a belief in many gods, and monotheism a belief in one god. But polytheism is not only a belief in many gods, but also and essentially a belief that *god is many,* i.e., that he is various in his forms and appearances, often in contradiction one to another, so that he is one in being although as unlimited in the diversity of his nature as is nature. Thus polytheism and henotheism are closely linked historically. In henotheism, many gods are recognized, and each is, for the moment, worshiped as the concentration of all the attributes of deity. Accordingly, we find, together with polytheism, a henotheistic identification, so that Astarte and Chemosh are closely linked or identified, although radically different, Jupiter and Zeus are easily merged, and the whole pantheon of gods seen as diverse aspects of the diversity of being. In periods of competing and warring states, the polytheistic aspect was paramount, whereas imperialism emphasized henotheism and monotheism. It is important to note also that modern philosophical and religious monotheism, by recognizing the "truth" in or of all religions, is strongly henotheistic and only a step removed from polytheism.

Rome moved from polytheism to monotheism and henotheism as it developed from republic to empire. Its religious policy enabled it to utilize fully every local faith, while doing it honor, and link it also to the empire and emperor. Thus, some of the most foreign of cities were also the most devout adherents to the emperor cult without any departure from their local cults, as witness Smyrna and Pergamos. The unity of empire went hand in hand with henotheism and monotheism, and these two led directly to the undergirding of the central Roman concept, law. Basic to this development was the Roman concept of natural law, which was *ius gentium,* the law of foreigners or law of nations, the legal analogue to religious henotheism. Foreign laws were absorbed by Rome, as were foreign cults, into the monotheism of the state. But legal henotheism and monotheism were as alien to biblical faith as religious henotheism. The Bible is neither henotheistic nor monotheistic, but rather trinitarian and theistic, and its supernatural conception of law makes invalid both Roman civil law and the law of nations. Rome's opposition to Christianity was thus grounded on more insight than was the compromising work of many Christian apologetes. The same tension exists today. A faith which puts African polytheism, Spinoza's pantheism, Unitarian monotheism, and Toynbee's modified henotheism all on an equal level as error is a cardinal offense to imperial man, whose empire must be all-inclusive and whose conception of truth and power is often closely linked with geographical extent and politico-religious inclusivism. Henotheism and monotheism, as aspects of one faith, are of the nature of empire as man develops it, and an aspect of the being of the state.

In terms of this, the Roman Empire could tolerate a diversity of faiths as long as their oneness in essence was recognized, and the cult of the emperor as the focus of and bridge between heaven and earth maintained. Christianity, biblical faith, was therefore doubly offensive because, first, it proclaimed another and an exclusive mediator, Jesus Christ, and, second, it seemed peculiarly and hostilely polytheistic by comparison to the deism which underlay all pagan polytheisms. The Greek and Roman believers and thinkers were not crude polytheists but sophisticated deists. The triune God was a standing offense, in that His self-sufficiency was so patent: He provided His own mediator or link, and His own Spirit, as against man's mediation, aspiration, and ascent. The ontological Trinity, Himself the fundamental principle of unity and multiplicity, creator, redeemer, and sustainer, undercut the autonomy of man and his religious effort and rendered all the magnificence of empire vanity in its effort to bring fulfilment to man and society and create the ultimate order. Accordingly, Arianism, subordinationism, monophysitism, nestorianism, and other heresies, and occasionally even Judaism (as with the Khazar kingdom), became men's vain refuges from the juggernaut of the triune God in its full-orbed and co-equal power, destroying as it did the claims of empire and religion to be the divine-human links and bonds. The kingship and priesthood of Christ undercut human kings and priests, and the finality of His office as prophet meant the end of religion as a creative and independent agency; all were now required to be ministerial or else criminal. Progressively, therefore, as the issue has come into focus, the patronage of true Christianity has been less and less possible for the state. The easiness with which Darius paid tribute to God becomes less and less practicable to men whose mediator and god is the state. In this respect, Soviet Russia manifests a higher degree of epistemological self-consciousness than those states able as yet to pay hypocritical tribute to God, whom they in reality war against. This hypocrisy was not present in Darius, in that the fundamental tension was not yet in focus. The tension of our era is witness to the existence of the problem, and is thus a forerunner of its solution.

DANIEL 7: THE COURSE OF DOMINION

The second half of Daniel is devoted to extensive and specific predictive prophecy, and the offense of the book comes therefore into sharper focus. Man, desiring to retain control over history in absolute fashion, is radically intolerant of any God who is more than idea and the ideal. Since the actual in history must be purely the domain of human activity, the ontological trinity is an offense by virtue of its creation and government of history. Again, the actual in history must be subject only to the prior interpretation of autonomous man, whereas the God of Scripture reserves unto Himself not only the creation but the ultimate and true interpretation of history. The natural man therefore will not tolerate a God who governs history but will have only a god governed by history and process and himself the product thereof. Every biblical depiction of God, therefore, is a standing offense, a presentation of a raw God who must be reshaped to conform to the narrowness of man's mind and subjected to man's radical demand for his own ultimacy and autonomy. Accordingly, predictive prophecy is ruled out of court on a priori grounds; it is adjudged to be religiously and historically offensive, as indeed it is to would-be autonomous man, and is supplanted with a picture of history as brute factuality, a chaos out of which man and cosmic processes coming to focus in man are bringing order, light, and meaning. The result is the conversion of history into myth, whereas Daniel gives us the rescue of history from the constructs of man the myth-maker.

In passing, it needs to be noted how absurd is the notion of a Maccabean date for Daniel. Not only does the book presuppose and require the knowledge of one contemporary with the events, and not only does it reveal on textual grounds its early date, but it moreover is an impossible book for a Maccabean Jew, indeed, any Jew except one under orders from God, to have written. And even then, Daniel was deeply grieved by the vision (7:15-28), which clearly declared the permanent by-passing of Israel as a nation. The intense nationalism of the Jews was apparent in Zerubbabel, Ezra, and Nehemiah, and by the time of the Maccabees was too intense and exclusive to be tolerant of a book which declared it to be the counsel of God to by-pass Israel.[1] It was briefly used for one point of interest in the Maccabean era and then again relegated to the background.

The date of this vision is "the first year of Belshazzar king of Babylon" (7:1). It portrays history as a great sea buffeted by "the four winds of the heaven" (7:2), an image repeated in Revelation 17:15, "And he said unto me, The waters which thou sawest, where the whore sitteth, are peoples, and multitudes, and nations, and tongues." History is thus a dark and turbulent sea, dark to itself, and acted on from without while having its movement and life within itself, an entity but by no means a self-sufficient and self-determinative entity. While to man, the sea of history is dark and hidden in its depths, from the throne of God it appears as "a sea of glass like unto crystal" (Rev. 4:6); there are thus no dark corners in history for God, who from His throne determines all things that come to pass and sees the end from the beginning.

Out of the depths of the sea came four great beasts, typifying the four great empires. Beasts of prey have been traditionally the symbols of state, intending to typify the national power and its ability to devour and destroy. Benjamin Franklin, in dissenting from this desire to choose a beast of prey as the American symbol, suggested the wild turkey, a useful bird and one representative of the profuse natural wealth of the continent, but was voted down.

The identification of the four empires has been more or less uniform, and dissent has been based on attempts to force a construction onto the text. "The first was like a lion, and had eagles' wings; I beheld till the wings thereof were plucked [or, torn out, according to Leupold, Calvin, etc.], and it was lifted up from the earth, and made stand upon the feet as a man, and a man's heart was given to it" (7:4). Thus, the Babylonian Empire is depicted as being checked in the course of its imperial dominion, by a humanizing force exerted from without; from the same source as all the government of history, God

[1] Wilson: *op. cit.,* p. 28.

Himself. This has reference to the humbling of Nebuchadnezzar, after whom the Babylonian expansive force never recuperated, despite Nabonidus' effort in that direction.

"And behold another beast, a second, like to a bear, and it raised up itself on one side [or, it raised up one dominion], and it had three ribs in the mouth of it between the teeth of it: and they said thus unto it, Arise and devour much flesh" (7:5). This command to destroy comes from God, who raises up the empire as an avenger and in terms of His end purposes. The Medo-Persian Empire is here depicted, with higher dominion going to the Persians, and vast conquests, as of Babylon, Lydia, and Egypt (the "three ribs," according to very ancient as well as contemporary interpreters), given to this huge and lumbering power.

"After this I beheld, and lo another, like a leopard, which had upon the back of it four wings of a fowl; the beast had also four heads; and dominion was given to it" (7:6). The rapid rise to power of the Macedonian Empire of Alexander the Great is fittingly depicted in the winged leopard or panther. "The symbolism indicates both the rapidity with which its conquests were made and also the width of the territory which it took. It had four heads, and thus the world-wide or ecumenical nature of the kingdom is stressed. Dominion is given to this beast from God, and thus we learn of this beast as of the first two, that it also is in the hands of God's all-controlling providence."[2] The four heads thus refer, not to the four successors of Alexander, his generals, but "representing the four corners of the earth, symbolize the ecumenicity of the kingdom."[3] The imperial dream of the kingdom of man, a one-world paradise apart from God, is thus the focus of imperial expansion and conquest, and represents man's desire to seize God's glory and realize it in history. To understand more clearly the impulse of these empires, let us note the summary comments of F. W. Buckler:

The Oriental monarch—the Great King—personally represents God on earth. His face is the face of God. He is the shadow of

[2] Edward J. Young: *The Messianic Prophecies of Daniel*. Delft, Netherlands, 1954, p. 30.

[3] Young: *Comm. ad loc.*

God on earth, and when he is seated on his throne, he is known as the threshold of the divine bounty. All this is in virtue of his possession of the divine Glory of the king, which "cannot be forcibly seized" but is the gift of God, to whom it must be ascribed, otherwise it will depart. In order to render apparent the Glory—or Grace, the alternative translation—to the eyes of the uninitiated, the king retains a long beard, avails himself copiously of cosmetics, wears magnificent robes and sits beneath a resplendent crown, suspended so as to appear to be worn, on a throne studded with precious stones. He is in this way the revelation of the Glory, if he possesses the Glory or the Grace. . . . But, however divine in his person, in virtue of the divine epiphany inherent in his kingship, he is human in his limitations by virtue of his being a son of man. . . .

For the eastern king represents much more than a mere arbitrary tyrant. He stands for a system of rule of which he is the incarnation, incorporating into his own body, by means of certain symbolical acts, the persons of those who share his rule. They are regarded as being parts of his body, *membra corporis regis,* and in their district or sphere of activity, they are the king himself—not the servants of the king but "friends" or *members* of the king, just as the eye is the *man* in the function of sight, and the ear in the realm of hearing.[4]

The institutional manifestations of this concept of kingship were, as Buckler pointed out, four: (1) the robe of honor, (2) the symbolic oath of allegiance, (3) common assemblies and common meals as the bonds of loyalty and sources of terms and symbols of loyalty, and (4) the terminology of officialdom and nature of appointment; whereby the officers of the king are his organic members rather than servants.[5]

This evidence reveals the very marked resemblance of the imperial dream to the kingdom of God, so that Babel parallels Jerusalem at point after point. This significance is commonly missed: Babylon is assumed to be immoral, and the true Jerusalem moral, the one wicked and the other righteous in moralistic terms. But the contrast is radically different: it is between *self-righteous* and *righteous,* be-

[4] F. W. Buckler: *The Epiphany of the Cross.* Cambridge, England: Heffer 1938, pp. 4f., 99.
[5] *Ibid.,* pp. 99-107.

tween *moralism* and *regeneration* as conflicting ways of salvation, or health and restoration, for man and society. The kingdom of God is the goal, but Babylon would seize God's glory and make the kingdom man's domain and possession, whereas the true Jerusalem in John's culminating vision is seen as "coming down from God out of heaven" (Rev. 21:2) and is all of grace. *The peril of condemning the empires of Daniel's vision, and the present pretenders to the kingdom, on moralistic grounds, is the necessity of repeating their error, for moralism is the very ground and spirit of man's pretensions to the kingdom, power, and glory.*

These Oriental empires appear and disappear, and a fourth rises with a more lasting impact on history:

> After this I saw in the night visions, and behold, a fourth beast, dreadful and terrible, and strong exceedingly; and it had great iron teeth: it devoured and break in pieces, and it stamped the residue with the feet of it: and it was diverse from all the beasts that were before it; and it had ten horns.

> I considered the horns, and, behold, there came up among them another little horn, before whom there were three of the first horns plucked up by the roots: and, behold, in this horn were eyes like the eyes of man, and a mouth speaking great things (Dan. 7:7, 8).

This fourth beast has no counterpart in the world of nature, i.e., no character of its own. In Daniel 2:40-43 this fourth empire is portrayed similarly, as a mixture held together by force but having no native binding power. The messianic character of this fourth or Roman Empire was no less prominent than that of its predecessors, as Stauffer's *Christ and the Caesars* makes clear. Its imperial power was more syncretistic than that of its predecessors in that less of the native force served as the point of amalgamation. Its concept of unity was less organic and more legal, and hence, while weaker, a more enduring concept and more readily transmitted to other cultures. The *pax Romana* or Roman peace was based on Roman law. This Roman law was well summarized in its spirit by Cicero in *De Lebigus,* echoing himself the fundamental temper of his heritage, in the statement: "The safety of the people shall be the highest law." Out of this principle came thereafter the "ten horns," i.e., the fulness of imperial and national impulse and power (horn being an ancient symbol of power and dominion). The goal of power became the establishment of *unity under law,* law not as an abstract and remote concept but law in a humanistic sense, in terms of human welfare and the rights of man. The revolutions of Western man, and now increasingly, the revolutions and aspirations of Asia, Africa, and the entire world are in terms of this anthropocentric concept, "the safety of the people shall be the highest law." The rights of man, human welfare, liberty, fraternity, and equality, all these things and more are the products of this, the *ultimate moralism: salvation and the kingdom of man by law.* Upon Rome and its world-wide heirs, "the ten horns," has fallen the mantle of the scribes and Pharisees! "Ten" as the number of fulness indicates the totality of man's statist devotion to this dream. (The numbers seven and ten, as terminal numbers in their respective systems of numerics, and the number four, representing the four directions, are used repeatedly to typify totality and fulness.) Another horn or power arises, uprooting all other powers in every direction (the three horns, or points of the compass), exercising dominion with particularly bold claims and pretensions, "a mouth speaking great things." Even as the others represent empires and dominions, so this last represents a like power, claiming a one-world dominion under the sovereign unity of law; it is no more a person than its predecessors, and, like them, it is the epitome of *the moralistic pretension to salvation by law.* Since this is *political* prophecy, the reference is thus not to the ecclesiastical area to which antichrist belongs, and hence not to antichrist.

The concept of salvation by law found particular expression in the concept and establishment of the United Nations, and its hope is ably summarized by a study of it entitled *World Peace Through World Law,* by Grenville Clark and Louis B. Sohn.[6] Can world peace be created by law, any more than murder be prevented by law? Is not the purpose of law to punish murder rather than to prevent it? Can the law change the heart or mind of any man? At

---

[6] Published by Harvard University Press, second edition, 1960. Sohn is a member of the faculty of the Harvard Law School.

best, the law by fear can only serve as a deterrent; it cannot exert a creative role. To expect that the law of the United Nations will somehow convert murderous nations into neighborly ones is moralism of the most vicious sort, and a moralism calculated to ensure the triumph of evil, as moralism always will.

The organic concept of society, on the one hand, seeks to effect salvation by the mystical experience of group absorption. Incorporation into the body politic, the great actual god on earth, is itself salvation. Thus, during the early years of Naziism, a brief revival of the organic concept, a Nazi agitator told a wildly cheering crowd of peasants, "We don't want lower bread prices, we don't want higher bread prices, we don't want unchanged bread prices—we want National-Socialist bread prices."[7] Here is a quest for meaning in a flight from meaning.

The organic conception absolves the individual of freedom and responsibility, whereas the legalistic conception of man and society places a burden of radical individualism on man which is more than he can bear, and ultimately shatters him and leads to a flight from freedom. Neither is able to effect any change in man or add to his being. Biblical Christianity, by its federal conception of man, sees two humanities, one in Adam, another in Christ. Its concept of man is thus federal and covenantal, and its conception of society, organic, but with it an insistence on individual responsibility to God the Judge. Each man bears the responsibility for his own life and destiny, but, as a member of Christ and a covenant people, he is never alone, and truly godly living is responsible and societal living, both individualistic and organic, with its full law in God's revealed Word, the Scriptures, and its true organic society, the Body of Christ. But, basic to all this, is *regeneration,* whereby man is rescued from the organic horror of Adam and the irresponsibile individuality of the covenant-breaker, made a new creature in Christ, and hence able to live both under law and in society, because Christ, the living word and righteousness of God, is now the new man in him and the law written on the tables of his heart, and he is a member of that great

[7] Peter F. Drucker: *The End of Economic Man.* New York: John Day, 1939, p. 13f.

organic new creation whose builder and maker is God. Thus, man is required to bear his own responsibility before God, but is not expected to exist in isolation and without societal bonds and nurture.

The heavenly judgment scene makes us aware of the sovereignty of God in all this course of dominion. God the Omnipotent reigns, and "the judgment was set" (7:10), or, literally, "the judgment sat."[8] From the throne goes forth judgment against "the little horn" (little in true power, though mighty in pretension), and it is consumed. "But with the destruction of the little horn, the power of the fourth beast disappears entirely."[9] The fall of Babylon is complete: the dream of salvation by law is fully and finally *in history,* for the triumph of Christ is not for eternity alone but by virtue of His resurrection is manifested in history, throughout history, and culminates history, and is thus both historical and also eschatological. The rest of the beasts (7:12), i.e., the other forms of the pseudo-messianic pretensions of politics and the state, remain barely alive after their disruption by Rome, but they too are now destroyed fully and completely.

Now the true kingdom becomes manifest, as "one like the Son of man came with the clouds of heaven" (7:13). This title, Son of man, in the same sense as Daniel's, Jesus applied to himself. Used in several contexts, "The dominant idea is that of sovereignty. The Son of man rules with divine authority. . . . 'Son of man' is a title pointing to deity rather than humanity . . . the Son of man is closely associated with a people. He is a societary figure . . . the connection between the Son of man and the saints of the most High is close."[10] "The clouds of heaven" refer to the glory of God whenever manifest (Ex. 19:9; 33:9; 34:5: 40:34, etc.), whether in revelation, as on the Mount of Transfiguration and the ascension, or in judgment, as in Isaiah 19:1. The last judgment is thus one such manifestation among many. The Messiah is himself the manifestation of God's glory, and was called by Jews either the Cloudy One, or Son of the Clouds. Not only did Jesus claim this title, but

---

[8] Young: *Comm., ad loc.*
[9] Young: *Comm. ad loc.*
[10] Leon Morris: *The Lord from Heaven.* Grand Rapids: Eerdmans, 1958, p. 28.

He claimed also the dominion accorded it, paraphrasing Daniel 7:14 in Matthew 28:18-20, issuing the great commission by virtue of His dominion as foretold by Daniel. This dominion, given Him in the days of the fourth empire (Dan. 2:34f.), reaches world-wide sway when the last manifestations of the false dream are fully shattered and crumble into ruin, reduced to impotence.

The grief of Daniel at the obvious setting aside of Israel made further interpretation necessary (7:15-28), and "the truth of all this" (7:16) is given him. The kingdom of the Messiah is not millennial but everlasting (7:18). The "little horn" prevails against "the saints" (7:21) until God intervenes in history to give dominion to the saints, the members of the true kingdom of God. The fourth empire was greater in power and influence, but not different in kind: "The whole point of the ch. is to show there is only one truly universal kingdom, and that the others could be called such in name only."[11]

"The little horn" "shall speak great words against the most High, and shall wear out the saints of the most High, and think to change times and laws: and they shall be given into his hand until a time and times and the dividing of time" (7:25). The opposition of the human kingdom to God's kingdom will be progressively more vocal. The "divisiveness" of God, and of His discrimination into saved and lost, is offensive to man's desire that "the safety of the people shall be the highest law." Thus, Dewey called Christianity an alien faith because committed to a fundamental discrimination and separation, to a "spiritual aristocracy": "I cannot understand how any realization of the democratic ideal as a vital moral and spiritual ideal in human affairs is possible without surrender of the conception of the basic division to which Christianity is committed."[12] *Salvation by law thus culminates in anti-law as the principle of democracy and the safety of the people!* Every man is his own god, and every man preserved from the possibility of challenge, insecurity, and consequence, this is the kingdom fulfilled! The attempt to "change times and law" is thus *the attempt of man's principle of law*

[11] Young: *Comm. ad loc.,* 7:23.
[12] John Dewey: *A Common Faith.* New Haven: Yale University Press, 1934, p. 84.

to deliver man from law, to make antinomianism law and *to deliver man from process and history.* Dewey, in seeking to obliterate "basic division" from life, is seeking to avoid and negate process and history and to escape from time and judgment. This is the political ideal of the kingdom of man; it affirms man, only to destroy him. It affirms history over eternity, only to flee from time and attempt to eternalize it. It deifies process in order to immobilize it. Its law is thus anti-law, and its life death. It turns first to process to escape from God, and then tries by man's own powers to turn process into a godless eternity.

The "time and times and the dividing of time" is an indeterminate but limited period of history. "Times" being plural, the scope and length of its reference is definitely beyond our knowledge. There is an avoidance of definite dating, but a specific statement of the fixed limitations of "the little horn's" sway. The half-time will mark a sudden collapse at the approach of seeming victory. "The little horn," lacking in the imperial pomp of his predecessors but surpassing them in pretensions, shall be succeeded by the kingdom of God, whose unbroken sway shall continue throughout time and eternity.

The seventy years of captivity were nearing their end when Daniel saw this vision. To his grief, instead of the restoration of the theocracy in Jerusalem, he saw a long sway of empire, succeeded by a messianic kingdom very clearly dissociated from Israel. It is no less dissociated from ecclesiastical pretensions and dreams. This is a political prophecy. The kingdom of God is not depicted as a political kingdom, but its unmistakable sovereignty in the political as in every other sphere is plainly affirmed. To separate that kingdom therefore from the economic, political, and educational aspects of world order, and from reference to the messianic pretensions of these and other activities of man, is to do violence to the kingdom and to misunderstand it. While the kingdom is not of this world in that it is primarily and originally an eternal order, its triumph in and over this world is set forth in the resurrection, a historical event, and shall be developed in terms of the whole of history.

DANIEL 8: THE PERSPECTIVES OF HISTORY

"In the third year of the reign of king Belshazzar" (8:1) another vision came to Daniel, one concerning the second and third empires. The vision was thus prior in time to the events of Daniel 5.

The locale of the vision is Shusan, or Susa, the chief capital of the Persian Empire in its days of power. Daniel 8:2 and 8:16 make clear that the entire vision, from the days of Medo-Persian power, through Antiochus Epiphanes, is from Shusan, a striking fact, in that the center of the stage *as far as action is concerned* is only briefly Shushan. The *perspective,* therefore, is Shushan, because the faith and philosophy of that fortress and seat of empire remained the perspective of its successors until Rome appeared on the scene.

The organic conception of kingship and its assertion *of the continuity of people with king, and of king with the divine,* is thus the governing principle of this vision, since this concept came into clearest focus in the Medo-Persian Empire and governed subsequent empires, influencing also Rome to a marked degree. However, in Rome, despite the very marked oriental influences, the legalistic principle triumphed as the abiding factor in subsequent Western and now world history, although not without conflicts, in that both concepts were transmitted to and through Rome.

The Greek contempt of Persian power was stated by Plutarch in his comments in his life of Artaxerxes II: "The Persian king and his empire were mighty indeed in gold and luxury and women, but otherwise were a mere show and vain display," but much of this contempt was based on envy, and the Greeks were not only concerned with conquest in the East, but power in terms of that golden East. Thus Alexander and his four successors took over the Medo-Persian concept of kingship to a marked degree. Plutarch cited a pointed example of the extremes to which the Persian concept of kingship was carried. Artaxerxes II married his own daughter, Atossa, declaring "her to be his lawful wife, overriding all the principles and the laws by which the Greeks hold themselves bound, and regarding himself as divinely appointed for a law to the Persians, and the supreme arbitrator of good and evil." These same ends, the overriding of good and evil by man the law-giver, and the deification of man, were also the ultimate goals of Roman legalism, but the Persian concept sought it in the organic unity of society in the god-king, the Roman heirs in the legal rights of individual man, for whose sake law, government, and society exist.

Daniel saw the Medo-Persian Empire as a ram, "and the two horns were high; but one was higher than the other, and the higher came up last" (8:3). According to Keil, "In *Bundehesch* the guardian spirit of the Persian kingdom appears under the form of a ram with clean feet and sharp-pointed horns, and, according to Amm. Marcell. xix.1, the Persian king, when he stood at the head of his army, bore, instead of the diadem, the head of the ram."[1] The power of this empire Daniel saw expanding markedly in every direction save the east: "He did according to his will, and became great"(8:4). "His will," Young has pointed out, means "he did exactly as he wished, indicating arbitrary, despotic power."[2]

However, a "he-goat" rises, Alexander the Great, who, Young observes, "came to be known as 'he of the two horns,' for he had himself represented with two horns to prove he was a son of the ram-headed Ammon of Libya."[3] Ammon, or Amon, of Egypt and Libya, also identified with Jupiter and Zeus by the classical writers, was represented either by a seated figure of a man with a ram's head, or an entire ram of blue; in his honor, the flesh of the ram was abstained from by the inhabitants of the Thebaid. His name appears on Egyptian monuments as Amn or Amn-Re (Amon the Sun). The Amon of Thebes had simply a human form, was called "king of the gods," and was virtually identified in one cult with the sun, in another with the Egyptian Pan. Judgment is pronounced on him in Jeremiah 46:25, "Behold, I will punish *the multitude* [of Amon] of No."

[1] C. F. Keil: *Comm. ad loc.*
[2] *Comm. ad loc.*
[3] *Comm. ad loc.*

The he-goat was an ancient deity, or symbol of deity, as Leviticus 17:7 indicates, being the "devils" whom the Israelites worshiped in the wilderness. The he-goat cult existed in Egypt, was present in the Pan worship, and was a recognized symbol of the Macedonian nation. Coins of Archelaus, king of Macedon (413 B.C.), represent on the reverse side a he-goat, and, much later, the conquest by Alexander of Persia is represented on a gem by an engraving of "two heads united at their occiputs, the one that of a ram, the other that of a one-horned goat."[4] Thus, Alexander was the great horn and founder of the Macedonian Empire, and the transmitter of the Persian Empire's life and rationale by his absorption of that faith into his own structure. The presumptuous and arrogant power of Alexander is depicted in 8:8, "he waxed very great" or powerful and successful in his own sight. The anger of the Greeks (8:7) was also notable, and the desire to overthrow Persia equated with an attempt to redress history. However, in the midst of his power, Alexander "was broken," dying at the age of thirty-three, and the empire divided among "four notable ones" (8:8), the four generals, a fifth, Antigonus, being early defeated at Ipsus, 301 B.C., so that twenty years after Alexander's death in 323 B.C. the kingdom fell to four generals. Lysimachus took Thrace and Bithynia, and possibly all Asia Minor. Cassander gained Macedonia and Greece. Ptolemy took Egypt and contiguous territories, and Seleucus gained Syria, Babylon, and the Eastern countries as far as India.

Out of the Syrian power, some generations later, from insignificance to great power and exaltation, "went forth one horn from littleness, and it became exceeding great."[5] This was Antiochus IV, Theos, Epiphanes, Nicephorus, as he called himself reigning from 175 to 164 B.C. Antiochus began life as a hostage of Rome, had little faith in any god save the Roman war god, and fortresses were his true temples. His policy with regard to the Jews seems inconsistent, in view of his usually liberal method of procedure, but sprang out of a passionate desire to consummate his concept of the state, the union of people and king as a divine and organic unity, the king

---

[4] John M'Clintock and James Strong *Cyclopaedia of Biblical, Theological, and Ecclesiastical Literature*, III, p. 899f.
[5] Young's trans.: *Comm.* 8:9.

himself manifesting this deity in his own person, the focus of historical and divine process. It is not surprising that Jerusalem and "the pleasant land" or, better, "The Desire" (8:9), as Canaan was called (Ezek. 20:26; cf. Jer. 3:19; Dan. 11:16, 41) should draw his attention, in that its faith was a radical offense to every aspect of his own philosophy. The Jews were in process of being Hellenized in terms of this Syrian Hellenism, and might have been radically syncretized, had not Antiochus supported flagrant corruption and murder by the Hellenistic priests. Antiochus Epiphanes, called also Epimanes, the Insane, by parody, sought to "stamp" out every trace of biblical faith (8:10, 11), ordering the adoption of Greek religion, consecrating, in December, 168 B.C., the Temple of Jehovah in Jerusalem to the Olympian Zeus, setting up his statue and sacrificing a pig in his honor. These actions precipitated the Maccabean revolt.

> V. 12. *And a host was given upon the Continual in transgression, and it cast truth to the ground, and it wrought and prospered.* In giving the above translation, I am merely setting forth what the text seems to mean. . . . Thus, an host (i.e., many of the Israelites), on account of transgression (i.e., apostasy from God), will be given up (delivered up in transgression) together with (i.e., thereon, at the same time) the Continual sacrifices.

> Further, the horn cast down truth (i.e., the objective truth, manifested in the worship of God) to the ground, and prospered in his actions. Cf. I Macc. 1:43-52, 56, 60 for the historical fulfillments.[6]

The length of this casting down is 2300 days (8:14), after which the sanctuary is cleansed. Keil rightly interpreted this time, a little short of six years, to mean not quite the full judgment of God on Israel, which full judgment fell in A.D. 66-70 for their culminating apostasy. The apostasy and punishment under Antiochus are described as coming near the end of time, i.e., the Old Testament era (8:17). It will be a manifestation of God's "indignation" (8:19) regarding Israel's apostasy. The "transgressors" of 8:23 are the apostate and compromising Jews. Antiochus is raised up by God

[6] E. J. Young: *Comm. ad loc.* For the extent of the Jewish apostasy, see Josef Kastein: *History and Destiny of the Jews.* New York: Garden City Publishing Co., 1936, pp. 94-102.

to punish Israel and is also thrown down by God (8:24, 25), "broken without hand," without human agency.

This vision, with its further statement of Israel's being set aside by God, had for Daniel the added horror of Israel's apostasy, with its hint of a culminating apostasy at the end, and it accordingly left him deeply disturbed and physically ill (8:26, 27).

What is the relationship of this "little horn" of the Old Testament era to that of the New Testament age, as depicted in 7:8, 24-26? The comparison of either, both *political* figures, to Antichrist, a *religious* and *ecclesiastical* figure, is, as we have seen, incorrect. The Old Testament "little horn," Antiochus Epiphanes, appeared as an off-shoot of the three great empires, Babylon, Medo-Persia, and Macedonia, and their organic concept of kingship, of heaven on earth by means of this concept of continuity which united heaven and earth. The "little horn" of the New Testament age similarly comes after the fulness of the development of the Roman concept of the kingdom of man and represents its idea of world peace through world law, salvation by law, and continuity with the ultimate powers of creation by means of entrance into their potency through legality and law. Thus, this first is viewed from Shushan, from the high point of Oriental conception of the fulfilment of man, and the second, from the perspective of Rome, the fourth monarchy, seen as powers emanating from the fourth empire. Each is an end product. Each forces the issue to its ultimate implications, and both are destroyed by God, and, with the second, its destruction is made the beginning of the mature and open power of the true kingdom of God.

DANIEL 9: "CONFUSION OF FACES"

Daniel 9 records a prayer and the answer to that prayer. Daniel, "in the first year of Darius the son of Ahasuerus, of the seed of the Medes, which was made king over the realm of the Chaldeans" (9:1), was in earnest prayer as a result of his study of Jeremiah, in particular of Jeremiah 25:11, and c. 29 (9:2), and also of Deuteronomy, as vv. 11-15 clearly indicate. The predicted seventy years of captivity were virtually ended, and deliverance accordingly nigh, so that, in terms of the promised restoration, Daniel could have rejoiced. Instead, he confesses his fear and grief for his people, acknowledging (vv. 1-19) that "all Israel," both northern and southern kingdoms, deserved their captivity, but, in spite of it, had learned nothing. Lacking true faith, for most of them adversity had begat no healing or redeeming experience, worked no repentance, so that, Daniel feared, more captivity and punishment was their only earned destiny. The indications are, indeed, that Phariseeism was a product of the captivity itself. The sin of Judah had been, predominantly, *syncretism*, a persistent attempt to unite faiths in the belief in a common core of religion in all religions. The most common form of syncretism was and is *moralism*, and, prior to the fall of Jerusalem, many of the earlier and flagrant practices of syncretism with fertility cults had given way to a cult of the temple and of moralism. In captivity, the contrast between Hebrew morality and pagan mores had deepened into an isolationist and proud moralism, the earlier obviously syncretistic moralism, and Phariseeism was the product. The judgment and fall of Jerusalem was already unique in history (9:2) as an instance of God's retribution to a privileged people. In view of their further contempt of God, Daniel was fearful for their immediate future, and, as one of the faithful remnant, prayed earnestly for grace (9:18). As a true believer and an enemy of moralism, Daniel knew that his righteousness was not in or of himself but entirely of grace: "O Lord, righteousness belongeth unto thee, but unto us confusion of faces" (9:7).

The expression, "confusion of faces," is a significant one. It is the confession of a godly man, and the beginning of his power. Moralism is not characterized by any such recognition, but rather by a *confidence of faces,* a self-righteousness which assumed that history is controlled by morality and works of morality. Thus, love is assumed to be capable of regenerating and controlling men, nations, and history. Liberty, fraternity, and equality—the moralism of the French Revolution and of subsequent humanism, politics, and revolt—are again instances of the self-righteous confidence that history is subject to man's dominion in and through works of morality. Communism and democracy are further instances of this same moralism in the area of politics, even as Thomism and Arminianism give instances of it in the churches. *Virtually all churches today are monuments to moralism, but the greatest monument is the modern state.* Fichte, lecturing in Berlin in 1804-1805, expressed the thesis of statist moralism: "A State which constantly seeks to increase its internal strength, is thus forced to desire the gradual abolition of all Privilege, and the establishment of Equal Rights for all men, in order that it, the State itself, may enter upon its true Right,—*to apply the whole surplus power of all its Citizens, without exception, for the furtherance of its own purposes.*"[1] Only thus, Fichte believed, could the great and righteous goal of humanity be fulfilled and the true order of man be ushered in. Therefore, all power to the moralistic state.

But righteousness belongs to God, and unto us confusion of faces, for man is by nature a sinner, a covenant-breaker, and, as redeemed man, walks only by faith and grace of God. History is not in his hands, nor can he see one step ahead. To him belongs confusion of faces. Responsibility is his, but responsibility is not the power to execute eternal decrees but is accountability to Him whose sovereign decree undergirds all creation. Only as man knows himself to be man, a creature under God, can he enter into this dominion as vice-

---

[1] William Smith, trans.: *The Popular Works of Johann Gottlieb Fichte,* vol. II. London: Trubner, 1889, p. 236, Lecture XIV, "Development of the State in Modern Europe."

gerent under God. Only as he grounds his words upon the word of God, can he speak with truth and assurance.

Daniel, praying in terms of this confidence in the sure mercies of God (9:9), was answered by God through Gabriel (9:21-27), whom he had previously seen in vision (8:16). Gabriel's statement has reference to Daniel's prayer concerning Israel, whose end had already been indicated, and whose course prior to that end is only incidentally dealt with now. The primary reference is Messianic. Accordingly, as Hengstenberg pointed out, "The announcement is essentially of a cheering character. This is true in a certain sense even of that part of it which relates to the destruction of the city and temple. . . . The sifting judgments of God are a blessing to the church. . . . Daniel had not prayed for the stiffnecked and ungodly, but for those who heartily joined with him in the penitential confession of their sins."[2]

Gabriel spoke of "seventy weeks" (9:24), or, more accurately, "seventy sevens" for Israel and Jerusalem, an expression again indicative of the fulness of a specified time. The purpose of the revelation is not a calendar of events, but warning, as well as hope in terms of the Messiah. Before the end of that period, six things will be accomplished, as Young has pointed out:

Negative
1. to restrain the transgression
2. to complete sin
3. to cover iniquity

Positive
1. to bring in everlasting righteousness
2. to seal vision and prophet
3. to anoint a holy of holies[3]

"To restrain the transgression," or apostasy and rebellion, was the work of Christ, who "shut up transgression by an act which He performed, namely, His atoning death. This is the only possible meaning of the words."[4] "To make an end of sin" has reference

[2] E. W. Hengstenberg: *Christology of the Old Testament*, vol. III. Grand Rapids, Mich.: Kregel, 1956, p. 86.
[3] Young: *Comm.*, p. 197.
[4] Young: *Comm. ad loc.*

again to the atonement, to removing sin out of sight. "To make
reconciliation for iniquity" means propitiation by the atoning blood
of the Messiah, the subject of the prophecy. Thus, the "seventy sevens" will be that period wherein God prepares the way and
then accomplishes the work of atonement. "Everlasting righteousness" will be brought in by the Messiah, the righteousness of God
unto salvation and a kingdom without end. "Vision and prophet"
will be sealed up or ended, the New Testament revelation of Christ
summing up and concluding the Scriptures. The anointing of "the
most Holy," i.e., Messiah Jesus, has reference to the full assumption
of His power and position with His ascension and the fall of Jerusalem in confirmation of His word and prophecy.

The "seventy sevens" are divided into three periods (9:25-27).
The first two periods are clearly dated from the permission to rebuild
Jerusalem to "Messiah the Prince," and the first "seven sevens"
covers the time from the issuance of the permission to the completed
work of Ezra and Nehemiah, and the second, sixty-two sevens, refers
to the long inter-testamental times from the rebuilding of Jerusalem
to the Messiah.

The third and last period, a single seven, shall cover the life and
work of the Messiah:

1. The Messiah shall be put to death.
2. The people of a prince (of the fourth monarchy) shall enter
   into Israel to destroy city and sanctuary, in a war that shall
   be as a "flood" and the end of it "desolations." This has
   reference to the war of A.D. 66-70 and Titus Vespasiamus.
3. The Messiah shall confirm or cause to prevail a "covenant
   with many," and this act shall be the end of the temple with
   its "sacrifice and oblation," both religiously and judicially,
   so that the temple will also be given over to profanation and
   destruction. "It is the Temple, itself, which is here mentioned as an abomination. Once the true Sacrifice of Calvary
   had been offered, the Temple no longer was the Temple of
   God but an abominable place."[5]

By this destruction, judgment is pronounced not only on the moral-
isms of history as institutionalized in the Temple cult, but also on the

[5] Young: *The Messianic Prophecies of Daniel*, p. 74.

legitimate function of the Temple as it sought to perpetuate itself as the sole vehicle of revelation. The exclusiveness of revelation cannot be arrogated by the historical instrument into an arrogance and pride wherein the vessel ascribes to itself the life of the potter. God, ever jealous of His honor, will not allow history to eternalize itself. The history of church, state, university, art, and society has been a lust for eternity that leads to the radical confusion of faces of desolation and judgment, whereas the confusion of faces of creatureliness and repentance alone leads to the life of "mercies and forgivenesses" (9:9) in terms of which alone man can stand and time have meaning and become itself a ground of joy and victory.

DANIEL 10: HISTORY AS LITURGY

The final vision of Daniel is dated "in the third year of Cyrus king of Persia," and placed at the Tigris (or Hiddekel) River on the 24th day of the first month, following three weeks of fasting on unleavened bread (10:1-4). Daniel's fasting included the Passover and the Feast of Unleavened Bread, and the remembrance of the great deliverance from captivity in Egypt brought to mind the captivity in Babylon and the recent deliverance. As the first event was followed by ingratitude, so apparently was the second now, as word from Jerusalem apparently indicated. Daniel was, therefore, in earnest prayer, like Moses before him, for his people.

The vision had as its purpose one similar to the Mosaic warnings of Deuteronomy 26-32, a declaration of the righteousness of God and His purpose.

Central to the vision is the description of the great priest-king (10:4-8), a description echoed in Ezekiel 1:26-28 and Revelation 1:13-15, both of which are further helps in the identification of this priestly and royal figure with God the Son. In Revelation, where the vision is given with greater details recorded, we see God the Son in the sanctuary, surrounded by the lampstands, declaring the meaning and course of history. All three visions are in agreement on three points:

1. This is a royal and divine person.
2. He is a priest.
3. His liturgy, or public work, is history.

The literal meaning of "liturgy" in its Greek original is public work, and the public work of God the Son is history. All things having been created by Him, and an eternal decree predestinating all things to their preordained and determinate courses, God the Son, by His personal appearance and incarnation in that history which He controls, asserts and demonstrates His lordship by His public work, His liturgy. The heart of this liturgy is indeed the atoning death on the cross and His resurrection, but inseparable from it is the whole warp and woof of history, whose every thread is His public work and manifest proclamation of His sovereign role as priest-king. The priest-king now as prophet declares the nature of His liturgy.

The degradation of the word liturgy to ecclesiastical ritual must not obscure the theological context of the word. For the believer, his liturgy is his daily life and his body his liturgical instrument (Rom. 12); for Christ the King, all creation, and history in particular, is His liturgy and the area of His open declaration of dominion. *Prophecy therefore, and specifically predictive prophecy, is an inimitable concommitant of the biblical doctrine of the priesthood of Jesus Christ.* A priest who is creator of and lord over all things, and whose liturgical role involves His entrance into history, will not only openly claim control over every facet and every last detail of that history, but assert His control by charting, mapping, and declaring its total course.

Such a claim will meet opposition from a fallen and rebellious creation. The fallen spiritual powers of creation challenge that plan and control. Their challenge, as manifested in the spiritual "prince" (not earthly kings) of Persia, is cited by the great priest-king (10: 9-14). In this struggle, He ordains that His human instruments have their role; thus, in His struggle with the prince of Persia, the angel Michael, "one of the chief princes" and prince or guardian spirit of Israel, came to His aid. While the sovereign and absolute control of history originates in the triune God, the ontological trinity, still the reality of the liturgical or historical role of man is real as the public work of Christ. Thus, while man's every step is predestined, and the very hairs of his head all numbered, his role is real, and no less earnest and historical, than the atoning death and resurrection of Jesus Christ. *Liturgy secedes to the church where history is surrendered to the devil.* Because of the totality of God's plan (10:14; Acts 15:18; Rom. 9, etc.), there is *a totality of liturgy: every aspect of history is a public work of the great priest-king, and only comprehensible in terms of Him,* and every grain of sand in all creation, and the totality of all things, can be known only in and through Him by whom all things were made. The true principle of interpretation is thus only in the sovereign God.

Moreover, God the Son speaks prophetically as priest-king to Daniel centuries prior to His incarnation, as indeed He does in the whole of the Old Testament, and in all creation. The significance of this fact must not be by-passed or obscured, for to do so is to undercut any valid Christian philosophy of history. The prophetic role of Jesus Christ and His public work, His liturgy, are not dependent on His incarnation, as neo-orthodoxy would have it, but are *the ground and condition of His incarnation.* The being of God cannot therefore be exhausted in His relation to creation, or seen as neo-orthodoxy does, as perpetually hidden because never prophetically vocal but only equivocal. The anthropocentricity of neo-orthodox historiography reduces God to the dimensions of man and accordingly surrenders time to chance and man to demons. But, long before the incarnation, God the Son spoke prophetically of those things decreed by the counsel of the ontological trinity, and His speaking was antecedent to and not conditional upon His epiphany. God's role is thus creative and determinative, man's role interpretative and analogical. The reality of man's role is the reality of creaturehood; those who see man's only possible role as autonomous and sovereign will invariably rebel against predestination as "destructive" of man, and indeed it is of autonomous man, the would-be god. But for man the creature, re-created by Christ in the image of God, there is a glorious role in the liturgy or public work of history as God's vicegerent, called to exercise dominion in His name over all creation. According to "the scripture [or writing] of truth," there is "none" who stands with the Lord in His warfare to maintain and develop His purposes "but Michael your prince," that is, Michael, the guardian of God's chosen people and, with him, those people. God's chosen ones today are the true believers, His people the true church, whose whole warfare is its glorious share in Christ's liturgy of history.

According to Revelation 12:7, "And there was war in heaven: Michael and his angels fought against the dragon; and the dragon fought and his angels." Only the true church wars effectually; only the true church comes to grips with the real and ultimate issues of history, and it alone knows both its enemy, its strength, and its objective.

DANIEL 11: LEGALISM AND ORGANICISM

The exactness of Daniel 11:2-35, minus only the names of men and sometimes empires, in its description of history from the Persian monarchy to Antiochus Epiphanes, is conceded by all scholars, but with a difference. For the higher critics, it is a cardinal ground for their late date for Daniel, and their claim that a Maccabean, familiar with the history involved, had written the book as a means of encouraging the persecuted Jews of his day. For the orthodox Christian scholar, this passage is another instance of predictive prophecy and came from Daniel's hand.

According to Daniel, the speaker is Christ, who supported Michael, and therefore His chosen people, during the aforementioned days (11:1), and He, God the Son, was instrumental in the overthrow of Babylon by Medo-Persia as a means of furthering His redemptive purpose for His people.

God the Son spoke then in terms of His promise (10:14) to make known the problems of the chosen people, i.e., the true church, "in the latter days," in the Messianic era (11:2). First, the Jewish church is prepared for her testing, and her experiences made basic to the perspective of the future. In addition to the current monarch, three kings would follow on the Persian throne, and then a fourth, "far richer than they all: and by his strength through his riches he shall stir up all against the realm of Grecia." Cyrus was then king; the three successors were Cambyses, Smerdis, and Darius Hystaspia, and the fourth, Xerxes. This attempted invasion of Greece was the height of Persian power.

Greek imperial power then came into focus in Alexander the Great (11:3-4), whose might, early death, and the fourfold division of his empire, "and not to his posterity," are foretold.

The next stage (11:5-20) is the struggle between Ptolemy and Seleucus, and their successors, *for Palestine.* Egypt, "the south," became powerful under Ptolemy Soter, 322-305 B.C., and Seleucus, put to flight when Antigonus took Babylon from him, gained support from Ptolemy and recovered Babylon in 312 B.C., gaining a realm extending from Phrygia to the Indus (11:5). Alliances, some years later, were formed between these two realms, Ptolemy Philadelphus' daughter Berenice being married to Antiochus II, Theos, who put aside his wife Laodiceia to marry her. When, two years later, Ptolemy Philadelphus died, Antiochus II abandoned Berenice and restored Laodiceia to queenship, with the revengeful Laodiceia reciprocating by murdering her husband first, and then Berenice, resulting in the prophesied failure of the alliance (11:6).

Berenice's brother, Ptolemy Euergetes, the third Ptolemy in Egypt, then invaded "the north," putting Laodiceia to death (11:7), and returning with much booty (11:8). Seleucus Callinicus two years later regained power "in the north," marched against Ptolemy, but was badly defeated, c. 240 B.C. (11:9). His sons, Seleucus Ceraunus and Centiochus the Great, restored the power of their realm and extended it through Palestine to Gaza (11:10). Ptolemy Philopator then attacked the Seleucids, or Syrians, and defeated them overwhelmingly at Raphia but was "not . . . strengthened by it," failing to have the character required to make use of victory (11:11, 12); one of the inevitable tests of victory is the ability to use it.

Antiochus returned to battle thirteen years later, after the death of Ptolemy Philopator, in league with Philip of Macedon and rebels in Egypt, and also "transgressors" in Judea who aligned themselves with Syria in the hopes of establishing their Messianic dreams or vision by the overthrow of Egypt (11:13, 14). Antiochus defeated Egypt at Sidon (11:15), only to fall victim to his own pride, but not without a full conquest over his enemies and his secure rule in Palestine (11:16). Antiochus married his daughter Cleopatra to the young Ptolemy in the hopes of controlling that throne, only to have her side with her husband against her father (11:17). Antiochus then conquered some of the islands of the Mediterranean, with no small contempt towards Rome, only to be defeated by Lucius Scipio Asiaticus, with the "reproach" or contempt turning upon him (11:18). The result was the eclipse of Antiochus (11:19), who was followed by Seleucus Philopator, who attempted, through Heliodorus, the prime minister, to seize the temple treasury in Jerusalem, only to fail, Seleucus himself soon perishing (11:20).

The next section clearly deals with Antiochus Epiphanes (11:21-35), who seized power, not rightfully his, "a vile person," who gained "the kingdom by flatteries" (11:21). By deceit and false peace, Antiochus Epiphanes stemmed the powers of his enemies, outflooding the floods of alien powers by his own means (11:22-24). There followed then the first Egyptian campaign, with victory for Antiochus, who then felt secure enough to begin his plans to overthrow the religious separation and independence of Judea (11:25-28). Another Egyptian campaign is also mentioned (11:29), occurring at "the time appointed," in terms of God's purposes. The persecution of the Jews for their religious independence is then described (11:30-35), coming after his failure, because of Rome's intervention (its ships coming from Chittim or Cyprus), to prevent Antiochus' capture of Egypt. The Temple was invaded, the daily sacrifice ended, and his idol established therein. The apostate or Hellenized Jews were in league with Antiochus, "but the people that do know their God shall be strong, and do exploits." The faithful would have their understanding increased and will give knowledge to others, but the faithful will find tragedy in these days nonetheless. As they make their stand and prosper, the hypocrites will quickly flock to their standard. The whole process, however, will be in terms of God's purging and refining process, to bring about understanding and historical maturation (11:30-35).

The concluding sections of Daniel 11, vv. 36-39, 40-45, are the points of radical divergence among commentators. Modernist critics, while arguing against any break in the narrative, nevertheless recognize a break of some kind. Thus, H. T. Andrews in *Peake's Commentary on the Bible* saw a break at 11:40, where "history ends and prophecy begins," an opinion which Driver also held. The reason for this opinion is the expression in 11:40, "And at the time of the end," taken to refer to some future era. And yet, in spite of this phrase, the balance of the passage goes on in perfect continuity with the foregoing! Moreover, even those who would refer 11:36-39 to Antiochus Epiphanes find it difficult to interpret it in the strict sense of fulfilment as with 11:2-35, where, with no trouble, events match prophecy, whereas in 11:36-39, the strict parallel becomes a forced one. Thus, certain things become apparent:

1. The entire nature of the chapter requires *continuity,* at 11:30 no less than at 11:36. Although 11:35 marks a close, "because it is yet for a time appointed," 11:36 begins on a note of continuity, and 11:40 likewise, by its return to "the king of the south," compels some kind of continuity.
2. At the same time, both 11:36 and 11:40 mark *new developments* and thus have an element of discontinuity, heightened by their more general nature, especially noticeable in 11:36-39.
3. There are precedents, in all biblical prophecies, most briefly and powerfully in Matthew 24, where specific incidents before the fall of Jerusalem are followed by very general descriptions of the time thereafter and the end times, for specific predictions to be followed by more general ones, for *events* to be described, and then *conditions.*
4. Antiochus Epiphanes is not, in 11:21-35, referred to individually as a "king," only once collectively so (11:27, "both these kings' hearts"), but is named simply as "a vile person," and then referred to as "he." There is thus an avoidance of dignifying him, whereas 11:36-39 refers specifically to "the king."

Keil, agreeing with most by referring 11:36-45 to Antichrist, remarked, "Essentially the reference of the section to the Antichrists is correct; but the supposition of a change of subject in the prophetic representation is not established." Keil thus held to continuity and development of a prophetic sort. "In the prophetic contemplation there is comprehended in the image of *one* king what has been historically fulfilled in its beginnings by Antiochus Epiphanes, but shall only meet its complete fulfilment by the Antichrist in the time of the end."[1] This is a most perceptive observation, although inaccurate in its reference to Antichrist. As we have seen, Daniel gives political prophecy, whereas Antichrist is a *religious* concept. And, while it is true that the politics is messianic politics, it is still clearly politics,

---

[1] C. F. Keil: *Comm. ad loc.*

civil activity, and by no means ecclesiastical. Thus, the reference cannot be to Antichrist, for such would be a radical break with the whole content of Daniel's prophecy. Calvin, as always a perceptive commentator, applied these sections to the Roman Empire. "By the word 'king' I do not think a single person indicated, but an empire, whatever be its government, whether by a senate, or by consuls, or by proconsuls." Such usage was already established in Daniel. Moreover, the four empires had been prophesied as rising and falling in relationship to the coming of the King Messiah.

> We lay this down at once; the angel did not prophesy of Antiochus, or any single monarch, but of a new empire, meaning, the Roman. We have the reason at hand why the angel passes directly from Antiochus to the Romans. God desired to support the spirits of the pious, lest they should be overwhelmed by the number and weight of the massacres which awaited them and the whole Church even to the advent of Christ. It is not sufficient to predict the occurrences under the tyranny of Antiochus; for after his time, the Jewish religion was more and more injured, not only by foreign enemies, but by their own priesthood. Nothing remained unpolluted, since their avarice and ambition had arrived at such a pitch, that they trode under foot the whole glory of God, and the law itself. The faithful required to be fortified against such numerous temptations, until Christ came, and then God renewed the condition of his Church. The time, therefore, which intervened between the Maccabees and the manifestation of Christ ought not to be omitted. The reason is now clear enough why the angel passes at once from Antiochus to the Romans.[2]

We can add, in confirmation of this, that "the king" or kingdom of 11:36 shall continue at least until (and, after that, its history is not *at the moment* of concern) "the indignation be accomplished" (cf. 8:19), i.e., the full wrath of God for apostasy be vented on Israel. This clearly has reference to the events of A.D. 66-70, and then both the apostasy manifested under Antiochus Epiphanes will have culminated and God's wrath or indignation will have been fully revealed. The wrath of God against Israel cannot be said to have culminated or ended under Antiochus Epiphanes, and hence

[2] John Calvin: *Commentaries on Daniel,* Lecture LXII, Daniel 11:36.

11:36 has reference to another "king" or kingdom, Rome. What is given here is, moreover, "a perpetual series," to use Calvin's expression (Lecture LXIII), whereby the true church is prepared for all the aspects of that fourth monarchy and its faith, salvation by law or legislation, which shall mark history during much of the Christian era as well as the concluding centuries of the Old Testament era.

According to 11:37, this new threat shall be marked by three characteristics:

1. Agnosticism or atheism will be the common religious attitude. Religion will be used, rather than believed. The organic societies were inevitably religious, and with pantheistic tendencies; the legalistic societies born of Rome are inevitably in their development alien or hostile to religion, having a rationalistic and legalistic approach to life, giving primacy to ethics over metaphysics at their best. This kind of formal agnosticism and atheism, while apparent in Greece after its fall, best flourished in Rome and in modern society, legalistic like Rome in orientation.

2. "The desire of women" shall be forsworn. The significance of this is that it constitutes a desire to transcend or to renounce creatureliness. Alexander the Great, who while having inclinations to various vices, sought by and large to avoid them, did so on the grounds of their indication of humanity. According to Plutarch, "He was wont to say that sleep and the act of generation chiefly made him sensible that he was mortal; as much as to say, that weariness and pleasure proceed from the same frailty and imbecility of human nature." The inscription on Cyrus' sepulchre moved Alexander deeply, "filling him with the thoughts of the uncertainty and mutability of human affairs," i.e., the horror of being human. Man today is filled with the same horror, and through science seeks to escape creatureliness, and by politics to create an eternal order. This *horror of humanity,* developed in antiquity, has come to sharper focus and formal power in the post-Roman states, wherein legalistic man hopes by legislation and by laboratory to enter into the kingdom of the gods. The goal in antiquity was *apathy,* to be passionless and hence

divine. The goal in modern life has varied between Hellenic romanticism, with frenzy and enthusiasm being divine possession, and cold, passionless legalistic rationalism and scientism, *abstraction,* as man's road to divinity, with the latter carrying the field by virtue of its command of science. In the Russian Revolution, which marked the triumph of scientific socialism and materialism, various leaders adopted new names to set forth their divine apathy, e.g., Stalin or steel, Molotov or hammer.

3. "For he shall magnify himself above all." Humanism, scientism, modernism, democracy, these and other developments of legalistic man constitute his modes of self-assertion and self-magnification. The Roman concept of law is the root of this assertion and its basic premise. It is the claim of man to autonomy.

This, then, was the new threat that arose in the form of Rome, in its first formulation, after the threat of Antiochus Epiphanes subsided. Antiochus had his followers in Israel (11:32), but by Christ's day, except for a remnant to be separated entirely from the old Israel, all were in apostasy. The line of division between Rome and Judea was a human one only: both were wedded to a radically legalistic concept of salvation. It was no accident of history, but its sure revelation of relationship, that the organization best perpetuating the Pharisaic doctrines calls itself the Roman Catholic Church, holding like the Pharisees to salvation by works, works of superrogation, the merits of the saints (or, with the Jews, of Abraham), etc.

Daniel 11:38, 39 speaks then of the devotion of this new empire to "the God of forces" and to imperialistic conquest and expansion, rewarding those who side with him in this program. To despise God means inevitably to despise man. Despising their own creatureliness, the sons of Rome despise also all other creatures and seek their self magnification through human destruction. There is always some Carthage that must be destroyed for some Rome to be free for its own brand of slavery. The modern imperial state insists on *neutrality* towards God, but *neutralism* with regard to the imperial state and its goals is intolerable, an affront to the majesty of the divine state. The United States, once the great international champion of neutralism, is today with Soviet Russia its great enemy.[3] No state can avoid making itself the divine touchstone of truth and character if it departs from the primacy of God and His word and law. The god of forces becomes the only god and the ultimate law, whether expressed in terms of the concepts of majority rule and democratic government, or openly avowed in the use of "forces" or "munitions" as the basis of law. It is a coercive and immanent power that is deified; it is the overwhelming of minority groups and of right and law in the name of the greater present power, the majority or the gun-wielder.

In Daniel 11:40-45, we have a further development of the prophetic perspective on history. Several things clearly appear:

1. "At the time of the end," the king of the South, Egypt, will attack the power of the fourth empire, as will also the king of the North, Syria, with the North triumphing in the empire.
2. He will also triumph over and absorb the land of the Delight, the chosen people or church.
3. The relatives of Israel—Edom, Moab, and Ammon—will be spared.
4   This renewed power will also overcome Egypt.
5. From thence he goes forth to overcome and overwhelm all rebellion and opposition.
6. His headquarters will be located midway between the sea and the mountain, i.e., the temple.

This passage is clearly symbolic, as is the preceding. To hold to a literal fulfilment in terms of Syria, Egypt, and Israel requires also the belief in the reconstitution of Edom, Moab, and Ammon, long-dead states and peoples. What, then, does the passage signify?

1. In the gospel age, the Christian era, repeatedly called the "end" or "last times" in the New Testament, not only will the legalistic state, with its concept of salvation by law, be the dominant power by and large, but it will also see a recrudescence of the organic state, pushing against and making inroads on, without overthrow-

---

[3] See Felix Morley: *Freedom and Federalism.* Chicago: Regnery, 1959, pp. 87-115.

ing or destroying, the legalistic state. The openly evil form, Egypt, the land of slavery and typical thereof, will not triumph, but the Hellenic form, as of Syria, will succeed.

2. This triumph will be especially notable in terms of the church, wherein an organic concept of man, the state, and the church, will cause many to stumble, as the concept invades and corrupts the church. Instead of the older legalistic rationalism, the Hellenic concept of the great chain of being will be the more basic concept in either realm. The slavery of the church will not be the obvious one of bondage in Egypt, but of Hellenic overlordship with the appearance of freedom.

3. The relatives of the church—those in the church but not of the church—will escape, since the corruption of the church does them no harm whatsoever.

4. Obvious evil, as of Egypt, gives way to the sophisticated evil and seeming good of Syria, i.e., its desire for social and religious unity, its affirmation of the apotheosis of man, its organic concept of man and society as set in the context, not of Scripture, but the great chain of being. The overthrow of Egypt is the triumph of moralism.

5. Evil triumphs, therefore, as a seeming good. Self-righteousness and the worship of man become virtues and are promoted as against all anti-social evils and all other-worldly faiths.

6. This position also means a radical syncretism, so that the order of the day becomes neither the open warfare of Antiochus Epiphanes in his attempt to absorb Israel into Syria, nor the outright persecution of Rome, or the radical and legalistic separation of religion and the state by the sons of Rome. Rather, it becomes syncretism. The sea is the world (Rev. 17:15, etc.), and "the glorious holy mountain" a frequent type of the true church. Thus, evil as it develops becomes more obviously self-righteousness and syncretism, becomes an attempt to have the power of God and the form of godliness in radical contempt thereof.

In the beginning of this vision, it was clearly stated that it was for "the latter days" and "for many days" (10:14). Thus, while it deals with the time from Daniel to Antiochus, its focus is clearly the

Christian era. The expression "latter days" is applied by the New Testament to the time from the first to the second advent (I Tim. 4:1). "Last days" is also frequently used (Acts 2:17; II Tim. 3:1; II Peter 3:3; Heb. 1:2, etc.), also "last times" (I Peter 1:20), and we are twice told, in a single verse, by John that "it is the last time" (I John 2:18; cf. Jude 18). The monotony of the history of Daniel 11:2-35 is the monotony of the bread of deceit. The note of progression in evil is introduced by Rome, with its legalistic concept of salvation by civil law, and then by the revival of the bastard Hellenic-Oriental concept of organic unity, as it invades the church from civil sources and creates a prevalence of its syncretistic faith. The organic state has not been without its triumphs in the area of politics. Hegelianism definitely furthered it in the modern world, and its influence on Marxism is marked, although the legalistic motive is definitely predominant in Marxist thought. Hitlerism was a definite revival of the organic state, as was fascism. But the clear-cut victory in the political arena belongs to Roman legalism. It is in the area of the church that the organic concept has triumphed, and existential and neo-orthodox thinking is obvious evidence of this victory. The Creator-creature distinction is basic to the Christian conception of the body of Christ and membership therein. *The union of the believer with Christ is not a sharing in His deity, but in His perfect humanity.* It is Christ as the last Adam, the new man who is the fountainhead of the new humanity, to whom the believer is joined. This distinction is circumvented in heretical ecclesiology, and man made partaker of the deity of Christ. The triumph of Antiochus Epiphanes and of "the abomination that maketh desolate," the symbol of man's continuity with the divine, is the modern church. The state Antiochus Epiphanes reigned over was a divine-human encounter, he himself the focal point of that encounter, and the necessity of organic unity made imperative the persecution of those separatist Jews who rejected the very premises of Syrian society. The modernist church today holds to an organic concept of itself in Hellenic-Oriental terms, and is a church in search of that divine-human state through which the redemptive order shall come. The revival, therefore, of the "north," of the divine-human society, and "the abomination that maketh desolate," while beginning as a *political* philosophy, has succeeded essentially in the realm of the church and has become the foundation of modern ecclesiology. It can speak the language of "the body of Christ," but its meaning has a radically different intent. Its headquarters is therefore fittingly between the world and the church. Even as the organic state and the legalistic state struggled for the Old Testament people and their land, with legalism triumphing imperially, and, from within Israel, triumphing religiously, so the two shall struggle for the Christian Church, with the triumph at first going to legalism, and then, but not finally, to organicism.

A further point must be noted. Both the first portion of Daniel 11 and the latter portion (v. 36ff.) have as their focus Jerusalem. Jerusalem is portrayed as the target of Syria and of Egypt, and it is also the target of the new kingdom of the latter days. Jerusalem here represents the people of God, the saints of God. At first, the hostility is not consciously manifested, but, with growing epistemological self-consciousness, as with Antiochus Epiphanes, it becomes open and direct. The people of God represent an alien power, and the kingdom of man therefore wages war against them. But the government is upon Christ's shoulder (Isa. 9:6), and He shall prevail, and His people with Him.

DANIEL 12: THE CERTAINTY OF VICTORY

The vast perspective of Daniel, historical and political prophecy with all time in purview, does not work, however, to the detriment of the personal perspective. Daniel's very private grief at the setting aside of Israel as a nation, and the creation of a new non-racial Israel to be the people of God, is always in view. It comes into especially sharp focus in 12:1.

The last prophecy began (10:14) with Israel's destiny and fall in view, and Daniel's concern and relation thereto. Again, with reference to "that time," the vision continues. Jesus' citation of 12:1 (Matt. 24:21, 22) with reference to the fall of Jerusalem (Matt. 24:21, 22 is otherwise interpreted by some, however), is of significance here. The fall of Jerusalem, and the public rejection of physical Israel as the chosen people of God, meant also the deliverance of the true people of God, the church in Christ, the elect, out of the bondage to Israel and Jerusalem, which were aspects of "the great city, which spiritually is called Sodom and Egypt, where also our Lord was crucified" (Rev. 11:8). Daniel is accordingly identified with the elect, and is to seek his identity therein, for "at that time thy people shall be delivered, every one that shall be found written in the book" (12:1). This new people of God shall not be confused with the remnant of Daniel's day; rather than a remnant, it is a multitude, ultimately the overwhelming majority, so that this description (12:2), setting forth salvation and pointing ahead to the general resurrection, can speak of the elect of God as the "many," and the reprobate as "some." Those who are wise or are teachers of the elect during the course of the oppression of the elect shall have all the greater reward and responsibility in the eternal kingdom (12:3).

Daniel's prophecy was given the status and dignity of Scripture, and was stated to be valid throughout time, as a means of true knowledge for men. The pursuit of knowledge, earnest but vain in that God is by-passed, will characterize human history. As Young translates it, "many shall run to and fro, that knowledge may be increased" (12:4).[1]

The conclusion of Daniel, 12:5-13, itself introduces, as Deane and Young have both noted, a new symbol, "the river" of verses 5, 6, and 7, a word in the original which indicates reference to the Nile, although the actual river is the Tigris or Hiddekel.[2] The double reference gives evidence of the generality of reference: every captivity of the elect, whether to Egypt, Babylon, the organic, or the legalistic states, will be in its entirety in the hands of the Almighty, and will be used by Him for His own glorious purpose. God is on both sides of the river with His angels, and controls every aspect of every step of history (Rom. 8:28), so that no captivity can end in other than God's glory and the destruction of the captors. Even as God miraculously delivered Israel from Egypt, and was about to use the Persian Empire to His glory, so in every age the wrath and treasures of men are made to serve Him.

The objective of all these events is the triumph of the saints, to be revealed with the collapse of the "little horn" at the end of "a time, times and an half" (12:7; cf. 7:25). With that collapse, Christian society shall triumph in every realm; then the suffering shall "be finished," that suffering which indeed is a cause for "wonders," since it seems to indicate the helplessness of God's people, and the failure of God to deliver (12:6, 7).

This answer failed to satisfy Daniel, who "understood not" and accordingly asked, "O my Lord, what shall be the end of these things?" The response is pointed: Drop the subject, go no further, for here the matter goes beyond your time and your concern, but it will be understood by those who need it, who are wise, redeemed, and mature in the Lord (12:8-10). Much as the suffering may seem to dominate the world-view, yet it is far from being the total picture. The daily newspaper may report fires, murders, and thefts, all in actuality far from depicting the day's events, in the main made up of worship, work, rest, and play, but the abnormality dominates the stage. Even

[1] *Comm. ad loc.*
[2] H. Deane, in Ellicott: *Commentary on the Whole Bible*, v. V. Grand Rapids: Zondervan, p. 400; and Young: *Comm. ad loc*

so, the tribulation of the elect seems to dominate the perspective, while far from representative of it. The persecution under Antiochus Epiphanes is compared to 1290 days, i.e., a little more than half of seven years, or the fulness of time, so that these grim days, not without their important revitalization of faith, can at best be said to represent the fact that the suffering of the true church, with every aspect thereof, will be only a circumscribed and limited element of history. Those who wait through these trials and attain their victories in Christ find the blessedness of the 1335 days, 45 days more than the earlier period. The two sums, 1290 and 1335, add up to more than seven years, and are not intended as proportionate representations of time and history. The first represents persecution; the second, blessing of a signal sort. History also has its eras of stagnation, development, groping, etc., and the depiction of these two periods as "days" indicates their limited nature in terms of the whole, and yet, by their relationship to seven years, their *importance* in terms of the meaning of the whole. Suffering or trial, and fulfilment, have both decisive roles in man's life and history. The culminating word is one of triumph in history, in the "1335 days" (12:11, 12).

The concluding word to Daniel is, "But go thou thy way till the end,"[3] or, as Young has interpreted it, "Go on as thou art until the end of life," and rest, and then "stand in thy lot at the end of the days," i.e., receive your eternal inheritance in the Lord (12:13).

Daniel is political prophecy, and it is confident prophecy, declaring the certain victory of the kingdom of God (*not* to be confused with or limited to the institutional church, which is one manifestation thereof), in history. If the victory of Christ is to be eschatological only, and in terms only of an eternal order, then Daniel is a monstrous piece of irrelevance. The sorry tribulation-complex of a smug and self-satisfied church, surrounded by ease and luxury, is certainly an amazing fact, one surely indicative of a masochistic desire for self-atonement by means of suffering. But the whole of Scripture proclaims the certainty of God's victory in time and in eternity, and the resurrection is the bold and uncompromising declaration of that victory in time. *There can be no retreat from victory without a corresponding*

---

[3] *Comm. ad loc.*

retreat from Christ. The Great Commission, with its confident command to make disciples of all nations (Matt. 28:19), was no mere hyperbole or vain expression of wistful hope, but the assured promise of Him who could say, "All power is given unto me in heaven and in earth" (Matt. 28:18), "Go ye therefore" (Matt. 28:19). Unhappily, since the day of Calvary, the church has all too often been concerned with embalming Christ, while His enemies, a little more realistically, have sought vainly to guard themselves from His power. It is high time to proclaim the power of His resurrection.

The resurrection is given in Daniel 12:2 as the keynote of the gospel age, i.e., of the latter days. The "day" or time of resurrection began with the resurrection of Jesus Christ, so that Christians live in the resurrection era. The age has its tribulations, its battles unto death, but its essence for the Christian is victory unto life. Because of the resurrection of Jesus Christ, it cannot be otherwise.

Part Two
Revelation

REVELATION 1: THE GREATER EXODUS

The biblical concept of history, as declared by Revelation, was given as a specific answer to the agonized cry of a suffering church, given, moreover, through a suffering man, the Apostle John, a prisoner on Patmos as a result of the Roman persecution of Christians. Being close to the events of Christ's earthly life, the Christians knew the amazing and miraculous power of His first coming, His triumph over death, the miraculous works in His name through the apostles, and knew as well the certainty of His coming again in full triumph and victory. This knowledge accentuated their present helplessness—persecuted, oppressed, miracles gone, "For thy sake we are killed all the day long; we are accounted as sheep for the slaughter" (Ps. 44:22; Rom. 8:36). The two great questions in the mind and heart of the church were, Why these things? And, How long, O Lord, how long? The cry from "under the altar" (6:9), from those redeemed by the atonement of Christ, was clear-cut: "And they cried with a loud voice, saying, How long, O Lord, holy and true, dost thou not judge and avenge our blood on them that dwell on the earth?" (6:10). Revelation, whose true author is identified as Christ (1:1), is the answer to this question of the church of every age.[1]

---

[1] Concerning the phrase, "must shortly come to pass," 1:1, Alford observed: "This expression must not be urged to signify that the events of apocalyptic prophecy were to be close at hand: for we have a key to its meaning in Luke xviii. 8, where our Lord says. 'Shall not God avenge His elect, which cry unto Him day and night, even if He is *long-suffering* with them? I say unto you that He will avenge them shortly': where long delay is evidently implied . . . we are driven to the very same sense of *shortly* as that in Luke xviii. above, viz., to *God's speedy time,* though He seems to delay." Henry Alford: *The New Testament for English Readers.* Chicago: Moody Press, p. 1781.

Revelation depicts the world as a turbulent sea, restless, always moved, not its own master but acted on by the winds of heaven, an area without foundation, security, or stability. The saints feel the impact of the world and its fever, are buffeted by its storms, and feel the fever of its restlessness, helplessness, lust for power and security, and its shapeless mutability. They feel driven, abandoned to the storms of a wild and restless sea, and wonder at the place of God in all this.

The salutation (1:1-6) identifies Christ and the Apostle John, declares the eternal power of God to the distressed church, the omnipotent and penetrating energy of the Spirit and His abiding presence, and the redeeming Lordship of Jesus Christ, who shall destroy His enemies. While seven specific churches are addressed (1:4), seven, as the symbol of completeness, indicates that these seven churches stand for the whole church of every age, even as "seven Spirits" means the Holy Spirit in the totality of His being and activity. Jesus Christ is "the faithful witness, and the first begotten (or, firstborn) of the dead, and the prince (or, ruler) of the kings of the earth" (1:5), the prophet, the life-giving high priest, and the true king of creation. He has made His people a "kingdom and priests unto God and his Father" (1:6), an important declaration. Concerning the Christ, Psalm 89:29 declared, "His seed [David's son, the Messiah] also will I make to endure forever, and his throne as the days of heaven." This was a triumph to be revealed in history, and the priesthood and the kingship of the believer likewise has reference to history as well as to eternity. To deny the triumph of Christ in time is to undercut the validity of the resurrection and its implications for history; it is to reduce Christianity to an other-worldly cult and to make a retreat from life the essence of faith.

This Christ comes continually in the clouds of judgment over history (1:7). He identifies himself as God: "I am Alpha and Omega, the beginning and the ending, saith the Lord God, which is, and which was, and which is to come, the Almighty" (1:8, RV; cf. 1:4; 4:8; 11:17). The inscription, according to Plutarch (*On Isis and Osiris,* 9) at the Temple of Isis or Minerva at Sais, reads: "I am all that has come into being, and that which is, and that which shall be; and no man hath lifted my vail."

The heathen inscription identifies God with the universe, making Him, not an ever-being, but an ever-becoming, from whom personality is excluded: the Christian description is of the personal, everlasting, self-revealing God—who is, who was, and who *cometh*. We should have expected after "is" and "was" "will be," but there is no "will be" with an eternal God. With Him all *is*; so that the word "cometh" is used, hinting His constant manifestations in history, and the final coming in judgment.[2]

Martin Rist has called attention to other parallels. Pausanias, in a *Description of Greece* (X. 12.5) mentions "a song of doves at Dodona: Zeus was, Zeus is, and Zeus shall be." The Persian *Bundahish* (1:3) declared, "Ormazd and the region, religion, and the time of Ormazd were and are and ever will be."[3] The declaration concerning Ormazd is in contrast to that concerning Aharman, who "is he who will not be," so that it has reference to continuity, of existence rather than absolute and unchanging self-sufficiency. "Both spirits are limited as to their own selves."[4] The Isis inscription and its parallels assumed a continuous potentiality in God; hence, the altar *To the Unknown God* (Acts 17:23), i.e., to the unknowable god, is the most fitting altar to all faiths in a god of continuity who is forever continuous with the universe and hence forever hidden because never capable of full self-consciousness. The god of the Isis inscription, like the god of Karl Barth, is a god with a future, because of his unexplored potentialities. The God of Scripture has no future, but only an eternal present, because, as the totally omnipotent and self-conscious Creator, all is under His sovereign control and completely apprehended in His eternal decree. He lives therefore in an eternal present, whereas futurity is the role of the creature, and of false gods. The eternal Now of God is also basic to His eternal decree: total self-knowledge and total sovereignty lead inevitably to the sovereign decree. "Known unto God are all his works from the beginning of the world" (Acts 15:18).

[2] W. Boyd Carpenter, comm. on 1:8, in Ellicott: *Commentary on the Whole Bible*.

[3] Martin Rist in *The Interpreter's Bible*, XII. New York: Abingdon, 1957, p. 368f.

[4] See Pahlavi Texts, trans. by E. W. West, Part I, vol. 5 of *Sacred Books of the East*. Part I ed. by F. Max Muller. Oxford: Clarendon Press, 1880, p. 4f.

The pagan gods, as gods expressive of the concept of continuity, cannot therefore be trusted. Indeed, apart from true biblical faith, no divine power can ever be *trusted*, only either *placated, bought off,* or *blindly submitted to.* Being full of potentialities, such gods are never trustworthy, often lacking in even an ascertainable character. Some assume the dual role of both devil and god. Apart from predestination in its biblical sense, no love or trust of God is possible. In paganism, the unpredictable nature of the gods was reflected also in the unpredictable character of men, in the inability to see an absoluteness as basic to deity or as the sub-structure of human faith and life. The epic poems and tales of antiquity are thus stories which emphasize *situation* above *character,* and, if character is presented, it is against the back-drop of an ironic and grim fate which is oblivious to man's nature, so that character is seen as futile against situation. This concept of continuity led in China to the radical and completely humanistic relativism of Confucianism, behind which stands a metaphysical doctrine, continuity, which overturns all standards in terms of the ultimacy of change. Taoism is continuity logically developed and formulated. Christ, however, as very God of very God, is the Alpha and the Omega, the a to z of all truth and power, all-inclusive in His total control of history. If history is thus in the hands of Christ, its issue is victory, not the surrender of time to Satan with the reservation of eternity to God. The statement, therefore, of a prominent American fundamentalist in 1953, attacking all attempts at social reform in the name of premillennialism, "You don't polish brass on a sinking ship," is arrant paganism and radically at odds with Scripture. Revelation begins with a promise of blessing to all who "hear . . . read . . . and keep those things which are written" in the book (1:3), and "those things" were not a promise of defeat but a declaration of the sovereignty, lordship, and victory of Christ in history.

In 1:9-20, John described his vision of Christ in glory, a prophetic vision, depicting Christ as Lord, having "the keys of hades and of death" (1:18), keys meaning total control, and describing Christ as surpassing the sun in His glory and as the source of all light and power (1:16). He appears clothed in robes of judicial and kingly power. "The girdle is not around the loins, as though ready for action and toil (Luke 12:35), but is worn as one who rests from toil in the 'repose of sovereignty' " (Carpenter, *Comm.* 1:13). Christ is seen as present in the world in the church, in the midst of the seven golden candlesticks, or lampstands (1:12, 20), alive and present in His body as well as in eternity. Christ is hidden now from the world, but present nonetheless not only as King of creation on His throne, but as the true church and the Head thereof. The purpose of this vision is to give comfort and assurance of victory to the church, not to confirm their fears or the threats of the enemy. To read Revelation as other than the triumph of the kingdom of God in time and eternity is to deny the very essence of its meaning.

A familiar parallel between Genesis and Revelation is instructive at this point in emphasizing the radically historical note of the book. It is *apocalypse* in the true sense, "revelation," and its concern is, as the very first verse asserts, an immediate and historical concern. The beleaguered saints are not told of an end to history, or a rapture out of it, but of the *coming* of the sovereign Christ and His New Jerusalem into history. The parallel, then, is instructive:

Genesis	*Revelation*
Paradise lost	Paradise regained
Creation of heaven and earth	A new heaven and a new earth
The curse enters: sin, sorrow, suffering, death	No more curse: no more sin, sorrow, suffering, death
Tree of life guarded	Tree of life restored
Four rivers watering the garden	A pure river of water of life
Communion destroyed	Communion restored
Work cursed	Work blessed
Man out of harmony with nature	Man at peace with nature

This parallelism is, of course, deliberate and prophetic. Even as God the Son came and, by His incarnation, made history the area of victory, so by His continued work, history shall see the further implications of His kingship. Christ, as the perfect man, did not thereby *end* history in fulfilling all righteousness, but rather opened up the "last days," the great era of the kingdom of God. His resurrection was not a surrender of history and the material world to the devil, but a declaration of His Lordship over creation and the promise, as the first-fruits of them that sleep, of His victory within it. By His virgin birth, his perfect obedience to the law, and His resurrection, He became the last Adam, the fountainhead of the new humanity, and hence the fulfilment of time and history, *not* the means of escape from it. Premillennial and amillennial thinking has implicit in it a latent dualism.

Again, Revelation, by its extensive echoes of Exodus, not only in the plagues on Egypt, the name of God, the deliverance from Egypt, and the overthrow of enemies in the mighty and miraculous wilderness care, but by many passing details, invites comparison to Exodus. According to Luke 9:31, Moses and Elijah, on the Mount of Transfiguration, spoke to Jesus "of his decease which he should accomplish at Jerusalem," the word *decease* or *departure* being *exodon,* or "exodus," in the Greek text. The death of Jesus was thus *the true exodus* of the people of God from slavery to freedom, from sin and death to life and righteousness in Him. Hebrews 9:15-23 made clear that "the death of the testator," Jesus Christ, made His testament law and opened up that inheritance promised and shadowed in the old covenant for the people of the new. The material and spiritual blessings promised therefore in the old covenant begin to come into true force by means of the death of Jesus Christ.

Exodus 3:14 is echoed in Revelation 1:4 and 8. The name of God, I AM THAT I AM, is basic to the declaration, "I am Alpha and Omega saith the Lord, which is, and which was, and which is to come, the Almighty." Again, Revelation 1:6 echoes Exodus 19:6, the promise of God that His people would be "a kingdom of priests, and an holy nation," being now *fulfilled* in the true church, and more broadly, in the kingdom of God. This reminder of fulfilment is a promise of even greater things to come shortly. The Sabbath, ordained in Exodus as the day commemorating redemption from Egypt and as therefore the day of worship, is now fulfilled in Christ, the true redeemer, so that worship is now on the day of resurrection, "the Lord's day" (Rev. 1:13, 20). His appearance is as burning fire, and He is, as in Egypt, the harbinger of plagues upon the enemies of God and His people. The golden candlesticks (1:20), are seen first in Exodus 25:37, and the plagues are hinted at in Revelation 1:7.

There is a further echoing of both Exodus and Matthew in the beatitudes of Revelation. The law was first given in Exodus; Jesus Christ, as the true law-giver, deliberately pronounced the fulfilment of that law in himself in the Sermon on the Mount, the law now being, to those in Him, not a curse but the promise and ground of life, and hence beginning with the beatitudes (Matt. 5:1-12). To declare emphatically this promise of life, and the conditions of its fulfilment, seven (the number of fulfilment) beatitudes are pronounced upon the faithful, whereas the curse of the law (Deut. 28:15-68) is unleashed against the ungodly as the seven vials of wrath are poured out upon the earth (Rev. 16:1). The seven beatitudes of Revelation are:

1:3　Blessed is he that readeth, and they that keep the words of this prophecy, and keep those things which are written therein: for the time is at hand.

14:13　And I heard a voice from heaven saying unto me, Write, Blessed are the dead which die in the Lord from henceforth: Yea, saith the Spirit, that they may rest from their labours; and their works do follow them.

16:15　Behold, I come as a thief. Blessed is he that watcheth, and keepeth his garments, lest he walk naked, and they see his shame.

19:9　And he saith unto me, Write, Blessed are they which are called unto the marriage supper of the Lamb. And he saith unto me, These are the true sayings of God.

20:6　Blessed and holy is he that hath part in the first resurrection: on such the second death hath no power, but they shall be priests of God and of Christ, and shall reign with him a thousand years.

22:7　Behold, I come quickly: blessed is he that keepeth the sayings of the prophecy of this book.

22:14　Blessed are they that do his commandments, that they may have right to the tree of life, and may enter in through the gates into the city.

These beatitudes declare that all the promises of the law and the beatitudes, and the curses of the law, are seen in their fullest sense in terms of Christ's purposes in and through history. To this end, Revelation gave assurance to the saints that

1. God sees their tears, 7:17; 21:4.
2. Their prayers are heard and used to rule the world, 8:3, 4.
3. Their death or suffering leads to glory, 14:13; 20:4.
4. Their final victory is assured, 15:2.
5. Their blood will be avenged, 6:9; 8:3.
6. Their Christ lives and reigns forever and is victorious in time and eternity, 5:7, 8; 21; 22.

It is further declared in many verses, as we shall see, that

1. The time is at hand.
2. Jesus Christ is the ruler of the kings of the earth.
3. He is the Alpha and Omega.
4. He holds the churches and believers in His hand.
5. God, the triune God, is sovereign.
6. Christ is the eternal God the Son.
7. The essence of the church is its faith in Christ, that it is the true Israel of God, inclusive of the saints of the Old and New Testament ages.
8. The world is not a picnic but a battle-ground, one, however, of assured victory.
9. In the midst of all the struggle, the church will sing "new songs" unto the Lord, "an Old Testament term for songs of thanksgiving expressly made for unexpected mercies" (Thomas Scott)

All this is inevitable, because Jesus Christ is, as Revelation 1 asserts,

1. The faithful witness (or martyr).
2. The firstborn of the dead.
3. The king of all the earth.

The earth is the Lord's, and the area of His victory. The issue of the kingdom's battle will be no more a flight from history than was the incarnation and the atonement. God the Son did not enter history in order to surrender it. He came to redeem His elect, assert His crown rights, make manifest the implications of His victory, and then to re-create all things in terms of His sovereign will.

Jesus came, moreover, as the greater and true Moses, and, in a double sense, fulfilled that role. First, He presented himself deliberately as the true law-giver in the Sermon on the Mount (Matt. 5-7), speaking from a mountain, declaring the true nature and scope of the law, and asserting himself as the source of law: "Ye have heard that it was said by them of old time. . . . But I say unto you." Second, He was the true and greater Moses in His capacity as redeemer, delivering the people of God from slavery to sin and leading them to the land of promise, the fulfilled kingdom of God. As such, therefore, His atonement marked the beginning of the greater exodus.

The proclamation of that exodus, and the summons to it, were made formally at the two miraculous feedings. As John clearly reported, Jesus proclaimed himself the Moses who gave bread from heaven of greater power than manna. "I am that bread of life. Your fathers did eat manna in the wilderness and are dead. This is the bread which cometh down from heaven, that a man may eat thereof, and not die. I am the living bread which came down from heaven: if any man eat of this bread, he shall live for ever: and the bread that I will give is my flesh, which I will give for the life of the world" (John 6:48-51). The old Israel, however, was, as Stephen declared, always "stiffnecked and uncircumcised in heart and ears" (Acts 7:51), seeking constantly to return to Egypt, either physically, as at the beginning, or spiritually (Ezek. chaps. 20, 23). The wilderness rebellion was fulfilled in Christ's time. The rebels who said, against Moses, "Let us make a captain, and let us return into Egypt" (Num. 14:4), obviously preferred slavery to freedom. They had therefore no love for the lawgiver or for His law, whose preface declared, "I am the LORD thy God, which brought thee out of the land of Egypt, from the house of bondage" (Deut. 5:6). The house of bondage was for them security. The declaration of Israel in the person of its chief priests, "We have no king but Caesar" (John 19:15), was an open avowal of its other captain, any captain but God's Messiah, and a return to the house of bondage.[5] The true exodus came in Christ, and the essential rebellion was against Him. Christ, as the representative man, broke the bands of slavery and the

[5] K. Schilder: *Christ on Trial*. Grand Rapids: Eerdmans, 1950, pp. 221-236. Trans. by Henry Zylstra.

law, and achieved the true exodus (Hos. 11:1; Matt. 2:14, 15), so that the true calling out of Egypt, of which Israel's was but the type and shadow, came with Jesus.

He appears, therefore, in the center of the camp, the new Israel of God, in the midst of the lampstands, or church. His appearance is as burning and consuming fire to the enemy, but as a pillar of protecting fire to the people of God. He is their true sanctuary and their strength.

As He begins the great exodus into the promises of God, He too first deals with a mixed multitude, with aliens in the camp, with men whose hearts yearn for slavery, and hence His manifesto, the letters to the seven churches, and the summons to victory. The people of God were assured the promised land under Moses, but not without struggle. The summons, therefore, is to open warfare, with the assurance of triumph, and to him that overcometh, a "crown of life" (2:10). Those in the midst of the struggle must hence never lose sight of two central facts concerning their status:

1) All the promises of the law and prophets, all the promises of life as created by God, are opened up by the atonement. "The death of the testator" (Heb. 9:15-23) opened up the inheritance to the people of God. The covenant law, violated by Israel upon its inauguration, could be restored into force only by the death of the testator, Jesus Christ, as the representative man both paid the penalty for the offense of the covenant people, and rendered perfect obedience to the law. Even as that death had been set forth in the typology of sacrifice, as a shadow of the reality, so all the fulfilled promises, material and spiritual, of the Old Testament, were shadows and types of the promises opened up for the members of the New Covenant. Warnings are therefore issued to the people of God (Rev. 2, 3) not to stray from the covenant and its promises, as did Israel of old.

2) This pilgrimage to promise is the greater and true exodus of the people of God, who are thus summoned to enter in and possess the land. They are not to tarry, as did old Israel, in fearfulness on the borders and thereupon die condemned in the wilderness. The "crown of life" awaits those who overcome.

REVELATION 2:1-7: FALSE HOLINESS

Revelation in its entirety is a general letter and "the Revelation of Jesus Christ" (1:1), who declares, "I Jesus have sent mine angel to testify unto you these things in the churches" (22:16). It is therefore no wonder that John, as the scribe (1:4), spoke, as Ramsay has noted, "with the tone of absolute authority. He carries this tone to an extreme far beyond that even of the other apostles, Paul and Peter, in writing to the Asian Churches."[1] Jesus Christ speaks to the church of John's day and of all time with absolute authority and finality.

Revelation 2 and 3 are thus letters within a letter, parentheses, particular statements to certain kinds of churches of all time, whereas the balance of the book is addressed to all churches generally. The form of address is especially revelatory: "Unto the angel of the church of Ephesus write." Ramsay's comments with reference to both the "angel" and the "star" are especially pertinent:

> It is fundamentally the same idea of a higher and lower plane of existence that is expressed in the symbolism of the Angels and the Stars in heaven, corresponding to the Churches and the Lamps on earth. The lamp, which represents the Church, is a natural and obvious symbol. The Church is Divine: it is the kingdom of God among men: in it shines the light that illumines the darkness of the world.
>
> . . . Thus the star and the angel, of whom the star is the symbol, are the intermediate stage between Christ and His Church with its lamp shining in the world. This symbolism was taken over by St. John from the traditional forms of expression in theories regarding the Divine nature and its relation to the world.
>
> Again, we observe that, in the religious symbolic language of the first century, a star denoted the heavenly existence corresponding to a divine being, or divine creation or existence located on earth. Thus, in the language of the Roman poets, the divine

[1] W. M. Ramsay: *The Letters to the Seven Churches of Asia, And Their Place in the Plan of the Apocalypse.* New York: Doran, 1904, p. 79f.

figure of the Emperor on earth has a star in heaven that corresponds to it and is its heavenly counterpart. So the Imperial family as a whole is also said to have its star, or to be a star. . . .

The star, then, is obviously the heavenly object which corresponds to the lamp shining on the earth, though superior in character and purity to it; and, as the lamp on earth is to the star in heaven, so is the Church on earth to the angel. Such is the relation clearly indicated. The angel is a corresponding existence on another and higher plane, but more pure in essence, more closely associated with the Divine nature than the individual Church on earth can be.[2]

The obvious defect of this perceptive comment is its Platonism, whereas here as elsewhere Scripture is markedly hostile to Platonism and its ideas. Biblical thought is *typological,* never abstract, as is Platonism. Moreover, typology sees the reality often as manifest in history, not in an abstract and transcendental universe. Thus, typology in Scripture is of three kinds.

1. In one form, there is a threefold division: shadow—image—body. Thus, in Hebrews 10:1, the law of the Old Testament is defined as "having a *shadow* of the good things to come, not the very *image* of the things," which image appears with Christ; the *body* of the law is in the triune God. Similarly, in Hebrews 8:5, the Old Testament priesthood was a *shadow,* and Christ's "more excellent ministry" in "the true tabernacle" "in the heavens" (8:1, 2, 6) is the *body.* Typology in this sense sees the *shadow* in the Old Testament, the *image* in the New, and the substance or *body* in God.

2. Again, there is type and antitype, antitype being that which a type prefigures. In this sense, the Old Testament *type* is a figure or parable of the *reality* which appears in the New Testament (Heb. 9:8, 9).

3. The primary emphasis, however, can fall on the Old Testament fact. Thus, Melchizedek is the *model* or *reality,* Christ the *copy,* "after the order of Melchizedek" (6:20). However, this same image becomes altered when we read that Melchizedek was "made like unto the Son of God" (7:3), the Son becoming the *type,* and Melchizedek the *antitype.*

[2] *Ibid.,* pp. 67-69.

Types, moreover, can *prefigure* and *predict*. Thus, whereas reality is reserved to the realm of abstract universals by Platonism, biblical faith, retaining always the priority of the ontological trinity by the sovereign and eternal decree, whereby the temporal order is predestinated and subordinated to the eternal, nonetheless makes that temporal order a domain of reality by means of typology. *Reality is seen as a past, present, and future fact and is both temporal ana eternal, whereas for Platonism, reality is never temporal, having neither past, present, nor future, and, in its eternity, is both impersonal and abstract.* The great assurance to the believer that "all things work together for good" (Rom. 8:28) is possible only in terms of the double fact that there is an eternal decree or absolute predestination, and that "all things" have a reality, in that neither time nor any eras in time are excluded from the presence and manifestation of, and integral relation to, reality. "The angel of the church of Ephesus" is thus not an abstract universal or "a corresponding existence on another and higher plane, but more pure in essence, more closely associated with the Divine nature than the individual Church on earth can be." The "angel" is the church as shadow—image—body, as type and antitype, as model and copy; it is a church totally grasped "in his right hand" (2:1), and yet not totally in Him. *Reality* is ascribed to its full position in Christ, and *reality* is similarly ascribed to its present state of service and shortcomings. It is the church whose past, present, future, and eternal states are closely interconnected, all possessing reality and yet shadowing and typifying one another. This is the church *in the fulness of its life and reality.*

Thus, the believer's life in the kingdom is not a nullification of the past but the fulfilment of it. The kingdom is "the times of the restitution of all things" (Acts 3:21) and their time of regeneration (Matt. 19:28). The contempt of history is accordingly neither godly nor tenable. Non-biblical thought has always culminated in a cynicism with reference to history, seeing it in terms of blind chance or determinism, or meaningless recurrences. By seeking to unite God and man in one great chain of being, it has destroyed the very ground of meaning. All being becomes one, equally divine and ultimately equally meaningless; the one and the many are alike meaningless, in that man is lost, either in a sea of particularity, or adrift in an un-differentiated ocean of being. The biblical doctrine of the ontological trinity, as Van Til has shown,[3] undergirds the equal ultimacy, reality, and unity of the one and many; the doctrine of creation, with its Creator-creature distinction, gives the principle of interpretation, in that the Creator is also the source of meaning, all facts being God-given facts. *Typology* is an essential aspect of this interpretation, in that inter-relationship of the temporal and eternal, but without confusion, is asserted. Marriage, for example, has more than its physical and temporal nature and is typical of the relationship of Christ and His church, even as human fatherhood is an image of the eternal re-lationship of the ontological trinity of the Father to the Son.[4]

Moreover, redemption involves, not the bare entrance of man's soul into the kingdom, but the entrance into the fulness of life, so that the redeemed order is the true order, that order in terms of which alone life has meaning. Life, family, society, law, government, and other spheres of human activity have no independent existence from God and cannot long exist without collapse into death apart from Him. Accordingly, the redeemed life is also the entrance into the opportunity for the fulness of life in every sphere, and the spheres are now seen as truly aspects of the kingdom. Thus Paul, in restating the fifth commandment, uses a new term for "honor": "Honor thy father and mother" (Eph. 6:2). "Honor" here means, in the Greek, "to pay a price and then to pay honor," and hence has reference to the price of blood. This statement is to the covenant people and declares that the very spheres and structures of life in the kingdom are God-given and a part of the redeemed order. Christ's atonement not only brought life to the people of God, but the covenanted con-ditions of life, so that family, society, school, state, and every sphere must be claimed by the believer as properly his realm in Christ. True honor to parents, and to every aspect of the covenant, is to see

[3] See C. Van Til: *The Defense of the Faith* (1955), *A Christian Theory of Knowledge* (1954), *Christian Apologetics* (1953), etc., all published by Pres-byterian and Reformed Publishing Co.

[4] See R. J. Rushdoony: *Intellectual Schizophrenia.* Philadelphia: Presby-terian and Reformed Publishing Co., 1961, pp. 21-37.

their status in terms of the Word of God and as aspects of the fulness of life in the kingdom.

This makes clear a point emphasized by Ramsay, and bypassed by many commentators, concerning the relationship of the church to Ephesus:

> He (John) assumes always that the Church is, in a sense, the city. The local Church does not live apart from the locality and the population, amid which it has a mere temporary abode. The Church is all that is real in the city: the rest of the city has failed to reach its true self, and has been arrested in its development. Similarly, the local Church in its turn has not all attained to its own perfect development: the "angel" is the truth, the reality, the idea (in Platonic sense) of the Church. Thus in that quaint symbolism the city bears to its Church the same relation that the Church bears to its angel.[5]

Again, Ramsay's perspective is Platonism and clearly wrong, but his perception of the relationship of the city to the church clearly on the right track. As Ramsay with others has noted, Revelation gives us the head-on conflict of two great invisible empires, Babylon the Great, and the New Jerusalem. Visibly, that conflict was manifested between Rome and the church. Rome steadily sought to exterminate Christianity, or at the least, to reduce it to the status of a Roman cult dedicated to providing social cement. Rome could not remain Rome and tolerate Christianity, a rival far more deadly to its basic structure than Carthage. Two very real empires were clearly in conflict. Ephesus was a central stronghold of that empire in Asia, and the church of Ephesus no less important as a visible center of Christ's empire. Neither was a shadow in the Platonic sense. *The two are rival empires, but Rome is dedicated to the hatred of God that spells death (Prov. 8:36), while the church is a tribe of the Lord, in exodus from the world of that empire to the land of promise and fulfilment. The Ephesus of Rome is the Canaanite who must be dispossessed, while the church of Ephesus is the true Canaan of God.* This conquest will be "little by little": "And the LORD thy God will put out those nations before thee little by little: thou mayest

5 *Ibid.*, p. 41.

not consume them at once, lest the beasts of the field increase upon thee" (Deut. 7:22). Social order requires the slow process, but it must be steady. The church cannot grow cold in its love and service (Rev. 2:4, 5). It is not surprising, therefore, that the language of the letters is "taken from military usage": "to him that overcometh" (2:7).[6] *Two empires are at war, each claiming title to the same cities and lands.*

"These things saith he that holdeth the seven stars in his right hand, who walketh in the midst of the seven golden candlesticks" (2:1). The seven stars and seven golden candlesticks both refer to "the seven churches," i.e., the church as a whole. William Barclay's comment with reference to the verb "holdeth" is to the point:

> In this sentence *kratein* is used, not with the usual genitive, but with the much more unusual accusative. The meaning is that Jesus Christ holds the *whole of the Church within his hand.* It is not any one church which belongs exclusively to Jesus Christ; no single church is the Church of Christ. He holds all the churches in his hand, for *all the churches* are his and all belong to him.

> Further, *he walks in the midst of the seven golden candlesticks.* That is to say the presence of the risen Christ is in every church. His presence and his power are not confined to any one church; he is there in the midst of them all.[7]

The "ascription of divine dignity," as Stauffer has observed, characterizes Revelation 2:1 as it refers to Jesus.[8]

"I know thy works, and thy labour, and thy patience, and how thou canst not bear them which are evil: and thou hast tried them which say they are apostles, and are not, and hast found them liars" (2:2). Barclay has called attention to the first and in this sentence, an *"expexegetic and"* which "explains what has gone before," so that, as Barclay translates it, the clause reads, "I know thy works—by that I mean your labor and your patience." *Labor* is *kopos,* the "toil which exhausts," and *patience* is *hupomonē,* triumphant fortitude."[9]

---

[6] See Martin Rist: *op. cit.,* p. 382.

[7] William Barclay: *Letters to the Seven Churches.* New York: Abingdon, 1957, p. 19.

[8] Ethelbert Stauffer: *New Testament Theology.* New York: Macmillan, 1956, p. 248.

[9] Barclay: *op. cit.,* p. 19f.

The patience of the Church of Ephesus, however, was not with reference to heretics, who were sharply tested and put out; it had reference to their own testing under persecution, as the Roman Empire sought to destroy this bastion of Christ's Empire (2:3). This persecution had weakened their love (2:4), in that believers had grown weary of trouble and weak in hope. Serving Christ had become all battle, and the important and necessary dimensions of hope and reward (Heb. 11:6) had grown dim and remote. But faith, hope, and love are different faces of a common fact, and a man cannot long remain in true faith without hope and love (I Cor. 13:13). The loss, under fire, of hope and love meant a corresponding decline of faith. A church without lively hope is a church soon to be uprooted by Christ (2:5), and a church that rejects history as a dimension of faith, hope, and love is likewise under judgment. The warning to Ephesus is therefore a very grave one: either move in the full confidence of faith, hope, and love, confident in Me as the ground of victory, or you move in terms of death and removal. Nevertheless, some of their "first love" remains in their hatred of "the deeds of the Nicolaitans, which I also hate" (2:6). This sentence is a qualification of the earlier statement, "I have somewhat against thee, because thou hast left thy first love" (2:4). *One cannot love God without hating all that He hates and all that which opposes Him. Men who cannot hate are beyond love also, and incapable of either action or hope.*

"He that hath an ear, let him hear what the Spirit saith unto the churches; To him that overcometh will I give to eat of the tree of life, which is in the midst of the paradise of God" (2:7). That paradise which was man's first estate before his fall shall in a fulfilled and new sense be his inheritance in Christ. The tree of life shall again be the principle of his life and the essence of his redeemed nature. That tree of life is Jesus Christ, who declared himself to be that "bread of life" which gives everlasting life (John 6:47f.), and to be the source of "living water," a "well of water springing up into everlasting life" (John 4:10, 14). Christ is thus the ground and condition of paradise. There can be no escape from the imperial war in the hopes of finding rest and refreshing on the sidelines or in the enemy camp: rest exists only in Him, and in overcoming, battling in the battle of empires, in His name.

Ephesus, titled the "Supreme Metropolis of Asia" and a city of great commercial and administrative importance (an assize town), was also a city of great religious importance as the locus of the Temple of Diana. Its river channel required constant work to be freed from silting. Even as the church in Ephesus was a type, so the city of Ephesus had a typical significance in its life and faith.

No church can exist in such a center without *either compromise or battle: the nearer the center, the nearer the heart of the battle.* Paul had accordingly given Ephesus much time and effort, as had John. Here, at the center, the battle must be joined.

The victory, moreover was assured if the church stood its ground in Christ. The religion of the world was well epitomized in the priests of Diana, called *Megabyzi*, eunuchs. Ephesus, on her coins called herself the *neokoros* or slave temple sweeper of the Temple of Diana. Here was a priesthood of escapism, of flight from the world, a priesthood of castrated men such as God declared unfit for His service. Only the whole man, meeting the whole responsibilities of life, is called to the service of God the Lord. The Temple of Diana also possessed the right of asylum, so that criminals poured into Ephesus and made it their haven. The right of sanctuary in Scripture is limited to cases of manslaughter, i.e., accidental killings, to protect men from vengeance. The Ephesian Letters sold at the Temple were magic charms to be worn by believers. In its every aspect, the cult of Diana represented escapism, a flight from reality, and the justification of evil in the name of mercy. It was committed to death and the ways of death, and *its holiness was only castration. Every faith which has a contempt of history eventually demands that its clergy become, physically or psychically, eunuchs as the measure of their holiness.* This heresy has extensively infiltrated the church.

But the call to the church is to gird for continued action, to stand, fight, love, and hate *as men.* Men cannot refuse to be men, to seek flight into eunuchism and be in any degree less than an abomination to God; neither can they seek to be more than man, to rise up into heaven and be as God. These *twin attempts of apostate man, eunuchism and divinization,* have only and always their outcome in death. The tree of life is only for those who, as men, *overcome* in battle, who enter in and possess the land under God. Man is called *through battle to victory.*

REVELATION 2:8-17: THE FUNCTION OF THE STATE

The cities and churches of Revelation 2 and 3 are alike typical in their significance, and only to be understood in their full scope, not as limited and restricted institutions and epistles.

Smyrna, a port city, was 35 miles north of Ephesus. An outstandingly beautiful city, it boasted itself as the "Glory of Asia." Its straight and wide streets included the famous "Golden Street." Smyrna claimed to be Homer's birthplace. A free city and an assize town, Smyrna was important to Rome, even as Rome was important to Smyrna. It was, accordingly, one of the great centers of Caesar worship, which, in Domitian's time, became compulsory throughout the empire, with legal certification of annual homage required of all peoples.

In Smyrna, Caesar-worship was adapted to serve as the capstone and fulcrum of local life and religion: adaptation was the essence of the state religion everywhere. The patron-goddess of Smyrna was a local variety of Cybele, the great Mother Deity of the Phrygians, and, among the Romans, the Great Mother of the Gods, or the Great Idaean Mother of the Gods (Magna Deum Mater, Mater Deum Magna Idaea). This cult was one of the central foes of Christianity and long its rival. Cybele was the universal mother of men and gods, and was closely linked with nature, orgiastic abandon, and wooded mountains. Her priests were eunuchs called *Galloi,* who dressed in female garb and wore their hair long. Attis (or Adonis) was the son and lover of Cybele; his death and rebirth cycle was observed ritually as the winter and springtime, fruition death and regeneration of plant life from Mother Earth. Cybele was thus the great Asiatic goddess of fertility. Swine were early associated with her in early Greek and Anatolian cults, and the flesh of swine was not eaten by the people of Pessinus. The cult entered Rome in 204 B.C. and was credited with helping Rome defeat Hannibal. It was only much later, under Claudius, that the cult, in particular its worship of the sacred tree, was officially and fully incorporated into the established religion of Rome.

The human priests of Cybele surrendered their manhood to the divine goddess, nature's principle of fertility, in order to receive back for mankind the fertility of nature. This was, of course, an assertion of the principle of continuity: nature was in itself barren until impregnated by man's great work and sacrifice and rendered fertile. The Day of Blood, March 24, apparently was an annual commemoration, and, perhaps on the part of novices, initiation into this sacrifice. On March 25, the revival of nature was observed, the Festival of Joy (Hilaria), and universal licence prevailed, all men free to do and act as they pleased. There was very early an attempt to fuse this observance with Easter, which was called by some the Sunday of Joy.[1] The high priest of Cybele, at both Pessinus and Rome, was called Attis.[2] The name Attis pointed, not only to the god Attis (or Adonis), but also to Atys, an early king of Lydia, so that Attis was not only the representative of man who, by his death released the fertility of nature, but also the representative of the king, so that the focal point of linkage between divinity and humanity may again have been the priestly king. Asia was the primary and strongest area of this faith, although Rome gave itself to the cult extensively.

The mother-goddess had a very close affinity to statism and was indeed the religious expression of a political faith to a very great extent. Man, by his political activity, brings out of a barren, but potentially great, nature all the fruition of the state's power and effects the development of the life and welfare of man. Although the effort and sacrifice is a very real one, the results for man are incalculable: the Day of Blood leads to the Festival of Joy. *The emasculation of man is the social salvation of the state.* Moreover, the state tends then to become the great mother goddess and the citizenry, Attis. In Smyrna, in 196 B.C., a temple was erected to Dea Roma, the goddess of Rome, and it was the first city to do so, priding itself then and always as the city which both served Rome

---

[1] J. Bingham: *Works,* vii. Oxford, 1855, p. 317ff.

[2] Sir James George Frazer, edited by Theodore H. Gaster: *The New Golden Bough.* New York: Criterion, 1959, p. 315.

and received of her bounty, playing proudly the Attis to Rome's Cybele. Smyrna as a city had been dead and had been made alive, and, under Rome, "had an almost unbroken career of prosperity."[3] Smyrna was thus politically and religiously closely allied to Rome and in fact and in spirit a center of emperor worship.

Christ, speaking to this church and city, began: "And unto the angel of the church in Smyrna write; These things saith the first and the last, which was dead and is alive" (2:8). Christ's self-identification is a direct assault on Smyrna. As "the first and the last," i.e., the totality of all sovereignty and decree, and of all deity, all participation in divine being by other men and gods was immediately eliminated, and both the emperor cult and the Cybele faith denied. Moreover, the vaunted resurrection of Smyrna as a city, and the mythological revival of life and fertility celebrated in the Cybele-Attis ritual, were alike relegated to contempt and outlawed from history by the emphatic assertion that it was He who "was dead and came to life again' (the preferred translation, according to many); "was dead" is forceful, meaning "became dead" or "became a corpse." History is here set bluntly against myth, as it is throughout Scripture.

But if the Lord commanded history, why then did Smyrna prosper and the church go in poverty? "I know thy works, and tribulation, and poverty (but thou art rich)" (2:9). *Tribulation* is literally *pressure,* and *poverty* is *destitution,* so that the difficulty of the church is stated plainly by Christ; they are, nevertheless, rich, in that they stand with Christ and in a sure command of history, as against Smyrna's flight from history and reality. The statist faith of Smyrna represented a cosmic "monism," a conversion of both nature and the state into a bountiful mother who spared or sought to spare her children from all unpleasantness, whereas God the Father gave His sons in Christ over to the harsh reality of maturation. Theirs was the richness of *life,* whereas Smyrna had only *death with flowers.*

"I know the blasphemy of them which say they are Jews, and are not, but are the synagogue of Satan" (2:9). In a masterpiece of fantasy, Rist characterizes this statement as "anti-Semitism."[4] In

---

[3] Ramsay: *op. cit.,* p. 265.
[4] Rist: *op. cit.,* p. 383.

actuality, the Jews of Smyrna not only opposed the church but worked with the emperor cult to bring Christians to trial and death. Much later, about A.D. 160, the Jews took an active part in the martyrdom of Polycarp of Smyrna, even bringing fuel to burn him, even though it was their Sabbath day. This was an especial horror to the Jewish believers, who, like Paul, yearned intensely for the old Israel's salvation (Rom. 10:1), for the ties of blood were strong. Against all this, the Lord stated the harsh reality: the "Jews" are not the true Jews or Israel of God any longer, but a synagogue or assembly of Satan, the opposer of God. They must be seen historically, not sentimentally or idealistically. The members of this synagogue, instead of being in any kind of relation to God, were in open blasphemy against Him through His saints and hence truly "the synagogue of Satan." The Jewish Christians of Smyrna must therefore see their kinsmen after the flesh, not in racial terms, but in religious perspective.

"Fear none of those things which thou shalt suffer: behold, the devil shall cast some of you into prison, that ye may be tried; and ye shall have tribulation ten days: be thou faithful unto death, and I will give thee a crown of life" (Rev. 2:10). In the face of the easy life of the unbelievers of Smyrna, Jesus promised the certainty of hardship. It is a perverted and vicious debasement of Christianity which some preach, promising all kinds of happiness in return for positive thinking, or affirming that Christ will rapture His saints out of tribulation. The pious who testify, "Thank God, I'm saved, and all my troubles are gone," may well not be saved, and certainly are not honest. Christ promises tribulation, trial, and testing to His people. It is *the dead who have no problems,* or the living dead, like the people of Smyrna and Ephesus, adherents of a faith which held castration to be holiness, the diminution of life to be life, and the absence of vice to be virtue. The salvation of Roman and Hellenic religion was a *deus ex machina* salvation, a miraculous rapturing or delivery out of adversity into a happy and luxurious situation. Biblical salvation, as the incarnation underscores, is in the context of life and is not a deliverance out of problems and conflicts but the promise of strength to battle and to overcome. The promise of tribulation by Jesus Christ is therefore more than a declaration of singular honesty: it is a revelation of the very nature of biblical faith as declared or exegeted by the incarnation and resurrection of Christ, by the totality of His life. The quest for a *deus ex machina* salvation by Christians is thus a radical error and an offense.

The "crown of Smyrna" was a familiar phrase for the hill Pagos, with its stately public buildings, and the phrase again suggested a floral or ivy crown or garland, often worn by worshipers of Bacchus and other deities on ritual occasions.[5] Against all this imposing display, Christ offers the true crown, "a crown of life," in and through tribulation, not in isolation from it. "He that hath an ear, let him hear what the Spirit saith unto the churches; He that overcometh shall not be hurt of the second death" (2:11). The call to suffering, therefore, was not for suffering's sake or in contempt of life: no false sanctification is proffered therein, nor is it asceticism. The open warfare between the two kingdoms or empires involves tribulation, and that tribulation and battle is an essential step to victory.

The church in Smyrna was uncompromising in its stand, however much distressed by the hostility of Jewish kinsmen. The church in Pergamos, however, despite some marked strength, was not without compromise.

Pergamos, northeast of Ephesus, was a capital city, historically the greatest city of Asia Minor. Its famous library contained over 200,000 books, and the word "parchment" comes from *he Pergamēnē charta*. Religiously, it was dedicated to emperor worship, and also took the title *neokoros,* temple sweeper to the divine Caesar. It was also prominently devoted to the worship of Dionysus, the bull god, and Asklepios, the god of healing, whose symbol was the serpent.

Dionysus or Bacchus is best known as the personification of ecstasy and intoxication. According to one form of the myth, Dionysus or Zagreus was slain by the Titans when occupying the throne of Zeus, and a ritual of annual revival was a part of the faith. He was a deity of vegetation who also appeared in animal form (bull and goat), doubly connected thereby with agriculture and fertility. However, Dionysus was not merely fertility in the same sense as

[5] Ramsay: *op. cit.,* pp. 256-258.

Cybele but the ecstasy of fertility and the intoxication thereof.

Asklepios, known as *Asklepios Soter,* Askelegios the Savior, was a god of healing, and his emblem was the serpent, often the intwined serpent. In his temple, tame snakes wandered freely, and the sick, left there overnight, were believed to be healed by the touch of snakes.

Thus, the cult of Dionysus offered salvation through escape into ecstasy, experiential religion, and the cult of Asklepios offered a healing cult, while the emperor cult offered man his link *through the state* to the divine order. The Roman law and peace were the foundation stones of that divine order, and the Caesars the visible manifestation of that order and *direction.* Valerian, who came to power in 253, proclaimed the nature of that direction on a coin declaring himself to be "Restorer of the earth," and his co-emperor and son Gallienus inscribed on another coin *Ubique Pax,* "Peace on earth."[6] Roman authority had therefore as its direction, purpose, and goal this divine-human order, whose foundation was law. The fundamental function of religion was performed by the state, and the subordinate religious functions by the cults. Against this *law* and *authority,* the word or *law* of Christ the King declared His *authority*: "And to the angel of the church in Pergamos write; These things saith he which hath the sharp sword with the two edges" (Rev. 2:12). Wherever any state assumes "the good life" to be its goal, and a messianic order its function rather than simple justice, it must of necessity declare war on the kingdom of God and in turn be the object of attack by Christians, and this is as true today as in Rome's time. There can be no concession: Christ calls such a state "Satan's seat" (2:13). Today as then much of the church dwells "even where Satan's seat is" (2:13). The modern state assumes, with the consent of compromising and false churches, the role of salvation and religion, and leaves the peripheral comforts and duties of religion to the churches. By and large, however, the church in Pergamos had stood faithful. It had moved into a direct challenge to the empire: "dwellest" (*katoikein*) implies the establishment of a

[6] Ethelbert Stauffer: *Christ and the Caesars.* Philadelphia: Westminster, 1955, p. 238-240.

fixed and permanent resident. The church was claiming the king-doms of this world for Christ, and witnessing faithfully even unto death, as in the case of Antipas (2:13). Conflict was inevitable, since "Satan dwelleth" (*katoikei*) at the same place, claiming the kingdom for Caesar. But the sword is not in Rome's hand but in the Lord's, whose very word (2:16) carries more authority and power than all the might of Rome. If they will not fight for the Lord, they must fight against Him (2:16). The sword He carries, more-over, is the Roman two-edged sword, not an Oriental weapon. The sword was the emblem of Roman authority. This authority Christ claimed as His own and challenged Rome on Roman ground. But it should be noted that Christ moves *first* against the derelict church and man. There were compromisers in Pergamos, followers of Balaam and the Nicolaitans. Balaam (Num. 24, 25, 31) led Israel through Balak into idolatry and fornication, into corruption as the means of overcoming faith rather than direct assault. These men were in effect accomplishing the same thing, seeking to merge the church and the world, to soften or eliminate the offense of the cross, and to make common cause with Rome in man's religious quest. Their primary sin was spiritual, and the consequences apparent also morally. But men cannot commit Christ to compromise, however much they may commit institutions to compromise, and the outcome of their compromise is not peace but war with Christ himself (2:16).

A twofold promise (2:17) is given to those who overcome:

1. "The hidden manna," supernatural sustenance, provision, and deliverance will characterize their daily life. Their endurance and success will be hidden from the world as to its cause but not in its effects.

2. "A white stone, and in the stone, a new name written, which no man knoweth saving he that receiveth it." The white stone had a variety of meanings in the empire. It was usually a cube or a rec-tangular block of stone or ivory. It was a symbol of victory, also of acquittal, again also a free ticket to food and entertainment. These and other meanings are all suggested by the usage here. The new name again was understood in the empire as having reference to the emperor and his title on assumption of power. With Antipas,

who was called by Christ "My faithful martyr," "Jesus Christ gave him nothing less than his own title. In Revelation 1:5 Jesus Christ himself is called the faithful '*martus*,' and that is the very title he gave to Antipas."[7] Thus, the imperial name of Christ is given to the triumphant believer and is his symbol of victory and token of entrance into the true realm of man, God's kingdom. This victory is hidden from others in that in its essence it is in terms of the relationship of the heart of man to his Lord, but it will be apparent in the integrity of his witness and the faithfulness of his stand against the kingdom of man.

It should be noted that these letters are summons to battle, not only in their technically military terminology but their outright declaration of hatred and war on both the enemy and the compromiser. David could declare, "Blessed be the LORD my strength, which teacheth my hands to war, and my fingers to fight" (Ps. 144:1; cf. also Ps. 18:34). War and conflict in any sense is both a product of a fallen world and a necessity therein. The capacity to fight is lost where meaning is lost, where evil becomes simply another facet of reality, or is relativized. As Robert Rendall has observed, "Why repudiate evil, if it be but part of ultimate reality?"[8] Rome had, by its faith, retreated from that basic war and was capable only of opposing those who disturbed its orderly death with hints of life. *If evil is as ultimate as righteousness, then death is as ultimate as life, and possibly more basic, since more prevalent.* Stoicism was soon to affirm this reign of death, and suicide became almost a virtue. The church's basic struggle, therefore, was to be with herself. The letters are written with this in mind. Today, as then, good and evil, life and death, all things, indeed, are equally ultimate for man, who thus stands unmanned increasingly by any hint of war. What can he war against, and where is his enemy? The modern post-Darwinian outlook is increasingly incapable of making any war other than *total war against all things.* Either everything is condoned, or all things savagely despised and stomped underfoot. The outcome, in either

---

[7] Barclay: *op. cit.,* p. 50.
[8] Robert Rendall: *History, Prophecy and God.* London: Paternoster, 1954, p. 47.

event, is death. The church's basic struggle is again with herself, and against compromise.

When men equalize good and evil, they hope with Adam to open up greater freedom to man, and to make *life* richer in its possibilities and actualities. But relativization is a two-edged sword: life, instead of becoming richer by the overthrow of moral law, becomes thereby on the same level as death, and no better. Nietzsche saw the consequences of this vaunted freedom and collapsed under its burden. Dewey could not explain why, having relativized all things, democracy should be held to have an especial value, or man's freedom and dignity be prized. The anarchy of values leads only to the frenzied hatred of and war against all reality, because reality has become the epitome of darkness by its equalizing absorption of all meanings. In this sorry equalization, the theology of the modern church has had no small share.

The progressive religious skepticism of the Roman Empire did not abate its religious nature but rather intensified it. *Man always insists on and seeks salvation, if not from God, then from the state, or some other agency which he divinizes.* The secularization of contemporary life is characterized by the rise of the state as the messianic order. The frenzy of religious revivals and experiences has given way to political fervor and revolution. The naive fervor of many earlier student religious movements has been succeeded by the passion of political radicalism, a *passion* in the religious sense, in that substitution, vicarious atonement, and intellectual stigmata are hall marks of the student devotee, whose capacity for capable and systematically positive action is as limited as his need for dramatization is great. Salvation is definitely the order of the day, and the state is the new god and juggernaut of secular and autonomous man.

REVELATION 2:18 – 3:6: DEATH AND CONTINUITY

Thyatira, a city of great antiquity, was a sentinel or garrison city to Pergamos and a major trade center. Its location was a poor one from a military perspective but an important one commercially. Its religion reflected its cosmopolitan character, in that it was radically syncretistic. The typological significance of Thyatira is readily seen in its economic life: "more trade-guilds are known in Thyatira than in any other Asian city."[1] This, the most notable fact in the life of Thyatira, was more than an economic fact: it was religious in significance. Certainly, the life of the guilds involved worship, and common meals at temple meetings, as well as frequent drunkenness and sexual immorality. It would be an error, however, to see the conflict in terms of moralism. Greek influence was sufficiently strong in Thyatira to color the guilds, and Greek guilds often had strict rules against disorderly conduct, were given to charitable relief to needy members, provided for funerals, governed themselves, made stated contributions to the general fund, and met and feasted at regular intervals. Corruption existed in the trade guilds then, even as it does in labor unions today, but it was not a particular character they shared in isolation from society. The guilds thus were not outstandingly evil in terms of general society, and much could be said in favor of their usefulness and their advantages. It can further be added that the trade guilds of Thyatira may well have been morally superior to those elsewhere, in that they appeared acceptable enough to the church to lead to compromise. The sin of the Nicolaitans of Thyatira was thus definitely not one of sexual immorality or a moral decline. Ramsay's remarks are here especially illuminating:

It seems therefore to be beyond all doubt that, as a rule, the Nicolaitans of Thyatira, with the prophetess as their leader, were still active and unwearied members of the Church, "full of good works," and respected by the whole congregation for their gen-

[1] Ramsay: *op. cit.,* p. 324.

eral character and way of life. The sentiment entertained with regard to them by the congregation is attested by the letter: "Thou sufferest the woman Jezebel, which calleth herself a prophetess, and she teacheth." It is evident that the lady who is here so rudely referred to was generally accepted in Thyatira as a regular teacher, and as a prophetess and leader in the Church. There was no serious, general, active opposition to her; and therein lay the fault of the whole congregation; she had firmly established herself in the approval of the congregation; and, as we have seen, she was so respected because of her liberal and zealous and energetic life she had deserved the public esteem. She was evidently an active and managing lady after the style of Lydia, the Thyatiran merchant and head of a household at Philippi; and it is an interesting coincidence that the only two women of Thyatira mentioned in the New Testament are so like one another in character.[2]

The sin of the church was thus closely connected with its virtues. The "works" or virtues of the church are very clearly cited: "Charity and service, and faith, and thy patience [endurance], and thy works; and the last be more than the first" (2:19). What then was its sin? The name "Jezebel" is a clear indication of its nature. Certainly, no sexual immorality can be associated with Queen Jezebel; rather, she dedicated herself to the advancement of an indecisive husband, and to the glory of his kingdom. Even the murder of Naboth (I Kings 21:7) was undertaken on her husband's behalf. Her hatred of Elijah and his adherents was based on the premise that they were a hindrance to the national welfare and a divisive influence. Baal worship was a deliberate act of political and religious expediency, designed to give common ground with neighboring states as the premise of a common alliance against alien powers. In this confederacy, the leadership would be assumed by Israel as a superior people. An uncompromising allegiance to Jehovah would be destructive of all social order, whereas a compromising Jehovah-worship had its due place in the kingdom, as witness the 400 false prophets gathered by Ahab in answer to Jehoshaphat's request for a prophet of Jehovah (I Kings 22:1-8). Jezebel came from *outside* the church, and was hence less acceptable; the Jezebel of Thyatira came from *within* the church,

[2] *Ibid.*, p. 336.

with every mark of sanctity, position, and honor. The goal, however, remained the same: *common ground as the basic principle.* The premise was simply this: *both Christian and unbeliever are working towards the same goal, the supreme good, and man's fulfilment therein. While Christians have the superior edge, it is basically one way the world over. There is no specifically and exclusively Christian goal, no Christian philosophy of history, concept of science or of society. The difference between Christian and unbeliever is a difference of degree, not of kind, and the same is true of their philosophies.* While not so baldly stated, this was the premise in Thyatira; it was certainly the premise of many Christian thinkers in the early church and throughout the centuries. So convinced were some early thinkers of the common ground, that Greek categories were used, and Christ was presented as their fulfilment. Plato and Aristotle became the cornerstones of Christian philosophy on the deeply rooted premise of common ground, the belief that differences cannot be of kind but only of degree. At Thyatira, the premise was manifested primarily in practical action rather than in theoretical thought, but it was no less real. These craft guilds, professional societies, and trade unions were concerned with the good society, with man's fulfilment and welfare. Despite their weaknesses and sins (and who is without them?), they were noble and moral in their purpose. Could the Christian isolate himself from them without being guilty of provincialism and without despising also God's general revelation? Cooperation must therefore be the principle of action, *morally circumspect cooperation,* but cooperation nonetheless. The respectable position of "Jezebel" of Thyatira indicated the dignity and morality of her participation.

The letter to Thyatira echoed the decision of the Council of Jerusalem (Acts 15). The purpose of that Council was not to put the yoke of Jewish legalism and *Jewish* separatism on the believers (Acts 15:5-11), but to insist on *necessary separation* (Acts 15: 28, 29). Much later, in Romans 15 and I Corinthians 10:15ff., it is apparent that Paul did not consider the statement concerning meat offered to idols to refer to meat eaten in the home, for no prohibition is made. The Council of Jerusalem *ended* the old Jewish separatism in favor of a common Christian separatism of Jewish and Gentile believers, whereby they as one body were *separated from the world.*

Thyatira was guilty of violating this separation and of seeking common ground; this was "fornication" and "adultery" by the church, the bride, against Christ, the bridegroom (2:21, 22), and, unless "Jezebel" and her followers repented, their hope in common ground would become the "bed" of their affliction (2:24) and death (2:23). Not all held this doctrine (2:24). Those who did, spoke of knowing "the depths of Satan" (2:25). This was quite apparently stated as a matter of pride, not of shame, by "Jezebel" and others who were all in good moral repute. It does not refer, therefore, to *moral* lapses or experimentation. It is a *spiritual* and *philosophical* principle, a *religious* affirmation. If common ground be affirmed, it is premised on the principle of the *continuity of reality,* so that God, man, and Satan are common and continuous aspects of reality. In terms of this, a religious profession which affirms a knowledge of the "deep things of Satan" will also affirm the possibility of knowing the deep things of God on the basis of continuity. Thus, the religious confession of the first involves the profession of the second as the goal of all being. This common ground concept, however, leads to a common bed of disaster and death for its adherents. (It is possible that the expression, knowing "the depths of Satan," refers to a Gnostic antinomianism, sinning that grace may abound, but the text does not seem to indicate two heresies in Thyatira, but rather one, namely, the compromise of common ground.)

Knowing "the depths of Satan" or the deep things of Satan meant also a concentration on the power of evil, studying conspiracies, Satanic forces, as though they represent the real power in the universe instead of God. For such a perspective, Satan is the present power and god, and the God of Jesus Christ is remote.

Apollo Tyrimnaios, the sun god, was worshiped at Thyatira. The line between Apollo's deity and humanity was a vague one: he was a god, but his tomb was at Delphi. His image in the sacred cave at Hylae near Magnesia gave men superhuman strength and rendered them sacred possessors of divine power. Helios Tyrimnaios Pythios Apollo was the union of diverse conceptions of the divinity and a union of the diverse elements of population in the city. This form of the name of Thyatira's deity is a forceful assertion of the principle of continuity. Apollo, the sun god, who wages war against Python, absorbs into himself, or reveals himself to be, at one and the same time that same Python. He is thus god and demon, good and evil, night and day, all things in turn as continuous with all reality. In the Apollo-Python myth, "the champion is the duplicate of his opponent."[3] Thus, Satan and God, in this view, are duplicates of one another, and all possibility and continuous potentiality exist in every form of being. The result is endless process without meaning, in that all possibilities are equally ultimate, good and evil, life and death, alike valid and alike invalid.

Against this infinitely mixed and perpetually grey concept of divinity, Christ revealed himself as both absolute and as light. He is that light which is a consuming fire to the enemies of God but the protecting and avenging pillar and cloud of fire to His people (2:18). He is "the Son of God," whose sovereignty over the nations is so absolute that none rules apart from Him (2:18, 26). This Christ demands the radical break of His people with the compromise of common ground and continuity: "I will put upon you none other burden" (2:24). To those who stand in terms of this faith and "overcome," keeping "my works to the end," He promises two things:

1. "I give power over the nations," to "rule them with a rod of iron; as the vessels of a potter shall they be broken to shivers: even as I received of my Father" (2:26, 27). The promise of Psalm 2:8-9 is thus fulfilled not only in and through Christ but in and through His people. This was a direct challenge to Rome, who held world power. The Pythian Apollo was also called Propator as the divine ancestor of the city, and linked the Roman Emperor as the ground of Thyatira's life and prosperity. The battle between the two empires seemed hopelessly uneven. Rome ruled the world;

[3] Joseph Fontenrose: *Python: A Study of Delphic Myth and Its Origins.* Berkeley: University of California Press, 1959, p. 470.

Christ's kingdom owned not even a single building into the third century, yet Christ won. Let men read history how they will, God not only governs it, but has always in all places manifested His dominion according to His word, to which all factuality testifies.

2. "And I will give him the morning star" (2:28). "The morning star was the symbol of world dominion,"[4] and Christ identified himself with "the bright and morning star" (Rev. 22:16). Power over the nations means world dominion, and this world dominion is inseparable from the great King, Jesus Christ.

This reality, however, can only be recognized by the living, the regenerate in Christ. Therefore, "He that hath an ear, let him hear what the Spirit saith unto the churches" (2:29).

The letter to Sardis is second only to the Laodicean letter in its harshness.

The history of Sardis is an ancient one. Once the capital of Lydia, its name called up echoes of King Croesus and untold wealth. It was one of the world's great trading centers and also a great natural fortress. The grim caution, "Be watchful!" (3:2), echoed an ironic fact of Sardian history. Its ostensibly impregnable fortress had fallen repeatedly because of appalling over-confidence. Because Sardis could be so easily defended, and attacked only with great and impossible odds, the Sardians were careless. But no enemy gave notice of its arrival: swift attacks took confident Sardis by surprise again and again. Ramsay called it therefore the "city of failure." Even as Sardis was careless in its watch, so was the church at ease with the world. Jesus warned the church that, even as the enemy took Sardis unawares, like a thief in the night, so would He bring judgment upon them unawares, and rob them of their false security.

The rich and easy life of Sardis made heedlessness a kind of natural religion. The very River Pactolus, as it ran through the city, was gold-bearing, according to Herodotus. Religiously, the city was devoted to Cybele worship, although the maiden Proserpine was extensively confused with Cybele or the Mother Demeter, and Cybele was the mother of the Sardian people, a healer, and a restorer of life to the dead. The assistance in the restoration of Sardis by

4 Rist, *op. cit.,* p. 390.

Tiberius after the earthquake of A.D. 17 attached that city more firmly to the emperor cult. Sardis, once a military power, lost its dignity with its empire, and, while remaining a wealthy trading center, became not only a secondary city but one identified with effeminacy and easy living. Herodotus characterized them as "The tender-footed Lydians, who can only play on the cithara, strike the guitar, and sell by retail." Barclay has therefore described Sardis as the city of "the peace of death," and "the church of the living death."[5]

"And unto the angel of the church in Sardis write; These things saith he that hath the seven Spirits of God, and the seven stars; I know thy works, that thou hast a name that thou livest, and art dead" (3:1). In Revelation 1:16, 20, Christ *holds* the seven stars or churches in His hand; now he *has* the churches in the very same sense as of the Holy Spirit. Even as He possesses the Holy Spirit in all His power and activity, so He has the whole church, and therefore is distinct yet inseparable from it. Man cannot therefore possess the true church or alienate it from Christ, any more than the Holy Spirit can be alienated from the Son. No church, therefore, can lay claim to the name of Christ and His Church without reckoning with Him in its every dereliction.

The reputation of the Sardian Church was good: it had a name or reputation and appearance of life, while in actuality dead for the most part. Its faith was clearly a form of Phariseeism.[6] The Sardian Church is summoned to be watchful or to awaken, "and strengthen the things which remain, that are ready to die." While its works seem outwardly good, they are not acceptable or mature "before God" (3:2). They must "remember" the faith they received, as against their present Phariseeism and appearance of life, and "repent." Failing this, the Lord will be, not their head but their enemy, who, even as Sardis' enemies took the city by stealth, will rob the church of her life and her privileges.

Those who are faithful and "have not defiled their garments . . . shall walk with me in white: for they are worthy" (3:4). The reference to clothing is twofold. First, garments could be defiling, according to the Mosaic law, in several ways: if mildewed by fungus or disease (Lev. 13:47), if made of diverse materials and hence in violation of the law of discontinuity and the principle of separation (Lev. 19:19; Deut. 22:11), and if belonging properly to the other sex (Deut. 22:5). Those who had not defiled their garments had therefore avoided the pollution of sin, common ground, and continuity, and transvestic perversion, in terms of their righteousness in Christ. Second, to walk now with Christ in white (Eccl. 9:8; Zech. 3:3; Jude 23) meant to walk in purity, festivity, and victory, in all three aspects being partakers of Christ's triumphant humanity.

Such overcomers will stand in "the book of life," the citizenship register of the kingdom (Ex. 32:32; Ps. 69:28; 136:16; Mal. 3:16; Dan. 12:1); they will remain forever citizens of life and of His empire, whom He will confess "before my Father, and before his angels" (3:5; cf. Luke 12:8; Matt. 10:32; Mark 8:38; II Tim. 2:12; John 2:23). The language is military; the robes are the garments of victory; without battle, no victory. The church that seeks the *form* rather than the *power* of life is in full retreat from life and from Christ.

REVELATION 3:7-22: FAITH OR SYNTHESIS

Philadelphia was founded by Attalus II (159-138 B.C.), called Philadelphus because of "truth and loyalty to his Eumenes," "as a missionary city . . . founded to promote a certain unity of spirit, customs, and loyalty within the realm, the apostle of Hellenism to an Oriental land. It was a successful teacher. Before A.D. 19 the Lydian tongue had ceased to be spoken in Lydia, and Greek was the only language of the country."[1] The city was also a gateway to the East and to an agriculturally rich area. While the Asiatic orientation was replaced with a Hellenic one, there was religiously a fusion of cultures. Dionysus was the chief deity, and Philadelphia was a wine center, among other things, but the Graeco-Roman forms and terms were united with Anatolian faiths. Sardis exercised the same unifying force among Lydians; Philadelphia also had a responsibility to Hellenize the Phrygians, who resisted the attempt in rural areas. The resistance was not integral but merely the persistence of the Phrygian language and ways within the context of Roman rule.

Philadelphia, like Sardis and Laodicia, was ruined by the earthquake of A.D. 17, and rebuilt by Tiberius, as a result of which, by permission of the empire, its name was in gratitude changed for a time to Neocaesarea. Ramsay cited four characteristics of Philadelphia which are pertinent to the letter: "first it was the missionary city: secondly, its people lived always in dread of a disaster, 'the day of trial': thirdly, many of its people went out of the city to dwell: fourthly, it took a new name from the Imperial god."[2] The second and third points have reference to the times of many earthquake tremors, during which the people lived outside the city for fear of collapsing walls.

Ramsay called Laodicea "the City of Compromise"; this title was no less true of Philadelphia. The concept of continuity which under-

[1] Ramsay: *op. cit.,* p. 391f.
[2] *Ibid.,* p. 398.

lay all non-Christian thinking made compromise of its very nature a virtue, in that it provided a bridge between man and man and between culture and culture. The more coastal cities were inevitably cosmopolitan and hence saw a blending of cultures attendant upon such a situation. Philadelphia and Laodicea, further inland and closer to populations of alien cultures, represented not so much cosmopolitanism and continuity within its context, as cultural synthesis.

Philadelphia, as the city of "brotherly love," had succeeded in fostering brotherhood between its area and the imperial masters. The brotherhood of Philadelphia was a pragmatic and relativistic one. The city was a missionary city in that its function was to bring about a pragmatic cultural synthesis, and its eminence rested on its successful discharge of this function. For the church to preach separation in terms of the faith, separation in terms of the truth, to a city founded on the premise of brotherhood and synthesis on pragmatic grounds meant that the church isolated itself and was of "little strength" in the face of a radically alien culture. Nothing seemed more impotent and futile in a city dedicated to synthesis than an emphasis on the antithesis of faith. But Christ nonetheless spoke of the open door and a great future for this faithful church.

Laodicea, on the River Lycus, was the gateway to Phrygia and was the meeting-point of three roads, from the seacoast, from the northwest, and from the northeast. It was a wealthy city, a banking center, had an important clothing industry, and was famous for its medical school and its widely sold eye powder for weak and ailing eyes. It was also a center of the emperor cult and received the Temple-Wardenship under Commodus, A.D. 180-191. Paul's concern for the Laodicean Church is reflected in Colossians 2:1; 4: 13, 15, 16.

Laodicea, founded in 250 B.C. by Antiochus II and named after his wife, was, like Sardis and Philadelphia, laid waste by the earthquake of A.D. 17 and restored with the aid of Tiberius. Again ruined by earthquake in A.D. 60, Laodicea refused aid, being now too rich to need it and too independent to receive it. There was thus much to commend in unbelieving Laodicea, and Philadelphia likewise represented the peaceful and cooperative synthesis of conflicting cultural strands. *The great temptation of the church in both places was to work in terms of congeniality to the local spirit of cultural synthesis.* In Philadelphia, this temptation was faithfully resisted, with the result that the church made seemingly little impact on men and their culture and had accordingly "little strength" (3:8). In Laodicea, however, the church had moved forward into the life of the city in terms of this strategy, and therefore felt "rich, and increased with goods" and in "need of nothing" (3:16). The church in Philadelphia was discouraged by her seeming lack of progress, while the church in Laodicea was confident of her destiny and importance in that city. The parallel to the modern church situation is a very marked one, in that the overwhelming majority of churches, including many ostensibly conservative ones, have either philosophically or culturally, or in both respects, effected a synthesis with the world as the means to power. The resistance to this movement is a slender line of protest, from John Calvin to Abraham Kuyper, and to Cornelius Van Til and others of the spiritual sons of Abraham Kuyper.

To Philadelphia Jesus the Messiah wrote, identifying himself: "These things saith he that is holy, he that is true, he that hath the key of David, he that openeth, and no man shutteth; and shutteth, and no man openeth" (3:7). This triune identification is in direct relationship to the situation in Philadelphia and the discouragement of the church. First, Jesus is "he that is holy," and whose often repeated commandment through Moses of old was, "Ye shall be holy: for I the LORD your God am holy" (Lev. 19:2). This was a requirement of radical cultural separation and dedication, a demand that man and society be premised exclusively on God's holy word and revelation. Second, Jesus is "he that is true," and, biblical truth being both absolute and personal because God who is truth is three persons, one God, the absoluteness of truth can be neither compromised by any cultural synthesis nor de-personalized and abstracted by an impersonal philosophy. Third, Jesus is "he that hath the key" of God and the absolute power thereof. The reference is to Isaiah 22:22; Eliakim, the faithful steward of Hezekiah, had been given the key to the royal palace, so that admission to the royal presence was possible only through him. Similarly, Jesus alone is the key and the door (John 10:9), the only way to God: "by me, if any man enter in, he shall be saved, and shall go in and out, and find pasture." Since that fulness of life ostensibly sought by all cultures is not attainable except through Jesus Christ, these words are a reminder to the church that no other attempt, however seemingly prosperous, can have any other end than death.

Accordingly, "I have set before thee an open door, and no man can shut it" (3:8). This open door is no way of escape but the way of fulfilment and of opportunity to victory in and through Him. Thus, not compromise, but a forward movement, a development of the presuppositions of biblical faith, is necessary. Not synthesis but the radical re-thinking of all life in terms of the word of God is imperative. The "works" of Philadelphia were not extensive, though godly: the church of Philadelphia has "kept my word, and hast not denied my name" (3:8). This is the *beginning* of faithfulness; development of the implications of the word and name for all of life must be pursued. To move in terms of this faith means victory and power: "the synagogue of Satan," the Jews whose thinking ostensibly represented hostility to synthesis but actually represented only moralism and pride, instead of triumphing over the church, would "come and worship before thy feet, and to know that I have loved thee" (3:9). This would be in fulfilment of Isaiah 49:23 and 60:14. Having kept "the word of my patience," they would be kept during the universal testing to come, one comparable in the cultural realm to the earthquakes which had shaken the city, but on a world-wide basis (3:10). Continue therefore to press forward in the race, moving in terms of your faith, that none other may seize that victor's garland or crown which properly belongs to you (3:11). Those in Philadelphia who were faithful servants of the culture of the state had their names inscribed on pillars in the temple of some god; for noted priests, a memorial pillar was added to demonstrate that they were the support of the edifice. Those who overcome in Philadelphia will be made pillars in the temple, house or kingdom of God; they shall receive a new name, the sign of ownership, a seal or brand declaring them to be the possession of God. They will also be identified by a new citizenship, "the name of the city of my God, which is New Jerusalem," paradise restored. They will also receive Christ's "new name"; as members of His glorified humanity, they share therefore in the name or nature of this new paradise man, the last Adam from above (3:12).

To the Laodiceans, who believed themselves to be successful in their relationship to the surrounding culture, instead of praise and encouragement there is undiluted rebuke from Christ. Again, there is a triune identification. First, He is "the Amen" (3:14) or truth of God "the God of Amen" or truth (Isa. 15:15). Second, He is "the faithful and true witness" or martyr. Third, He is "the beginning of the creation of God," beginning (*arche*) here meaning *origin*.[3] Christ shares His position with none; He and He alone is the truth, the way, and the fountain and creator of life. There can therefore be no common ground between Christ and the world except on the premise of His status as creator, redeemer, and absolute lord, the sole source and principle of interpretation in and through His word. Men stand on common ground as sinners in rebellion against their Creator, or as men saved by sovereign grace and now members of His humanity. To seek common ground on any other basis is to seek both a mediation apart from Christ and a God in antithesis to Him.

As a result, the Laodicean Church, instead of being the successful church it deemed itself, was neither hot (at boiling point, *zestos*) nor cold, but only repulsively lukewarm or tepid, fit only to to be spewed or vomited out (3:15, 16). The independence and wealth of Laodicea might be commendable traits of man in relationship to man, but they were no basis of relationship to God, who must be approached by the poor in spirit, they who feel their spiritual need or nakedness (Goodspeed), who mourn over their sins, and hunger and thirst after righteousness (3:17). True wealth is in the refining processes of God, a process of burning and chastening or education which destroys dross. There is no pure gold without the refining fire, nor true spiritual wealth and wisdom without the furnace of affliction and testing. It means putting on "white raiment." the

[3] Barclay: *op. cit.*, p. 97.

righteousness of Christ as our sovereign law and power rather than synthesis with the world. It means that true sight comes not from human science but from the radical acceptance of Jesus Christ and His word as the premise and presupposition of all thinking, including all science (3:18). Those whom Christ loves, He rebukes, i.e., brings conviction to them.[4] "Chasten" is *paideuo,* education and discipline. The church in Laodicea had sought to avoid His way in favor of a "simpler" path, and is now summoned to be zealous and repent (3:19).

The concluding word to Laodicea, and to all the churches, is directed to the individual members thereof: "any man" (3:20). To those who hear His "voice," who are in subjection to His word, Scripture, rather than to mystical experiences, human expediencies, and syntheses, the richness of full communion and the dinner table will be opened (3:20). These shall reign with Christ, who, in His humanity, "overcame" and is therefore "set down with my Father in his throne" (3:21). At no time is the believer ever summoned to the *imitation of Christ's deity,* but rather to *participation in Christ's humanity* and the victory thereof. It is the radical subversion of biblical faith when the two natures are confused, and man's goal thereby made deification. Man is never asked to be more than man, and he can never be more nor less than man. Man he was created, and he will always be either man in rebellion and apostasy or man in Christ and His grace. Philosophies which assume that man is, was, or can be less than man also assume that he can be more than man. The fall of man was based on this presupposition, and every such thesis is an exemplification of the fall.

Jesus had to overcome, and only so could reign. His people are *saved* by His atoning work but not spared from *life* thereby, and life means, in this fallen world, struggle and trouble. Acceptance into Christ's army means, not deliverance from battle but deliverance from defeat. There is now a necessity to do battle, to overcome, and only so to reign. The condition of victory is always battle. The modern lust in religion and all of life for a battle-free victory is only escapism of the ugliest sort. Salvation is never deliverance from conflict but the

[4] W. Boyd Carpenter: *op. cit.,* p. 550, see John 16:8.

assurance of power and victory in the conflict. Accordingly, salvation, by reversing defeat, intensifies the struggle and revives the ancient warfare wherever it occurs.

"He that hath an ear, let him hear what the Spirit saith unto the churches." These words occur in every one of the seven letters. They have reference, not to the physical ear, but to the heart (Jer. 6:10; John 12:37-40), which alone hears, and hears only when regenerate. Thus, while a warning to the reprobate, they are truly heard only by the regenerate.

REVELATION 4: THE THRONE OF GOVERNMENT

The letter to Philadelphia (3:7-13) spoke of Christ as the Door, and Christ promised "an open door" to His people. The letter to Laodicea (3:14-22) concluded with a summons to open the door to Christ the King and Savior. Then, wrote John, "After this I looked, and, behold, a door was opened in heaven: and the first voice which I heard was as it were a trumpet talking with me; which said, Come up hither, and I will show thee things which must be hereafter" (4:1). This "first voice" is the same heard from the beginning (1: 10ff.), even Jesus Christ, who now declares that "things which must be hereafter" will be revealed to the church through John. Thus Christ, the Door to God, the way, the truth, and the life, is moreover of necessity the open door to a knowledge of the future, since He is the key to all history. The *details* of history were often stated by the prophets; the *course* of history, its goal, and meaning, is now declared by Jesus Christ. The Christian has no right to be surprised by history; he is in command of it in Christ, and thereby knows its nature and destiny. Having revealed the true nature of the historical church (Rev. 2, 3), Jesus Christ now reveals the nature of history from the standpoint of the Throne. The purpose of this revelation is not the satisfaction of human curiosity but the preparation of His church for battle and victory. He will not permit His people the luxury of compromise with their own nature, with the world, or with despair. Compromise with despair is still compromise, however much it calls itself the grief of faith. The purpose of the unveiling is to leave the church without excuse, and to give the believer strength and joy in his stand.

John, when heaven was opened to him by vision, saw, first of all, "a throne." The central fact of heaven is not angelic bliss but the absolute authority of God over heaven and earth as symbolized in the Throne. God on the Throne governs absolutely the whole of creation. This fact is underscored throughout Revelation. "He is represented as being on his throne in every chapter, save ch. 15, where he is in the temple, and chs. 2, 9 and 10, where there is no occasion for any mention of the Throne."[1]

"And he that sat was to look upon like a jasper and a sardine stone: and there was a rainbow round about the throne, in sight like an emerald" (4:3). The jasper is probably our diamond, and the sard, the blood-red carnelian.[2] The whole universe is seen in a blaze of light going forth from the Throne, But God himself remains hidden in that light. The knowledge of God remains eternally inexhaustible to man, even in heaven, so that His very revelation underscores His inexhaustibility and incomprehensibility. He is the fountain of life; in His light alone we see light (Ps. 36:9), so that the true understanding of anything is impossible without the explicit or implicit presupposition of God the Creator. He is the sun, by the light of which we see all things, but we cannot look directly and immediately upon the sun. He is not the object of knowledge, but the necessary presupposition to all knowledge. We know God truly, but not exhaustively. However, the clearer that understanding, the clearer the knowledge of His incomprehensibility. The mind of the creature cannot comprehend the mind of the Creator; to claim that comprehension (i.e., to understand fully) is to claim either a mind equal to God, i.e., a status of autonomy and of divinity also, or to assert participation in that one deity.

But, although God remains eternally inexhaustible and hidden, the very hiding is a glorious revelation of Himself, because He is hidden from view by the gem-like glory of His being and by a flashing rainbow of emerald green. This rainbow not only sets forth His glory, but it is a perpetual reminder to man of God's covenant of peace, His covenant to restrain His wrath from man on earth (Gen. 9:13). The rainbow which hides God at the same time reveals Him to be the God of grace, the God who chooses whom He will and out of His mercy sustains them throughout all time and eternity. Moreover, the green rainbow is a promise of spring, a declaration that the

[1] Rist: *op. cit.,* p. 401.
[2] R. C. H. Lenski: *Interpretation of St. John's Revelation.* Columbus, Ohio: Wartburg, 1943, p. 171. Harry Buis: *The Book of Revelation.* Philadelphia: Presbyterian and Reformed, 1960, p. 27.

destiny of His people, the people of the ark of salvation, is paradise restored.

With reference to 4:4-8a, Bowman's comment is of interest:

> The *twenty-four seats* for the *elders* were set up after the mode of the Jewish Sanhedrin in *a semicircle* about the throne. These elders represent the Church which sits in rule or judgment over men and history (Luke 22:30; Rev. 3:21). The physical phenomena proceeding from the throne express God's power and Majesty (Ex. 19:16ff). The *seven flaming lamps* here stand for the Spirit of God, as did the seven-branched candlestick of the tabernacle (Zech. 4:2ff). The *sea* is the laver of the latter (Ex. 30:17ff)—a symbol of that purity without which man cannot approach God. The *four creatures* represent all creation and their *eyes* God's intimate knowledge of all his works (Ezek. 1:5ff.).[3]

"Elder" is a term in the New Testament for God's ministry and here typifies the Messianic people of both dispensations, the old and the new, the fulness of God's people giving Him praise and reigning in Him. They are "clothed in white raiment," in the righteousness of Christ. The "beasts," more accurately "living creatures" (Ezek. 1:5), are called in Ezekiel 10 *cherubim*. The lightning which goes forth from the throne is the justice and judgment of God, as it illumines the darkness of history, clears the air, and brings new and fresh power to the earth.

The crystal "sea" is a point of some difference of opinion. Some, with Bowman, refer to I Kings 7:23, to the laver used for ceremonial cleansing and called "a molten sea." Others refer it to Isaiah 57:20, "But the wicked are like the troubled sea," or, more generally, to the world or creation. In Revelation 13:1, the beast rises up out of the sea, or out of creation; the new creation means the passing away of the old: "and there was no more sea" (21:1). On the other hand, the sea is associated with the "molten sea," the laver, in 15:2, "a sea of glass, mingled with fire." Moreover, the laver itself refers to the world, to creation, and to the futility of

---

[3] John Wick Bowman: *The Drama of the Book of Revelation*. Philadelphia: Westminster, 1955, p. 43.

the cosmos. The "sea" in Mesopotamian thought (*apsu*) is a term used both for the temple basin of holy water and for the subterranean fresh water ocean, the source of life and fertility. This is the cosmic sea, and, as it stands before the Throne, represents creation under the absolute authority and government of the Creator. It is also the necessary corollary of the altar. Salvation is through the sacrifice of atonement, through Jesus Christ, but the ceremonial washing at the sea is indicative of the presupposition of all regeneration, the recognition of creatureliness and the abnegation of Satan's temptation and man's original sin, his desire to be as God (Gen. 3:5 RV). In salvation, the once would-be gods accept joyfully their status as creatures, as men in and under the perfect Adam, Jesus Christ, so that regeneration involves the *baptism into humanity,* the new humanity of Jesus, "the last Adam" (I Cor. 15: 45), and the renunciation of man's apostate plan of salvation, self-deification. Baptism is thus the death of the old Adam, and our dying to the old man and his humanity. Baptism is moreover our baptism into the *humanity* of the new Adam, it is baptism into *Christ,* the true and perfect man, very man of very man.

The sea therefore is the cosmos, seen by apostate man as his ocean of potentiality, but seen by God and the people of God as His domain, absolutely transparent to Him, however dark and potential to man. In this inspired philosophy of creation, we are shown the entire universe as governed from the Throne of God. Creation is not man-centered or nature-centered; it is God-centered. The whole universe is seen in the blaze of light that goes forth from the Throne, and it is immediately apparent that there are no dark corners in God's universe. This means that there are no brute facts in creation. Every fact is a created fact and has existence and meaning only in terms of the creative will and purpose of the triune God. In view of this, no fact need give us despair, because *all* facts are God-given facts and are to be interpreted, not in themselves, but in God only. Romans 8 is a declaration of this same faith, as indeed all Scripture is.

The cherubim "full of eyes" depict a creation, to use Torrance's phrase, "beyond chaos," i.e., so established in knowledge by their holiness in the Lord, that they see, not chaos, but the glorious purpose of the King of creation.

> Instead of a dark and iron destiny we see a creation symbolically full of eyes for no longer do men see through a glass darkly but worship the Creator and behold His glory, seeing Him as they are seen. The eyes of the One upon the throne have always been and always are upon His handiwork. Here is no blind fate but an all-seeing Creator on the Throne, and the Throne is upon and over and in the midst of all creation.[4]

Moreover, as Beasley-Murray has pointed out, "The song of the cherubim implies that the certainty of the future triumph of God is rooted in His very nature, the Lord, who is holy and almighty, *is to come*."[5] The cherubim, by their varied nature, sum up the creation, including man, and typify it. This creation, groaning and travailing under the fall, looks to the glorious redemption in Christ for its fulfilment (Rom. 8:18-23). The whole creation, having been created by God for His pleasure (4:11), finds its own health, pleasure, and being only in glorifying and serving God. Its liberty is in creaturely submission, and its glory is inseparable from its destiny in Christ.

Thus the Church and the Christian find themselves and fulfil their nature in submission (casting down their crowns), and in ascribing all glory, honor, and power to the triune God, who as Creator is alone worthy of taking pre-eminence in creation (4:11). Man *knows* only as he knows by submission to God, by thinking God's thoughts after Him. Man reigns and exercises dominion again only by submission to the Creator-Redeemer, apart from whom is neither life, power, nor authority. All creation is governed from the Throne, and man can have knowledge and dominion only in terms of the Throne. Creation and its history appear as a sea of glass from the Throne, not because it appears smooth and unruffled, for such a concept is alien to the vision, but because it is absolutely transparent, totally under, and comprehended by, the eternal decree. God's provi-

---

4 Thomas F. Torrance: *The Apocalypse Today*. Grand Rapids: Eerdmans, 1959, p. 32.
5 G. R. Beasley-Murray, "Revelation," in F. Davidson, A. M. Stibbs, E. F. Kevan: *The New Bible Commentary*. Grand Rapids: Eerdmans, 1953, p. 1177.

dence in history seems to men dark and unfathomly complex, mysterious, and almost without pattern. But from the Throne all history is crystal clear; His providential government and authority go forth from the throne in an unbroken circle of dominion and light. There are no dark corners, no brute facts, in God's providence.

In terms of this, therefore, the expectation that history will culminate in the triumph of antichrist is not only a dualistic surrender of the material world to Satan, but also a direct offense against the announced power and supremacy of God in, through, and over all creation and history. Premillennial and amillennial interpretations are tainted with the background of Manichaean heresy, with its surrender of matter to darkness. A further heresy clouds premillennial interpretations of Scripture—their exaltation of racism into a divine principle. Every attempt to bring the Jew back into prophecy as a Jew is to give *race* and *works* (for racial descent is a human work) a priority over *grace* and *Christ's work* and is nothing more or less than paganism. It is significant that premillennialism is almost invariably associated with Arminianism, i.e., the introduction of *race* into prophetic perspectives is accompanied by, and part and parcel of, the introduction of *works* into the order of salvation. This is the essence after all, of the Phariseeism which crucified Christ and which masqueraded, as it still does, as the epitome of godliness. There can be no compromise with this vicious heresy.

This, then, is a vision implicit with victory because explicit in its view of total sovereignty. The framework of reference further reveals this fact. According to Burch, "the Apocalypse was inspired from and conceived within the context of the Feast of Tabernacles" and reflects also the Feast of Pentecost. The synagogue lectionary for the Feast of Tabernacles was Zechariah 14, which gives us a vision of the transformed and New Jerusalem, "no night there," seen in essence in Revelation 4 and then declared at length later. The lesson for Pentecost was Ezekiel 1, also used in Revelation 4 (Ezek. 1:4-10, 26, 28; cf. Ezek. 10:1, 12-15, 20-22).[6]

---

[6] V. Burch: *Anthropology and the Apocalypse, An Interpretation of "The Book of Revelation" in relation to the Archaeology, Folklore, and Religious Literature and Ritual of the Near East.* London: Macmillan, 1939, pp. 18-20.

The Feast of Tabernacles was a harvest festival commemorating Israel's sojourn in the wilderness, and a type of the ingathering of the Gentiles into the kingdom of God. For both Jew and Gentile, it was a feast of remembrance, recalling their wilderness wandering in sin and their glorious entrance into the kingdom, the promised land. Pentecost celebrated the giving of the law to Moses. The Christian Pentecost celebrates the writing of the law on the tables of our hearts by the indwelling Spirit. They are alike glorious feasts and fittingly echoed in this chapter.

REVELATION 5: TESTAMENT AND EXECUTOR

Central to the biblical doctrine of history are two important factors, both manifested in their relationship to one another in Revelation 5; the first is the book, or roll, the second, Jesus Christ, the Lion of the Tribe of Judah, the Lamb of God. Jesus is the Lamb of God with respect to His sacrificial role; it is *not* a description of His nature, as sentimental Arminianism would have it, with its lamb-like Jesus "meek and mild." In His nature, Jesus is the Lion of the Tribe of Judah, the self-assured and authoritative ruler.

The book or roll is "sealed with seven seals." This at once indicates the nature of the book. The central problem, however, is not so much the content of the book, although this is to be revealed by its opening, but who is able to open the book. The book is extended toward the church, the four and twenty elders, by God, in His right hand: it is His gift to them. The right hand is the hand of action, power, and blessing: all this is offered to the church. The book is written over completely, "within and on the back side" (5:1); with no room for additions: God's providence and decree are clearly total.

The seven seals on the book or roll indicated immediately to the church that this document was a testament. "When a testator died the testament was brought forward, and, when possible, opened in the presence of the seven witnesses who sealed it; i.e., it was unsealed, read aloud and executed."[1] This testament or inheritance which God offers to the church is the promise of the kingdom. Man had once destroyed the kingdom God had given him: Adam's apostasy and rebellion turned him out of paradise and brought sin and death into the world. God's promise of a redeemer who would destroy the power of the adversary and restore man to paradise was given to Adam and Eve, covenanted to Abraham, fulfilled in the coming of

---

[1] T. Zahn: *Introduction to the New Testament,* vol. 3, p. 393f.

Jesus Christ, and to be manifested in all its fulness in His glorious return. But, to the early church, suffering as these saints did, and not fully aware of the implications of Christ's priestly work, as Hebrews reveals, the kingdom and the glory were very remote: they lived under the power and authority of Rome, and no other kingdom seemed to avail. Thus, to the saints of the Old and New Testaments, it has often seemed as though, while God indeed offered the kingdom, it was remote and unavailable. No man was able to restore paradise, no man able to execute the testament and give man his inheritance: "And no man in heaven, nor in earth, neither under the earth, was able to open the book, neither to look thereon" (5:3). The promise of God and His providential purpose were extended to man; the kingdom by testament was given to man, but no man was able to seize the inheritance, and none qualified as executor of the testament.

No man was qualified to open the book, because all men have sinned and come short of the glory of God. None have earned the kingdom; none have kept the commandments; none are able to save themselves or cleanse themselves. None can make themselves righteous. Thus the church of both Testaments feels its radical helplessness as it stands on the threshold of the kingdom, as it faces the promises of God and man's great and appointed inheritance, the kingdom of God.

God offers the kingdom: man must receive it, but no man is qualified to receive it. John feels the frustration of the centuries and weeps. The promises of life, the hope of the kingdom, the body's potentiality and hope, the soul's longing, to what end do these move other than the grave? Man seeks his own kingdom, and its end is sin and death. He tries to create his own decree and destiny, and they are revealed to be only hell and the grave. God offers His kingdom to perishing man, but how can man receive it?

At this point, the Kinsman-Redeemer steps forward. The family is not only central to biblical law, faith, and typology, but enters into its doctrine of redemption. Revelation gives us the fulfilment of the Old Testament law of the kinsman-redeemer, the basic texts of which are Leviticus 25, Ruth, and Jeremiah 32:1-15. The responsibility to one's blood and kin was basic to society. To break bread with another man, or to eat his salt, meant to be incorporated into his life, his body or family. Every meal was sacramental. The woman's role as bread-maker emphasized her importance in the family covenant; the man's role as the host who alone extended the family's protection to another, or barred the transgressor, emphasized his headship in the community of the family.

To redeem, in its basic meaning, means to buy back, buy again, or re-purchase, "and always refers to property which has passed out of the hands of the original owner; whether by sale, by security, or of a loan, and which he buys back under the laws governing such cases. Only the original owner, or some one acting on his behalf, has a right to redeem pledged property."[2]

There were certain obligations that rested upon a kinsman-redeemer:

1. He must be next of kin to the one whom he redeemed.
2. He must pay all accrued charges, and satisfy every legal claim.
3. The redemption of an inheritance might require marriage.
4. He must avenge the wrongs his kinfolk have suffered.

A kinsman-redeemer was to redeem a forfeited inheritance (Lev. 25:24-28).

A kinsman-redeemer was to ransom his kinsmen from bondage (Lev. 25:47-54).

A kinsman-redeemer was to avenge the death of his kinsman (Num. 35:12, 19).

> Adam forfeited his inheritance, and sold the race into the slavery of sin. Jesus took upon himself flesh and blood, thus becoming next of kin to Jew and Gentile; paid the price and ransomed the captives. And he will in due time take vengeance on Satan the great enemy of his people (Rev. 20:1-3).[3]

Thus Jesus Christ enters history as our next of kin to redeem us from the power of sin and death and to restore us to paradise, to the kingdom of God. Our salvation is not merely negative, but positive, not merely from sin and death, but into righteousness, holiness, knowledge, and dominion in His eternal kingdom, into re-creation in His image, and into re-establishment in our calling as kings, priests, and prophets of God the Almighty. This is God's declared

[2] M. M. B.: *Revelation*, vol. 1. Pittsburgh: Silver Publishing Co., n.d., p. 62.
[3] *Ibid.*, p. 62f.

purpose from the beginning, made known to man by the revelation of His word. As God said to Abraham, whom He called in terms of the Kinsman-Redeemer and the redeemed humanity, "Shall I hide from Abraham that which I do: Seeing . . . all the nations of the world shall be blessed in him?" (Gen. 18:17, 18).

Jesus Christ, our next of kin, redeems us by His atoning work on the cross. The mediator is thus invested with the office of King over the universe (Rev. 5:7-14).[4] He is seen as the God-man, the Lion of the tribe of Judah, the heir of the throne of David. His lineage and family is truly man. But He is not only the fulfilment of David and of Judah, its culmination and Branch, but also "the Root of David" (5:5), the Root and Branch of the House of David, its divine creator and source, and its human son and heir. He is the Lamb of God, the atoning sacrifice, and the Passover lamb fulfilled, but a Lamb with seven horns, the totality of omnipotence and power, and with seven eyes, omniscient, all-seeing in His purview of the ages and possessing the fulness of the Spirit of God in His control of "all the earth" (5:6).

Jesus declared himself to be this Kinsman-Redeemer, declaring the Scripture (Isa. 61:1, 2) to be fulfilled in himself, but the people of Nazareth, mindful of the poverty of His family, despised His claim, despite the compelling quality of His words (Luke 4:16-21). In announcing himself as the Kinsman-Redeemer, He proclaimed that the great jubilee of liberty came only through His person and work.

Christ Jesus attained His power as King of the universe and of tne eternal kingdom of God through His victory at Calvary, and now, as next of kin to man, "he came and took the book out of the right hand of him that sat upon the throne" (5:7). Christ is the key to history and the gateway to the kingdom. He alone opens up the kingdom to man and reveals the meaning of all history.

When the omnipotent and all-seeing Lamb, the God-man, takes the book and assumes the responsibility as executor of the estate and Kinsman-Redeemer to man, heaven and earth and all creation resound with the joy of all created being at this first act of restoration

---

[4] See W. Hendriksen: *More Than Conquerors.* Grand Rapids: Baker, 1939, p. 111.

and fulfilment. Three mighty hymns are sung in His praise, as is to be expected, since all creation finds its fulfilment only in Christ.

1. The first hymn is sung by the four living ones and by the twenty-four elders. The Church, typified in the elders, is the church of all time, not those in heaven, but those on earth, who offer up "golden vials full of odours" or incense, the prayers of the saints (Ps. 141:2), thus discharging their God-given function as priests in Christ. They sing a "new song," i.e., a song of gratitude for a new, unexpected and undeserved blessing. Theirs is the hymn of joy for redemption, a universal redemption calling the elect out of every "kindred, and tongue, and people, and nation" to be made "unto our God kings and priests: and we shall reign on earth." The RV reading states: "unto our God a kingdom and priests; and they shall reign upon the earth" (5:8-10). The Church reigns today in Christ, because He rules and over-rules in all things by His total providence and makes even the wrath of man to praise Him.

2. In the second hymn (5:11, 12), the hosts of heaven chant the praises of the Lamb and His worthiness, who "was slain to receive power." The Son of God died that we might live, and we must die to ourselves that He might live in us. The whole of creation finds its true life and fulfilment in Him, so that it is not man alone, but the hosts of heaven as well who rejoice in the coming of the great executor and the restoration of the forfeited estate.

3. The third hymn (5:13, 14) is the mighty chorus of all God's creatures in heaven, earth, and sea, praising the Lamb "for ever and ever." Paul in Romans 2:20-22 gives us a like glimpse of the universal praise of God, and also in Philippians 2:10f. This joy is inescapable, "Because the creature itself also shall be delivered from the bondage of corruption into the glorious liberty of the children of God. For we know that the whole creation groaneth and travaileth in pain together until now" (Rom. 8:21, 22). In view of this great redemption, it is only to be expected, and inevitable, "That at the name of Jesus every knee should bow, of things in heaven, and things in earth, and things under the earth; And that every tongue should confess that Jesus Christ is Lord, to the glory of God the Father" (Phil. 2:10, 11).

REVELATION 6: THE EXECUTOR AND THE ESTATE

We have seen that the sealed roll was a testament declaring the inheritance of the saints. This testament was *released* to man by Christ through His atoning death and *opened* to man by Christ through His resurrection.

Sometimes, however, the possessors of a forfeited estate and inheritance refuse to vacate the property or to surrender the enslaved persons. In like manner, the powers of darkness refuse to surrender the world to Christ the King or to yield believers to their God. They insist on trying to retain title to both. The City of Man emphatically rejects the legal claims of the City of God and refuses to be dispossessed.

Action must be taken, therefore, to oust the powers of darkness from the Lord's possession. Jesus Christ as true man is also the true heir, and His saints are heirs in and through Him.

This action to dispossess the enemy the Kinsman-Redeemer takes. The Book of Revelation gives us the nature of this action, both as it affects the world and as it affects the Christian. Part of the action is directed against the Christian himself, because every believer, by virtue of the old Adam in him, clings to an extent to his slavery and is unwilling to assume the full stature of his manhood and liberty in Christ. Thus, the action is directed both against the powers of darkness and against the Christian in his participation in that old humanity.

In the following chapters we have three visions: seals, trumpets, vials. Each vision has seven parts, because each vision is God-given and complete. Each seven is subdivided into six and one, the one being final, the six present in all history. It is thus apparent that the visions are in a sense repetitious in that they cover the same ground, while new, in that they cast further light on the same subject.

Christ is the executor of the estate, of the kingdom of God, which He restores to man by His work and by His grace. As executor,

Christ must dispossess the false heirs, who, under the influence of
Satan, have seized the earth in defiance of God and declare the kingdom to be man's, not God's.

The full significance of this sevenfold action cannot be understood
without reference to God's first great deliverance of His people, the
deliverance of Israel from Egypt. To effect this salvation, ten plagues
against Egypt were proclaimed by God. The first three plagues
struck both Egypt and Israel or Goshen equally. The six that followed struck only Egypt, although throughout that process Egypt's
hatred of Israel was only intensified. The tenth plague was directed
against all, of Egypt and of Israel, who were not under the blood of
the Passover lamb, the type of Christ. This tenth plague signified
that Israel together with Egypt was under condemnation of death
for her sin, but that God in His mercy extended grace and pardon
to all who found refuge in the chosen substitute, in God's atoning
sacrifice.

The seven seals, trumpets, and vials of Revelation are God's
plague on "Egypt," on the kingdom of man which has laid claim
to the earth as its "rightful" inheritance. The false heir persecutes
and seeks to kill the true heir. The very fact of inheritance makes
the Christian the target of the world's hatred and hostility. A rich
inheritance, wrongfully seized, is not lightly surrendered. The word
spoken concerning Jesus is still spoken concerning His people: "This
is the heir; come, let us kill him, and let us seize on his inheritance"
(Matt. 21:38).

Against these wicked ones Christ takes action, to dispossess and
punish them, and to give the kingdom to His people:

At the close of the seal judgments John sees 12,000 out of Israel,
and a great multitude whom no man could number from among
the Gentiles. *The Kinsman Redeemer has redeemed His people.*

At the close of the trumpet judgments, great voices in heaven
said: "The kingdom of the world has become the kingdom of the
Lord and of his Christ." *The Kinsman Redeemer takes possession
of His inheritance.*

At the close of the bowl, or vial judgments, the marriage of the
Lamb. *The Kinsman Redeemer takes the bride.*

After the Lord returns in glory, Satan is put in his abyss. *The Kinsman Redeemer avenges His people.*[1]

The nature of the dispossession, and of the action to dispossess, is indicated in part in the following verses:

V. 1. When Christ opened the testament, the four living ones cried out in a voice like thunder, Come and see. Psalm 47:4 declared of the Lord, that "He shall choose our inheritance for us." Not only is the inheritance chosen for us, but the action to recover our inheritance is the work of Christ.

V. 2. Four horsemen emerge from the sealed roll, from God's testament, and ride across the stage of history. The first one, crowned and riding forth conquering and to conquer, is Jesus Christ, as Revelation 19:11 makes plain. He, as the executor, goes forth in judgment against the false heirs. All four horsemen ride simultaneously, but Christ is cited first of all because all other facts of history are subject to and subservient to Him. There are no brute facts in history, no events that occur apart from Christ or in isolation from Him. All events occur as part of the eternal plan and are to be interpreted in terms of Him. This is certainly true of the fact of judgment. Thus, Christ is the first horseman, because all that follows, from the second to the seventh seal, can be understood only in terms of Christ. His purpose and direction govern absolutely. The other riders and the remaining seals are not before but behind Him as He moves through history as executor of the will, to destroy the enemy, and to drive out slavery from His once-enslaved people. Christ not only evicts the enemy but prepares His own people for liberty.

Vv. 3, 4. The second horseman follows immediately, representing war. Christ brings not peace but a sword. He is the principle of perpetual warfare to a world that seeks an unregenerate and unprincipled peace. He is thus a sword and warfare to the world around us, but also the enemy world as it exists within the true believer, who too often expects the profit of both Christ and the world to accrue to him. Men cannot find peace in Christ until they

---

[1] M. M. B.: *op. cit.*, p. 68f.

accept the necessity for war with the fallen world, and Christ as the principle of this warfare. It is a part of His shaking of the things which are, so that the unshakeable might alone remain. In the words of Moses, "Thou turnest man to destruction; and sayest, Return, ye children of men" (Ps. 90:3).

Vv. 5, 6. The third horseman is economic hardship. "A measure of wheat for a penny" means that a day's wages (in terms of the wage-scale then) hardly sufficed to buy the necessities for satisfying one's hunger. "See thou hurt not the oil and wine" has been variously interpreted. Some refer it to a Roman edict prohibiting the manu-facture of wine at the time, because of near-famine conditions, on the premise that the farm lands should be put to use for basic necessities. Others refer it to an edict designed to protect Italian wine-growers by ordering half of the vineyards of Asia Minor to be uprooted. In either case, the reference is to statist interference in agriculture. "A measure of wheat for a penny" refers clearly to inflation; the second statement refers to controls, and inflation and controls are twin measures which are basic to economic hardship. A problem also faced by Christians in the church, and again a matter of conscience, was membership in the labor guilds or unions. Mem-bership required not only a surrender of liberty but of religious faith. Economic hardship strikes the entire world; thus it also affects the Christian. To the unregenerate, the economic hardships come in mockery of their dreams of paradise on earth, their utopias without God. To the people of God, who are warned of them by Revelation, they are a hardship, but they are also a sign of judgment against their oppressors.

Vv. 7, 8. The fourth horseman is Death, with Hades, the place of the dead, riding in his train as his esquire. In Death's train come war, hunger, death at the hands of the beasts of the field, and deso-lation through war. All four horsemen are riding relentlessly ahead, lunging towards the goal of their warfare, the dispossession of the false heirs.

Vv. 9-11. The fifth seal is now opened. John hears the martyrs of the faith crying out to God, "How long, Lord Absolute, the Holy and Genuine One, does thou not judge and avenge our blood on those dwelling on the earth?"[2] The word here translated as God is the same as our English word "despot," which is derived from the Greek original. God is the only true and genuine despot: the saints cry out against man's flagrant challenge to His absolute power and authority. They are told to "rest yet for a little season" until the fulness of suffering and death be fulfilled on the Lord's people! White robes were given them, that is, they were clothed with the righteousness and person of Christ. This, for the time being, is all. The saints are justified, and are being sanctified. But the fulness of the inheritance must wait on God's time. The saints are portrayed as "under the altar." The imagery is drawn from the sacrificial service of the Temple (Ex. 40:29); the blood of the victims or sacrificial animals being received by the priest was poured out at the foot of the altar. All suffering of Christians, because they are in Christ, is connected with the expiatory suffering and death of Christ. In themselves, the expiatory sufferings and death of Christians have no meaning. Paul spoke of himself as being poured out, i.e., his blood as an offering, in II Timothy 4:6. The meaning is that our labor is not in vain in the Lord (I Cor. 15:58).

Vv. 12-17. The sixth seal gives us a great shaking (rather than earth-quake), so that all heaven and earth are shaken. This signifies God's continual shaking of the things which are, so that the things which cannot be shaken may remain (Heb. 12:27). The four horsemen are aspects of this shaking. Men react to the shaking by God in every age with the same flight and hiding. Even as Adam hid from God when he heard His voice, so men are constantly running from God and trying to find hiding places down here from His judgment

The seven seals give us Christ as executor of the inheritance of the saints, taking steps to restore the paradise and to prepare man for his freedom under God. The kingdom Christ is repossessing is His own kingdom, and He moves against it in absolute power and sovereignty. The process of recovery is a difficult one for the people

[2] Lenski: op. cit., p. 231f.

of God. As St. Paul told the early church, "We must by much tribulation enter into the kingdom of God" (Acts 14:22).

The expression, "wrath of the Lamb" (6:16) is significant, in that it represents a seeming paradox. One would expect reference to the wrath of the Lion of the tribe of Judah. But the wrath of the Lamb is apparent in the first Passover in Egypt, when the blood of the lamb saved those under it, while those rejecting it felt His wrath and the destruction of their firstborn. This aspect of the atonement is generally overlooked. The Passover was the judgment of Egypt; the cross was the judgment of Satan and the reprobate of this world, as well as the atonement for the sin of God's elect, and it unleashed the great shaking of the nations, beginning with the fall of Jerusalem. Atonement includes restitution and restoration, according to biblical law. Phineas, in the only voluntary and human act of atonement, i.e., not prescribed by God, in Scripture, effected an atonement for his people by his execution of justice (Num. 25). It was accordingly imputed to him for righteousness and made typical of Christ's eternal priesthood (Num. 25:10-13; Ps. 106:28-31). Christ's atonement involves therefore the destruction of the kingdom of man and the full institution of the kingdom of God. Restitution and restoration are basic to atonement. Both in time and in eternity, this restitution and restoration will be effected.

To cite the Passover again, this great act of atonement was also accompanied by restitution. On the orders of Moses, the Israelites *asked* the Egyptians for gold, silver, and clothing in recompense for their labor, and they "spoiled" the Egyptians. (KJV reads "borrowed" but the Berkeley Version translates "asked." The intent was to secure just wages, Exodus 12:32-36.) The atonement of the Passover was thus followed by restitution, and, finally, on entrance into Canaan, by restoration to the land, Israel's inheritance.

REVELATION 7: THE HEIRS

The cry of the world, "Who can stand?" (6:17), is an insistence that *no one* can stand on God's ostensibly unjust terms. God indicts the world for its rebellion and prosecutes a world that attempts to seize God's kingdom on its own terms, and the world responds with a counter-indictment, a charge of injustice against God. The exclamation, "Who can stand?," involves a resolution, since it is an unrepentant cry, that Christians must not be able to stand. The world wants justification, and it wants to justify itself against God by declaring God's plan of salvation and God's law to be monstrous and impossible. If Christians cannot stand, then God's justification is rendered null and void. Hence, justification is sought in cutting down the saints, even as Satan sought to cut down Joshua's stand before God by citing Israel's sin (Zech. 3). Hence, every attempt is made to cut down the believer and reduce him to a level lower than apostate man, who can then justify himself by comparison with the saints. But, even as Joshua stood by God's grace, so the saints stand in God's prior act and grace.

The heirs, the saints of God, have an inheritance in Christ which cannot be repossessed without a devastating shaking and destruction of all things, and this shaking will leave even the believer shaken. In the face of the totality of God's justice, the king's, the great men, rich men, chief captains, mighty men, and every bondman and every free man hide in terror, crying out, "Who is able to stand?" (RV). This fear finds an echo in the hearts of believers, and therefore to the troubled, persecuted church a mighty answer is given.

In the midst of the judgments, another vision intervenes. The storms of judgment have been let loose on the earth; John now sees the storms held in check, and the wind not permitted to breathe, until the Lord seals His own (7:1, 2). Thus, in the midst of the storm and wind, there is peace where God makes secure His elect, and judgment cannot begin until the elect are sealed.

The word "seal" has an important meaning in Scripture. A seal

1. Protects from tampering. The tomb of Jesus was sealed and guarded (Matt. 27:66; Rev. 5:1).
2. Marks ownership. It is a brand (Song of Solomon 8:6).
3. Certifies genuine character (Esther 3:12).

The seal thus signifies that the believer has the assurance of salvation and is eternally secure in Jesus Christ. He is protected from tampering and branded as Christ's own man, a true believer. St. Paul speaks also of the seal of the living God, which bears two declarations: "The foundation of God standeth sure, having this seal, 'The Lord knoweth them that are his,' and 'Let every one that nameth the name of Christ depart from iniquity' " (II Tim. 2:19). The seal of God asserts therefore His electing grace and our justification, and requires of us holiness of life and sanctification.

The answer to the question, "Who is able to stand?," is clear-cut: the sealed of God. His saints are able to stand, because their strength and security are not in themselves but in the Lord. But if the saints have security, then why are they exposed to the wrath of the world, to the fiery darts of the devil, to the temptations of the world, the flesh (i.e., human nature), and the devil? Why does the hatred of Egypt fall upon the saints of God? The answer is that God's conception of security is different from man's. Man's conception of evil too often revolves around the fear of defeat, tribulation, and suffering. For the Lord, the real evil is sin and compromise with sin, as all Scripture makes clear. God makes His people eternally secure from the destruction of sin, and He protects His people from being overcome by sin. And very often the means to this security involves defeat, tribulation, and suffering.

Revelation 7 gives us a picture of the sealed church in its ultimate victory. In Revelation 21 we are shown Jerusalem, symbolically portrayed as a perfect cube, the symbol of perfection. Jerusalem has twelve gates, twelve foundations, the walls are 144 cubits in height, and the population numbers 144,000. That this is a symbolic figure 7:9 makes clear. The twelve tribes of Israel give us a type of the whole church. Dan, the first tribe to introduce idolatry, is dropped, and Levi, having no longer any priestly function, takes its place in the tribal register. Ephraim, having used its eminence for apostasy under Jeroboam, is replaced by its father, Joseph.

This Israel is the true Israel of God, the true church. As Romans 2:29 stated it, "But he is a Jew, which is one inwardly; and circumcision is that of the heart." This is "the Israel of God" (Gal. 6:16), the true church, the body of Christ, who is "Abraham's seed," and whose members are "heirs according to the promise" (Gal. 3:29), i.e., are the true Israel of God.

The sealing of the saints recalls the protecting blood upon the lintels of the houses of Israel in Egypt. Even as the plagues of death, devastating Egypt, left unharmed those sealed by the blood of the Passover lamb (Ex. 12), so the sealing by the blood of the Lamb now preserves the true and chosen people of God. The tribes are named to indicate that the true Israel now exists as the church. The sealing of the elect no more raptures them out of tribulation than did the marking of the elect in doomed Jerusalem spare them from the horrors of the siege (Ezek. 9).

In 7:9, we see the saints, with palm branches, singing hymns of joy; the Feast of Tabernacles is recalled and echoed. The parallels between Exodus and Revelation are many. Jesus is both the true Moses (the Song of Moses is cited in Rev. 15:2ff.), and the greater Joshua. He is the deliverer of God's people. Simeon at the temple declared that his eyes had seen God's salvation, having seen the infant savior (Luke 2:30; cf. Isa. 52:10), for he was one of those "who were looking for the redemption of Jerusalem" (Luke 2:38), i.e., its deliverance from captivity, from spiritual Egypt. Pharaoh's killing of the infants is paralleled by Herod's murderous order (Ex. 1:16; 2:15; 4:19; Matt. 2:16). The infant Christ is called the true Israel called out of Egypt (Matt. 2:14f.; cf. Ex. 4:22; Hos. 11:1). Israel's 40 years of temptation in the wilderness, and its failure, is matched by Christ's 40 days of temptation in the wilderness, ending in victory; Jesus resisted by quoting Moses. Jesus sent out 12 disciples, to be the new Israel of God, the new heads of a new nation or people. Jesus also sent out 70 (Luke 10:1ff.), even as Moses gathered 70, to whom God gave the Spirit (Num. 11:16ff.). We are given parallels to the conquest of Canaan, and the destruction of its cities by the fire of judgment (Matt. 10:15; 11:20ff.; Luke 10:12ff.; Deut. 9:1ff.; Matt. 24). The old Jerusalem now has the role of Canaan and is to be destroyed (Matt. 24). The whole world is the new Canaan, to be judged and conquered: "Go ye into all the world. . . ." Both Exodus and Revelation conclude with the Tabernacle, the first with the type, the second with the reality.

In Revelation 7, the rejoicing saints are pointed out to John as those who have been justified by the blood of Jesus Christ; they have been sealed by God. This means that their salvation is not of works but of God through faith. Their security is therefore not in themselves but in the Lord (7:13-17). They are seen in their ultimate victory, and in that vision their present victory is manifested. They neither hunger nor thirst any more, nor do the desert sun and heat oppress them. They are delivered from these afflictions, not merely because the wilderness is behind them, but positively, because the Lamb of God feeds them, gives them to drink, and God himself wipes away all tears from their eyes (Isa. 49:10; 29:8). Their victory is therefore not a negative relief but a positive presence, Jesus Christ.

The word here translated as *victory* by some[1] and *salvation* by others (7:10) is *soteria*. Salvation does mean victory, and any doctrine of salvation which omits the fact of victory is not Christian.

---

[1] G. B. Caird: *The Revelation of St. John the Divine.* New York: Harper and Bros., 1966, p. 99f.

REVELATION 8: INHERITANCE OF THE FALSE HEIRS

Before an inheritance can be received, a true and approved will must be forthcoming, and a contested will or testament is not an uncommon fact in legal history. Essential to religious history is the same controversy: Which "word" or testament constitutes the true will of God concerning man's inheritance? The first contesting of this testament came in Eden, when Satan declared, "Yea, hath God said?" (Gen. 3:11). According to the tempter, God, like a fumbling and foolish testator, needed correction, and this Satan offered to do. His version of the terms of the testament of the kingdom constituted the true light, the true righteousness, and true inheritance of man. Thus, in the temptation in the wilderness, Satan tried to point Christ to that "true" kingdom, to His role as executor of the "true" testament as revised by Satan. Not only the false religions but heresies within the church are attempts to revise the nature of that testament and "correct" God's foolishness in terms of modern wisdom, or in terms of autonomous man's consciousness of god in himself. Moreover, the "correcting" of that testament is also undertaken subconsciously by ostensible champions of Scripture when they neglect the Old Testament, or undervalue or by-pass segments of Scripture, or simply relegate some doctrines, such as predestination, to a limbo of neglect or indecision. Hence, a major problem of history is the revisionist philosophy of history held by autonomous man, the attempt to alter the inheritance in terms of his own autonomous consciousness and dictates. This constitutes fraud and forgery and it must be dealt with accordingly. Thus, the Kinsman-Redeemer, the great executor of the kingdom, must not only redeem His kinsmen and drive out the enemy from their possession of the kingdom, but He must also establish the true testament in its authority and its truth.

The false heirs work in two directions. First, they claim to have the true testament and therefore the rightful title to the earth, and, second, they claim to be the true church of God. The invasion of the church by the false heirs is thus a continual problem, as they seek from every direction to seize the kingdom.

It is essential therefore for the church to understand the nature of the situation and pray for judgment against the enemy and against all his revisionist attempts.

Before inheritance comes the dispossession of the false heirs and their judgment. Accordingly, Christ (8:1) now opens the seventh seal on the will and testament which gives man his forfeited inheritance. As He does so, silence fills heaven. All heaven is silent, as the prayers of the saints are received, their petition for the kingdom. At one side stand the seven angels with seven trumpets. The trumpets sounded, in the Old Testament, for assembling, for journeying, and for war. Here they are trumpets of war, trumpets of judgment against the world. God waits, in His judgment, in part perhaps with patience toward the sinner (Ezek. 33:11), but essentially to allow the petitions of the saints to rise up before acting.

In the silence, an angel approaches the altar of incense, the altar of gold, the altar of intercession, to offer up "the prayers of all saints" (8:3). The prayers immediately ascend to God, and then descend upon the earth as judgment. The church is thus given a vivid picture of the power of prayer, and also of the necessity for praying for judgment and for justice. The church is too often remiss in this central aspect of intercession. Its prayers are pietistic and humanistic, unconcerned with God's justice and unduly concerned with escape rather than battle.

Torrance has observed that "the real cause of the world-disturbance is the prayer of the Church and the fire of God!"[1] But it is not enough to speak of this text as an instance of the "power of prayer." Even more, it makes clear that the true church must pray for judgment as well as for salvation. Until then, there is "silence in heaven." Judgment and salvation go hand in hand, and the cry of the saints for deliverance (6:10) must be also a cry for vengeance.

Then four trumpets are sounded by four angels. Judgment begins

[1] Thomas F. Torrance: *The Apocalypse Today*. Grand Rapids: Eerdmans, 1962, p. 60.

to descend as fire upon the earth. These four judgments echo the judgments on Egypt:

1st trumpet: vegetation;
2nd trumpet: sea;
3rd trumpet: land, waters; and
4th trumpet: sun, moon, stars (darkness).

This world is thus likened to Egypt, hardening its heart against the Almighty and refusing to release His saints from bondage. The wrath and judgment of God therefore descend upon the world to destroy the world and to release the saints for their exodus to the promised inheritance. As Caird noted,

> John likens the disasters of his own times to the plagues of Egypt. This is the first statement of a typological theme which he will develop in great detail in subsequent chapters. Like the other New Testament writers he believes that the church is the New Israel (i. 6) and its redemption the new Exodus (xv. 2-3).[2]

Joel 2:30 declared that these signs or wonders would follow the day of Pentecost and precede the second coming, that great shakings, convulsions, of heaven and earth, i.e., of nature and of nations, would leave the world in a perpetual crisis and in continuing destruction. The sea becomes blood, a natural phenomenon which has occurred in earthquake areas, and a sign reminding us of Egypt's plague. The fountains and rivers are smitten, and the sources of health, joy, prosperity, and life are dried up. The star Wormwood (Absinthos) falls, polluting the waters. At Marah, during the Exodus journey, a tree cast into bitter waters sweetened them, a sign of grace. Now the waters become poisoned, a sign of judgment. The four trumpets give us a picture of the progressive disintegration of the City of Man, as it opposes the City of God, and the growing terror of man.

According to Barnes, "A STAR is a natural emblem of a prince, of a ruler, of one distinguished by rank or by talent. See Numbers 24:17 and Isaiah 14:12. A star falling from heaven would be a natural symbol of one who has left a higher station, or of one whose character and course would be like a meteor shooting through the

---

[2] Caird: *op. cit.*, p. 115. Caird's restriction of the action to John's day is, of course, not the opinion of this writer.

sky."[3] The sun, moon, and stars typify the powers of this earth. When Scripture speaks of their fall and darkness, it declares that the powers that be are shaken or destroyed by the judgment of God. The association of the heavenly bodies with earthly powers is an ancient one. In Genesis, we find superior powers typified as such, and, when Joseph dreamed that the heavenly bodies would bow down to him, his father and brothers recognized that this meant that they were to humble themselves before Joseph (Gen. 37:9-11).

This process of judgment is a hard and bitter one. Every judgment brings about great dislocation and a tearing of lives and a rending of hearts. The early church prepared for the fall of Jerusalem, but it was not easy to see their relatives and friends go down in blood. The Christians of the empire suffered brutally under Rome, but they wept when Rome fell, and the entrance of the barbarians was sometimes their grief also. As Ellicott pointed out, "No great institution, or nationality, or evil principle is overcome without some corresponding disadvantages. The falling mountain carries evil in its fall, the sea becomes blood, the ships are destroyed."[4] The Christian is in the world, and too often in some measure of the world as well, so that the judgment affects him also. But, for the City of Man, these judgments bring ruin, and, ultimately, damnation. For the people of God, the purpose of these judgments is clearly given in Romans 8:28, i.e., all things are made to work together for good by the Lord, and their ultimate outcome is victory, and no separation from Christ. These judgments separate the saints from the world so that the saints might not be separated from Christ. The heirs are readied for their inheritance. The Exodus journey has as its purpose deliverance, and the purging of the remnants of slavery from the ex-slaves.

Basic to an understanding of this chapter is a recognition of the meaning of the "one third" which is twelve times (RV) cited as "destroyed." This has reference to the laws of inheritance. As Laetsch pointed out, with reference to Zechariah 13:8f., "Two parts,

[3] Barnes on 8:10, cited in J. P. Lange: *Revelation*. Grand Rapids: Zondervan, p. 208.
[4] C. J. Ellicott: *Commentary,* vol. VIII, p. 573.

literally, two mouthfuls, portions, the right of the first-born inheriting a portion double that of any other child (Deut. 21:17; II Kings 2:9)."[5] Here in Revelation, the two parts are the first-born of God, i.e., those who are begotten in Christ, who have the promise and the birthright as did Jacob. They are the heirs of the kingdom. The rest, the *third part*, are the unregenerate, and they are given over to destruction, twelve times pronounced on them, so that the false Israel, the false chosen people, is clearly connoted, among other things. Thus, for the profane, for the Esaus, the curse, already upon them, is intensified. This means the parallel blessing of the first-born, i.e., their clearer blessing in the sight of all the world. The wheat is revealed to be wheat.

The world believes that it can inherit the kingdom on its own terms. Its inheritance proves to be judgment and death, a blasting of its every hope in every area of its life. The Executor renders a judgment against the false heirs: dispossession and death.

[5] Theo. Laetsch: *The Minor Prophets.* St. Louis: Concordia, 1956, p. 492.

REVELATION 9: THE PLAGUES AGAINST BABYLON

When the executor begins His judgments against the false heirs, against the spiritual Egypt and Babylon which hold in captivity the people of God, the response of the false heirs is a counter-attack against the true heirs. But as Revelation 9 makes clear, even these attacks are within the providence of God and part of His judgment of the world. Thus, the very attempt of the world to destroy the true church becomes an element in the destruction of the City of Man.

In Revelation 9, we have the fifth trumpet and first woe, and the sixth trumpet and second woe. In 9:1-11, the first trumpet and first woe, we are given a report of a star or power fallen out of heaven. A great power or authority, or a ruler fallen from authority, is both humbled and yet given the key of "the pit of the abyss." This fallen power, Satan, unleashes plagues against God's order by means of his now perverse authority. The purpose of his action is to corrupt the heirs and to destroy them. A plague of locusts covers the earth for five months, the usual life span of locust plagues, thus indicating that the judgment will cover a life span, thus perhaps a generation. This plague cannot be interpreted in terms of any physical plague of locusts, nor any disaster to food supply. The "locusts" have no power to destroy or harm the grass or plant life. They cannot kill people. The locusts set loose by Satan affect only "those men which have not the seal of God in their foreheads" (9:4). These men, the false heirs, are tormented all their lives, so that they "seek death, and shall not find it; and they shall desire to die, and death shall flee from them" (v. 6). The evil accomplished by these "locusts" is in the realm of the human spirit. The "locusts" arise out of the smoke of the pit, which darkens the sun and pollutes the air, i.e., clouds human authorities and poisons the life of society.

This plague echoes both the eighth plague in Egypt (Ex. 10:4-15) and Joel 1:2-11 and 2:1-11, but it differs in that not only are the godly spared but all plant life as well. In other words, the earth, the Christian man's inheritance, is not destroyed.

Normally, a locust plague strips the lush green earth of all growing things and makes a rich valley barren and desolate. Feast is turned into famine. When Satan looses sin into the world, hoping thereby to frustrate man's submission to the kingdom of God, instead of afflicting the heirs, he afflicts only his own followers. Even as locusts destroy the earth, and sulphur fumes darken the sun and pollute the air, so sin and demonic influences reduce the rich promises of life to nothing and darken the light of life. Sinful men, frustrated by the very things which hold so much promise, find the hope of life turning to desolation. In the place of the will to live, a suicidal will to death begins to rule their lives.

In 9:1-11 we have an echo of Luke 10:19. Jesus saw Satan fall like lightning from heaven and declared, "Nothing shall by any means hurt you. . . . I give you power to tread on serpents and scorpions, and over all the power of the enemy."[1] This is not a promise of freedom from danger, pain, or death, but it is clearly a promise of victory over Satan and over sin. Jesus had plainly stated the problem of faith: "And the brother shall deliver up the brother to death, and the father the child: and the children shall rise up against their parents, and cause them to be put to death. And ye shall be hated of all men for my name's sake: but he that endureth to the end shall be saved" (Matt. 10:21f.). The promise is clearly one of victory over sin and preservation from its power. In peril, nakedness, and sword, we are told that we shall be more than conquerors.

In 9:12-21 we have the sixth trumpet, the second woe. Here we are given a symbolical geographical setting. A great army of horsemen, two hundred million strong, pours across the Euphrates River. They ride thus from Babylon and Assyria toward the promised land. This is clearly a world army, a world-wide power, moving in hostility towards the kingdom of God, determined to destroy the heirs and thus solidify its claim to the inheritance. Their purpose is the destruction of the heirs, but it is "the third part of men" (i.e., the false heirs) who are killed instead. The horses kill the false heirs; the

[1] The two sentences are here transposed.

weapons of social revolution unleashed by the City of Man are destructive to its own welfare and existence. The survivors of this judgment are not repentant; they continue in their idolatry (v. 20). Christ judgment is not reformatory here; rather, it is vindicative and vindictive.

A very obvious fact appears in this chapter. The Euphrates River formed the "ideal limit" of the promised land (Gen. 15:18). Across the Euphrates were the great enemies of the people of God, Assyria and Babylon. The river was a great natural barrier, a defense, and a point of separation. When the sixth trumpet sounds, the barrier disappears. A characteristic of Christian history thus appears. There is a progressive breakdown of the physical line of division between the church and the world and between the kingdom of God and the kingdom of man. The world has always tried to destroy the boundary between God's people and itself; the world claims total right to the earth and denies the claims of Christ's heirs. By compromise, concession, and invasion, the world seeks to reduce the kingdom of God to a captured province. Here, by God's permission, we see the world being allowed to do this, and we see it as a part of God's judgment on the world. The evils unleashed by the kingdom of man become more potent than the men who unleash them. Forces are set in motion which destroy their creators. Not the horsemen but the horses become the terror. The evils begun by the false heirs find their most vulnerable mark in the false heirs themselves. When the City of Man seeks to destroy the City of God, it destroys itself instead. The people of God have a sanctuary in Christ, but the citizens of Babylon have no refuge. The attempt by the City of Man to destroy the City of God becomes God's judgment on the City of Man and leads to the world's will to suicide and to its own destruction. In all this, the true kingdom, like Israel in Egypt, stands protected and secure even in the enemy's hands.

A few notes on some of the symbols of this chapter are in order. The ruler of the abyss (v. 1) is named in Hebrew "Abaddon," and in Greek "Apollyon," meaning *Perdition*. The basic effect of Perdition is on the hosts of Perdition, i.e., his God-ordained power cannot extend beyond his sway.

With respect to Babylon, Ellicott has noted,

> The two cities, Babylon and Jerusalem, are the types of two radically different sets of ideas, two totally antagonistic views of life; and the meaning and mystical import of the River Euphrates must be determined by the relation to these two cities.

> . . . if Babylon be mystical and Jerusalem mystical, it is hard to see why Euphrates should not be also.

> . . . The loosing of these four angels, then, seems to indicate that the issues at stake have become more distinct; that the conflict which had gone on under veiled forms begins to assume wider proportions and to be fought on clearer issues. The issues have been somewhat confused: the world spirit has crept into the Church, and against the world spirit, wherever found, the trumpet blast declares war.[2]

[2] Ellicott: *op. cit.*, vol. VIII, p. 578f.

REVELATION 10: PEACE AND JUDGMENT

God's tabernacling glory, Jesus Christ, the pillar and the cloud of the wilderness journey of Israel, now appears only partially veiled by cloud and by fire. Whereas then He dwelt in His little flock in the desert, now, by virtue of the world-wide extent of the church, He covers land and sea and overshadows the entire world. The rainbow over His head reveals Him to be the principle of peace and the ground of God's covenant with Noah. In dominating the entire world by His covenantal claims and promises, He heightens the tension in the world and makes sin progressively more high-handed as His own crown rights are progressively asserted and made manifest.

A principle of peace is at one and the same time the principle with reference to the infraction of peace, and hence the principle of judgment. The Roman peace meant Roman power and judgment. Peace means the prevalence of an order and the tranquility of that order. Jesus Christ, thus, is not only the prince of peace but the lord of judgment. The two are inseparable. *In order to eliminate judgment, man must of necessity eliminate peace.* To hate judgment is to hate peace; it means the creation of perpetual warfare as the condition of man. The so-called peace-lovers who wage war against Christian law and order are seeking not peace but perpetual revolution. *Judgment* exists only as the *maintenance of order.* The Last Judgment, as total and absolute judgment, ushers in absolute peace. To eliminate judgment, it is necessary to eliminate every form of order. As men, therefore, religiously, socially, and juridically, exorcise and seek to abolish hell and judgment, they attain, not the tranquility and peace they profess to long for, but that very *descent into hell* they seek to avoid, for hell is the absence and negation of every principle and law and is the chaos of total affirmation of will and being. In the perfection of God, such total affirmation is an inevitable and necessary consequence of His being. God, as absolute holiness, righteousness, and truth, in the total affirmation of His will

and being, is proceeding in terms of that which He is, holiness, righteousness, and truth. But for man to affirm his will and being as the
absolute and total order is to affirm hell. Man's continual attempt
to exorcise, to abolish judgment and hell, is hence an integral part of
his claim to be as God. It is man's claim that He is his own universe
and law. Because man is a creature and under law, not himself
law, and because man can sin and has sinned against God, hell is
a reality. If there were no hell there would be no man. A creation
without hell is an impossibility and a contradiction. The attempts
therefore to abolish hell mean also attempts to abolish man, to create
an ideal order in which men are nothing but chess pieces to be
moved by a group of self-appointed gods; man is denied the privilege of being a man; this is reserved to the new gods of being.

The rainbow signifies the covenant of grace. Christ appears to
the church in the person of John, but His message is to the entire
world. He declares (v. 2) His title to the entire world by planting
one fiery foot on the sea and another on the land while towering into
the skies. He proclaims the fulness of judgment, the seven thunders.
John is in haste to record this, desiring the end and the full deliverance of the saints. It is the end of history John longs for, the great
consummation. He is restrained from his haste: "write them not."
But, lest John be impatient at God's time, he is told "that there
should be time no longer, but in the days of the voice of the seventh
angel, when he shall begin to sound, the mystery of God should be
finished, as he hath declared to his servants the prophets" (vv. 6, 7).
The most literal reading of "time shall be no longer" is "there shall
be no more delay." Man sees God as delaying: God assures man that
the time of delay is past in the Christian dispensation.

John is then given a little book, and he is asked to eat it. This
is a familiar prophetic symbol for mastering God's requirements of
us, of digesting the meaning of His word, of making His purpose so
much a part of our life that it is like food assimilated and become our
life. At first blush, the calling of the evangelist John seems to be
a glorious and a happy one, but he is made to realize that it involves
not only the sweet but the bitter also, persecution and sorrow. This
John had already experienced, and He sees it now as the providence

of God and the necessary price of His calling. Only those who make God's will part and parcel of their lives can know either the bitterness or the sweetness of obedience. Both are there, and John is permitted no illusions concerning his calling. The inheritance is being restored, the promised land is being reclaimed for the saints, but not without its demands of us. Only when John accepts both the bitterness and the sweetness of his calling can he be truly commissioned with power. "Thou must prophesy again before many peoples, and nations, and tongues, and kings" (v. 11). This is the order to John, as the representative of the church. Our power as Christians is in eating the little book, in accepting our calling both in its bitterness and sweetness.

As Torrance has ably stated it,

> Surely there is a question here we must ask of ourselves. If there is no wormwood, are we really in touch with the Word of God? If our message is not disturbing and even sometimes tormenting, may we not wonder whether we have ever really eaten God's holy Word? This chapter tells us quite plainly that we cannot partake of God's Word in this world without bitterness. Why does the Church of Jesus Christ today sit so easy to her surroundings? Why do Christian people live such comfortable and even undisturbed lives in this evil and disturbed world? Surely it is because we are not true to the Word of God.[1]

[1] Thomas F. Torrance: *The Apocalypse Today*. Grand Rapids: Eerdmans, 1959, p. 70.

REVELATION 11: THE KINGDOM MILITANT

This chapter concludes the first half of the Book of Revelation. It gives us a summary picture of the church and of the kingdom of God throughout the whole Christian era, and it is a picture in terms of the vision of the little book.

In 11:1, 2, 3 we see the security of the church in the midst of battle, and the security is the security of victory. We see the temple at Jerusalem, a type of the church, measured off, together with its worshipers, for protection in a period of trial and a time of sackcloth, i.e., of mourning because of deaths and losses in battle. To measure is to fence and to separate. The measuring is of three things:

1. The temple itself is measured, and the court of the Gentiles is left unmeasured and given over to the Gentiles to tread for 42 months. Thus, the true church is measured or set apart by God's protection, and the unbelieving members are given over to destruction.

2. The altar of incense is measured. The altar of incense represented intercessory prayer. Thus, the whole domain of intercessory prayer is set apart. Its place in the providence of God is so significant that the security of the true church involves intercession.

3. Then the worshipers themselves are measured. We cannot limit the measure and extent of our obedience and service: God himself establishes the measure thereof. The measure of man's life is the work of the Lord.

The preservation of the church throughout the Christian era, to the very last, is seen as a saving, not "out of" trial and sorrow, but rather "in the midst of" tribulation.[1] Pagan salvation is *deus ex machina;* the hero is snatched out of trouble by the gods and placed in a situation of luxury. Thus, in *The Iliad,* when Menelaos and Paris fought before the walls of Troy, the goddess "Aphrodite snatched up Paris, very easily as a goddess may, and hid him in thick darkness, and set him down in his fragrant perfumed chamber." The adulterer,

[1] Bowman: *Drama of the Book of Revelation,* p. 71.

Paris, is thus saved from the wrath of the husband, Menelaos, and
then Helen is brought to him and Paris declares, " 'I snatched thee
from lovely Lakedaimon and sailed with thee on my seafaring ships,
and in the isle of Kranae had converse with thee upon thy couch in
love—as I love thee now and sweet desire taketh hold upon me.'
So saying he led the way to the couch, and the lady followed him."[2]
In all non-Christian religions, salvation has this character: it is
essentially escapist. It is an evasion of life and responsibility, a
flight from consequence. Every weakening of the biblical doctrine of
salvation, from a belief in restoration into responsibility under God
into a doctrine of escape from responsibility is paganism and a perversion of Scripture.

In 11:1-4, we are given an account of the two witnesses. Originally, the two witnesses were Moses and Elijah, the law and the
prophets, typifying the Old Testament in its fulness and witness. The
plague on Egypt, under Moses, and the great drought, under Elijah,
make the identification clear. To them is given power for 42
months, 1260 days. They are also the "candlesticks" of God. Their
identification as two witnesses recalls Deuteronomy 17, and the fact
that in biblical law two witnesses alone give validity to prosecution.
Here they typify the kingdom of God in its fulness, the Jerusalem
which is from above. This heavenly Jerusalem, the kingdom of God,
is set in contrast to that Jerusalem "where also our Lord was
crucified," which "spiritually is called Sodom and Egypt" (v. 8), i.e.,
the City of Man or Kingdom of Man. The City of Man thus takes
into itself all who oppose the City of God, and the historical Jerusalem of Christ's day is clearly identified as part of the City of Man.
The heavenly Jerusalem, typified by the two witnesses, seems small
by contrast, but, like Moses and Elijah of old, the people of God,
through intercessory prayer and the providence of God, have "power
to shut heaven, that it rain not in the days of their prophecy: and
have power over waters to turn them to blood, and to smite the
earth with all plagues, as often as they will" (v. 6). And although
the City of Man believes itself victorious over the City of God, so
that it slays the saints and leaves their bodies unburied, the crowning

2 Homer: *The Iliad,* Bk. III (Lang-Leaf-Myers trans.).

indignity to man, yet God revives His people with such great power and at the same time brings such judgments upon the City of Man, that men (v. 13), without believing, still say these things are beyond man and must come from God.

Moses and Elijah, the law and the prophets, represent the kingdom of God in the forms of state and church, or, more broadly, the ministry of justice and the ministry of grace. Apart from these ministries, the world faces only chaos and judgment: by destroying the God-given orders, it brings destruction upon itself.

In 11:14-19, we have the seventh trumpet and the third woe. This is a proclamation of the end, and yet at the same time a revelation of the beginning. It shows us the triumph of the kingdom of Christ, and yet it also reveals that which rules in power from the first coming to the end of history. Thus, it is a revelation of the first coming by a revelation of the end. The kingdoms of this world become the kingdoms of our Lord, and of His Christ, at the first coming, and His kingship is openly revealed and its fulness manifested at the second coming. But the destruction within history of the forces of the City of Man is in its every occurrence an opening of the end and a revelation of the true kingship. When Christ was crucified, the veil of the temple was rent in twain, because now the old temple was finished, and a new temple, the Body of Christ, revealed. Revelation 11:19 now shows us the temple of God opened in heaven. The stronghold and refuge of the saints is revealed, and their names made manifest, as storm and judgment overwhelm the world. The ark of the covenant is seen, containing the tables of the law, the rod of Aaron, and the manna. Here are the sources of the saints' courage and strength: they have been fed by the true temple, the Body of Christ. The mercy seat is revealed, from whence there is renewing for the saints and eternal grace. When the law was given at Sinai, voices, thunderings, earthquakes, and storm surrounded the mount: judgment was proclaimed against all who fail to keep the law. Only those who find Christ through the sacrifice of the substitute shall stand. Now the "habitation of God is an open sanctuary to faith; it is a clouded and lightning-crowned Sinai to faithlessness."[3] The end is a revelation

3 Ellicott: *op. cit.,* VIII, p. 590.

of the beginning, and its unveiling and fulfilling.

Thus, a summary view of the history of the world from the first to the second coming is given. It is governed by Christ the King, and it sees

1. A measuring of the true church, so that the correct boundaries of God's people are progressively manifested.

2. The true saints, the true heirs of the kingdom, shall witness mightily during the period of the false heirs, when salvation by politics is prevalent. Against the humanism of the City of Man, the City of God proclaims the lordship and kingship of Christ.

3. The City of Man shall war against the true witnesses and shall "kill" them. It will believe itself to be trumphant and shall congratulate itself on its victory.

4. The witnesses shall stand again in power, and judgment shall overwhelm the wicked as the people of God openly trumph and ascend into power through their inheritance.

5. Christ's world-wide kingdom shall prevail, and there shall be Christian order throughout the earth.

A note is in order with respect to the numbers of Revelation 11. The first is in 11:2—42 months for the treading of the outer court and the holy city. This is half of seven years, i.e., the fulness of time. The 1260 days of 11:3, the time of the power of the two witnesses, is the same time span, 42 months, or half of seven years. The time of the "death" of the two witnesses is three and a half days, again half of seven, but indicating a greatly shorter period, i.e., 1260 days against three and a half days. The period of power is thus vastly greater than the period of "death" (11:9). The number of the slain (11:13) is seven thousand, the number of fulness, indicating that opposition to the two witnesses collapses and is destroyed. The purpose of the numbers is symbolic. We are not given a chart or a time-table. We are given the assurance of victory and a description of the general course of battle.

REVELATION 12: CHRIST VERSUS SATAN

Revelation 12 marks the beginning of the third section of the Book of Revelation. In a sense, it covers the same ground as chapters 4 – 11, but with a difference. The conflict is now seen from the standpoint of God himself, not merely as a struggle on the part of the saints against the world, nor as the dispossession by the executor, Jesus Christ, of the false heirs to the kingdom. The battle is between Christ and Satan, and the conflict between the true heirs and the false heirs is an aspect of this greater battle. This is therefore the major section of the book; here we see the dimension, scope, and direction of Christian history more clearly.

Without this viewpoint, the perspective could easily have been perverted. It is the temptation of men, including Christians, to moralize Christianity, to see the struggle as one between good and bad, between love and hate, between good people and wicked people. All other religions are moralistic: they reduce religion to the dimensions of man and his man-centered moral concerns. Christianity is hostile to moralistic religion, and this section of Revelation is designed to make a moralistic interpretation of Christianity impossible. It is very easy for men to feel good and holy; self-righteousness is a basic part of man's original sin. It is easy to "get religion" by approving of love, honesty, fidelity, and the other virtues: there is not a man living who does not believe in these things in some sense and desire them for himself and for others. Non-Christian religions make it easy for man to be moral. If in his heart man harbors hatred, he of course does so with good "moral" reasons. If man is not honest, it is because he has very good reasons to be otherwise. If he lacks faithfulness, it is because this was the righteous thing for him to do under the circumstances, because faithfulness would have been "foolish" or "immoral" in view of his wife's nature, the needs of the moment, the requirements of the situation. All men are in favor of morality: the question is, whose morality? The morality of situation ethics is not the morality of the Bible, nor can biblical ethics be equated with those of any other religion. All men are for morality— of a kind. Thus, when MRA (Moral Re-Armament, or Buchmanism) sought to organize the world before World War II in favor of moral- ity, it gained the backing of such diverse persons as Franklin Delano Roosevelt, Admiral Tojo, and the Nazi hierarchy. Every last one of them favored moralism. Moralism is a religion of self-deceit and self-righteousness. Men who preach love and virtue too much are dangerous men from the biblical perspective, in that they proclaim a morality which is not grounded in the absolute law of God, nor motivated by the new man in Jesus Christ. All moralistic religion and all moralistic preaching and teaching encourages hypocrisy. Christian preaching destroys it. It would have been easy for the troubled Christians of John's day to take refuge in moralism and find comfort therein against the wickedness of Rome. Their mor- ality seemed obviously far superior to Roman morality. But the ground of the Christian's strength was not in their morality but in Jesus Christ, and the Christian's true morality is the outworking of his salvation. The battle is revealed by Revelation 12 to be between Christ and Satan: the governing power therefore is not of man, and hence moralism is out of the question.

We are given a picture of a woman clothed with the sun, clearly a cosmic figure. She is the true Church of God in every age, cosmic in its government and therefore in its scope, because Christ is the head of the Church. The Church is described in symbols denoting sov- ereignty under God, with images derived from Joseph's dream (sun, moon, and stars, Gen. 37:9). Through the true people of God, Christ originally came into the world, and through them He con- tinues to come to the world. True, while this incident reflects also the historical event, the nativity of Jesus Christ, it reveals even more the continuing event from the first to the second coming, the bringing forth of Christ to the world. W. Boyd Carpenter very ably described this fact:

> There is an anguish of the Church which Christ laid upon her: it is the law of her life that she must bring forth Christ to the world; it is not simply that she must encounter pain, but that

she cannot work deliverance without knowing suffering. This the Apostles felt: the love of Christ constrained them; woe it would be to them if they did not preach the Gospel; necessity was laid upon them; they spoke of themselves as travailing in birth over their children till Christ was formed in them. This, then, is the picture, the Church fulfilling her destiny even in pain. The work was to bring forth Christ to men, and never to be satisfied till Christ was formed in them, i.e., till the spirit of Christ, and the teaching of Christ, and the example of Christ were received, loved, and obeyed, and men transformed to the same image, even as by the Spirit of the Lord. But there was to be opposition: the enemy is on the watch to destroy the likeness of Christ wherever it was seen.[1]

The dragon (12:3, 9, 13) is identified clearly as Satan, the slanderer, and his point of origin, heaven. In the Old Testament he is sometimes used to represent Egypt (Isa. 51:9; Ezek. 29:3), out of whom Israel had come in order to become the people of God, i.e., forsaking the principle of autonomy for obedience to the covenant God. Satan's unrelenting purpose is the destruction of Christ and His Church. Against this persecution, the people of God find refuge (v. 6) in "a place prepared of God" for 1260 days, or 42 months. This same period is described in verse 14 as "a time, and times, and half a time," i.e., three and one-half years, again 42 months. Satan is filled with wrath, because he knows that against the backdrop of eternity his time is very short. The "war in heaven" described in verses 7-10 and the casting out of Satan signal the great victory accomplished by Christ in His sacrifice on Calvary: Satan's claim on sinful man was broken by the substitutionary sacrifice of Christ. The elect are delivered from Satan's power. The saints overcome Satan "by the blood of the lamb, and by the word of their testimony" (v. 11).

The dragon pursues the people of God and seeks to destroy them. Failing to destroy Christ, Satan seeks to destroy Christ's people. "And the serpent cast out of his mouth water as a flood after the woman, that he might cause her to be carried away of the flood" (v. 15). The delusions coming from his mouth are every kind of

---

[1] W. Boyd Carpenter, in Ellicott: *op. cit.,* VIII, p. 591.

false doctrine and teaching, every delusion of religion and science whereby men try to infiltrate and destroy the true Church of God. But verse 16 reveals that such attempts are frustrated: the earth, that is, the world apart from Christ, so welcomes these delusions that the dragon's flood of falsity only overwhelms his own people, while the true Church is delivered into safety by God. As C. H. Little expressed it,

> To the earth and its earth dwellers the river of delusions spewed out of his mouth by the devil was so welcome that it was at once absorbed, while the Church on her powerful eagle wings flies away so swiftly that these waters do not reach her. This out-pouring of delusions is continuous, and is not limited to any particular time or event in the history of the Church.[2]

Again it is clear that we cannot force chronology onto Revelation: we do not have a sequence of before and after events, but a description of events or states of warfare which characterize the Christian era.

The dragon is described as having seven heads, and ten horns, and seven crowns upon his head (v. 3). In Daniel's vision, the seven heads were divided among the four beasts, while here, at their source, they are seen in one total concentration of evil. The four empires of Daniel represented the power here seen in all its nakedness, and in all its pretension, for the numbers seven and ten are symbols of fulness and totality, and Satan, in claiming fulness and totality, is challenging God's title to the same. In drawing "a third part" of the stars of heaven in his attempt to destroy the Church and her Redeemer, Satan uses the powers of this world, the stars, in his effort to overwhelm and destroy the true people of God. In this he fails, and the Church is nourished because of this opposition (v. 14), and so he seeks to "make war with the remnant of her seed, which keep the commandments of God, and have the testimony of Jesus Christ" (v. 17). The true Church is not destroyed by Satan's efforts. The false church can be captured and made a tool of autonomous man's pretensions, but the true Church, the remnant of God, although the object of warfare, cannot be destroyed.

[2] C. H. Little: *Explanation of the Book of Revelation.* St. Louis, Mo.: Concordia, 1950, p. 127f.

In verse 5, Christ is described as the one who comes to rule the nations with a rod of iron. Buis notes,

> Rule means literally "shepherd." The words come verbatim from Psalm 2 which is evidently Messianic. "Thou art my Son; this day have I begotten thee. Ask of me, and I shall give thee the heathen for thine inheritance, and the uttermost parts of the earth for thy possession. Thou shalt break them with a *rod of iron*" (vv. 7-9).[3]

[3] Harry Buis: *The Book of Revelation.* Philadelphia: Presbyterian and Reformed Publishing Co., 1960, p. 69.

REVELATION 13: ANTI-CHRISTIANITY
IN CHURCH AND STATE

The direction of history is twofold in its historical manifestation. Apostate man moves towards establishing a radically humanistic social order, in which God is abolished and man is his own law and law-giver. Apostate man works to create a paradise on earth without God, law, or morality. The morality of humanism is that man is his own law, and that no moral law beyond man can govern man. On the other hand, regenerate man works to re-establish the law order of God among men, to establish church, state, and society in terms of the word of God, and to manifest the kingdom of God in its every meaning. History thus is in tension between these two warring forces, but the tension is more than the natural, historical tension. There is also the tension which apostate man inescapably feels by virtue of his rebellion against his sovereign, the triune God. There is the tension of epistemological self-consciousness, as apostate man comes to know himself and his implications more fully. And there is also the tension of failure, as apostate man finds that his every effort is frustrated and works towards his own confounding.

In Revelation 13, the nature of the opposition to Christ and His church, and to Christ and His law order, is given to us in greater clarity. A beast rises out of the sea, i.e., out of the unbelieving world, having seven heads and ten horns, whose horns rather than his heads are crowned, and upon whose heads are names of blasphemy. The fact that the horns rather than the heads are crowned signifies that in this world, power is the source of authority and sovereignty, and men give obedience, not to legitimate leadership, but to power as such. "Might makes right," and might is worshiped and obeyed in its every implication. The names of blasphemy indicate that human governments arrogate to themselves the authority and sovereignty which properly belong to God. This is true not only of kings and dictators but of democracies also, with their blasphemous doctrine, *vox populi, vox Dei,* the voice of the people is the voice of God. Majorities are thereby equated with righteousness, and appeal beyond the government and its courts is rendered null and void: "god" has spoken only through his approved voice, the government!

The beast, symbol of human government and empire, of anti-Christian states and cultures generally, represented the Roman Empire of St. John's day, and all other anti-Christian orders. The beast represents the totality of all such empires in the ancient world, and all to come. Its seven heads and ten horns emphasize totality. In this image is concentrated the opposition to God by apostate man. This opposition, more diffuse in antiquity, becomes more self-conscious and more concentrated as history progresses. Bowman clearly stated the meaning of this symbolic figure, the beast, writing,

> . . . this *Beast,* the Dragon's messiah, stands for the secular world culture generally. . . . That the Dragon has *committed* its *authority* to the Beast means that the world culture has become Satan's messiah and is dedicated to bringing out his rule in the affairs of men—hence man's *worshiping* of both figures.[1]

This world is clearly Satan's messiah. Man is man's own and only savior for humanism. The humanist therefore delights in the centralization of power into the hands of human government, because this is his hope. The pretensions of apostate culture are his glory and hope. The humanist holds to the limitless possibilities of human culture and to the sovereignty of man's rule, and he declares proudly, "Who is like unto the beast? who is able to make war with him?" (v. 4). Power is given by God (v. 5) to the beast to speak great things and utter much blasphemies for 42 months, throughout his appointed time. Power is given to him, moreover (vv. 6, 7) to attack not only the saints, "and to overcome them; and power . . . over all kindreds, and tongues, and nations," but also to attack God with blasphemy and insult. There is thus a seeming outward victory by humanism over Christianity.

But the reality of the situation is disclosed in verses 8-10. Those

---

[1] J. W. Bowman: *Drama of the Book of Revelation,* p. 85.

who have not been saved by the "Lamb slain from the foundation of the world" worship the beast, seek salvation in human culture by statist action, and make the very source of their damnation their hope of salvation. But to the suffering saints comes this word: "If any man have an ear, let him hear. He that leadeth into captivity shall go into captivity: he that killeth with the sword must be killed with the sword. Here is the patience and the faith of the saints." The absolute and final court of the Almighty renders a full and just judgment to the pretensions of human culture and to the works of apostate man. They cannot escape: they shall pay to the last penny.

St. John, in verse 3, speaks of one of the heads of the first beast being slain, and yet the wound unto death healing, so that, "all the world wondered after the beast." Albertus Pieters pointed out, in summarizing the views of Sir William Milligan, Hengstenberg, and Lenski, that

> Since the wild beast is the symbol of the antichristian power, the coming of the Redeemer into the world was its death-stroke; but yet it seems to continue. The deadly wound is healed. In the days of St. John it was evident that the brute was by no means dead, and this healing of the wound was, no doubt, a sore trial to him and his friends.[2]

The next section, verses 11-18, deals with a second beast, this time coming up out of the earth. To understand its meaning, we must realize that biblical symbols are fluid, not stereotyped; some maintain that the meaning of symbols never varies: this is definitely not so. For example, Satan is compared to a lion (I Peter 5:8), and Jesus Christ is also compared to a lion (Rev. 5:5). "Dove" means "silly" in Hosea 7:11, but its meaning is "harmless" in Matthew 10:16. "Earth" in Revelation 12:16 means the unbelieving world, because it is contrasted to the woman, i.e., the true Church. But in Revelation 13, earth is used in contrast to sea; thus, the sea is the symbol of the unbelieving world, and the earth here represents the unbelieving church. The two beasts are thus the apostate state and the apostate church. The second beast is false religion which serves

[2] Albertus Pieters: *Studies in the Revelation of St. John.* Grand Rapids: Eerdmans, 1950, p. 220.

human culture and whose messiah is human culture rather than Jesus Christ. It is false religion whose kingdom is this world, and whose salvation is secular and social. It appears to the world (v. 11) like a lamb, like a Christian Church, but its voice is the voice of the dragon, of Satan. It exercises its authority (v. 12) for one purpose, to subordinate man to human culture, to the state, to humanism, and to direct man's hopes from Christ to society, from salvation through the atonement of Jesus Christ to salvation by social action. For the second beast, the kingdom of God is this world in all its human hopes and pretensions: it is the world of Adam in revolt, attempting to build a tower of Babel in opposition to God, a one world order without God. And this beast comes out of the church and is the apostate church.

The second beast, this false religion, the Christianity which is moralistic and Christless, deceives people (vv. 13, 14) with great wonders and a tremendous display of power. It seems to possess the power of Elijah of old, to make "fire come down from heaven on the earth in the sight of men," that is, to bring down judgment upon those whom it opposes, but its power is not supernatural; it is not derived from God but from the beast, from statist power and from human culture, and its object is not the glory of God and the sovereignty of God, but that "they should make an image to the beast, which had the wound by a sword, and did live" (v. 14). This has reference to the worship of the first beast, human culture, the state. The new god of the false church is the state, with which it is in union. The false beast, false Christianity, sees as its enemy all true Christianity and seeks to force its conformity to a man-centered doctrine, to a faith centered on the fulfilment of Adam's ideal, the self-deification of man, on all men. This enthronement of fallen Adam, however, is not sought as a conscious rebellion against God; it masks itself as true piety and true faith; it is now a highly moralistic religion in that it believes in man's works and man's law.

Those who refuse to participate in the worship of man, those who refuse to surrender to man's complacent satisfaction with man and man's society, are increasingly branded as aliens. All who do not have the mark of the beast, all who do not surrender to the humanistic social order, are refused permission to buy and sell, that is, they are the objects of social, political, and economic ostracism. Every kind of subtle and direct pressure is employed to force the true believer into conformity with the City of Man and the creed of Cain. Concerning the mark of the beast, we are given to understand that it is the same as his name or number (1. 17). In verse 18, we are told that this is "the number of a man," or, more literally, "a human number." The number is 666. Attempts have been made to equate this with Nero, but it can be done only by reading Nero Caesar, and by misspelling it. Every generation has seen equally fantastic attempts to give a like reading.[3] But Revelation gives us the very simple answer: 666 is the number of a man, the human number, raised to its highest degree. Seven is the symbol of totality, of divine fulness; six is the human number. Man was created on the sixth day. The number 666 represents the essence of man's messianic pretensions as well as their futility: at its highest, it constantly falls short of the divine totality and sovereignty. Neither 6 nor 66, nor 666 can ever become 7, or 77, or 777 in itself. Man is a creature and always remains a creature: his messianic dreams concerning himself cannot change the fact of his creaturehood or remove from him the divine judgment that faces his rebellion and sin. In verse 14, the faith of this beast, of this false Christianity, is clearly revealed: for all its moralism, it believes basically that "might is right" and exalts human culture because it exalts man. Self-exaltation, self-justification, and the blind worship of power are behind all moralistic doctrines. Humanism becomes progressively a naked viciousness, man confirmed in his depravity. Moralism always reveals itself as basically immoralism.

---

[3] See, for example, Oswald J. Smith: *Is the Antichrist at Hand? What of Mussolini.* New York: Christian Alliance Publishing Co., 1927, seventh edition, p. 24f., "Mussolini may not be the Emperor (the Beast) himself, but if not, he is certainly a remarkable foreshadowing of the one whom the Bible predicts will reign." Others were more ready to identify Mussolini as the Beast, and in every generation such foolishness has been in evidence.

REVELATION 14: THE DISPOSSESSION

We have seen the dimensions of the satanic attack on the kingdom of God, the nature of the spiritual issues at stake, the blasphemous extent of the power of evil, and the suffering of the saints. But is this all that God's people do in history, suffer? As Carpenter noted,

> The sealed ones of God have suffered: but have they done more than suffer? Has theirs been only a passive endurance of evils? Have they wielded no weapon against these foes, and used no counter-influence for good? The chapter before us will answer.[1]

Tragically, the church has too often felt that its only role is to suffer and to wait. Too often the role of the Christian, according to the church, has been defined as passive; the church has allowed the world to act, while it has passively suffered, "waiting" on God. The influence of asceticism and pietism has been to withdraw the Christian from the world. But such "waiting" on God and such passive suffering are not marks of holiness; they can be described only as *sin*. The church is not merely a victim in the world struggle, but it must be an active and aggressive army.

The reduction of the kingdom of God to a spiritual realm is in effect a denial of the kingdom, whose claims are total. It surrenders the world to the enemy and retreats into defeat as though it were victory. It is not surprising that alien creeds then take over. Reinhold Niebuhr, himself a representative of a newer creed, observed early in his career how irrelevant the church's role had become:

> The church is like the Red Cross service in war time. It keeps life from degenerating into a consistent inhumanity, but it does not materially alter the fact of the struggle itself. The Red Cross neither wins the war nor abolishes it.[2]

Niebuhr's point is well taken, although his view of the church's role

[1] W. Boyd Carpenter, in Ellicott: *Commentary*, VIII, p. 601.
[2] Reinhold Niebuhr: *Leaves from the Notebook of a Tamed Cynic.* Chicago: Willett, Clark, & Colby, 1929, p. 113.

is in error. The work of the church, which is not to be identified as the kingdom of God, but simply as a part of the kingdom, is to proclaim the whole counsel of God, to administer the sacraments, and to establish discipline within its framework. The church must instruct its members concerning every aspect of the Christian's responsibility, in every sphere of law and life. But Niebuhr is right in comparing the role of the pietistic church to the Red Cross. Such a conception of the church visualizes its role as that of *the grand neutral* on the human scene: this is a fearful perversion of the role of the church, and it labors under an illusion. The church is in Christ's army, and there is no neutrality in this warfare between Christ and Satan. This warfare is in process in every sphere of life. The church is the main contender, humanly speaking, on the world-battlefield, and it cannot retire to the sidelines without conceding defeat and effecting its own execution. And this Christ will never permit His Church to do without inflicting fearful judgment upon her.

The concept of neutrality is an invalid one in any sphere, and certainly never less appropriate than when held by the church. The church is not a political organization, but it must instruct men in the fundamentals of godly politics. It is not a welfare agency, but it must teach men the meaning of godly charity. If the church confines its teaching to spiritual matters, it must neglect most of Scripture, which speaks to man's condition in every area of life. Christian faith is either relevant to *all* of life or it is relevant to *none* of it: the claims of God are either total, or He is not God. To ask Christianity to stay in its own territory is to ask it to stay in all of life. Religion as the Bible conceives of it and declares it has no *separate domain* apart from the rest of life: it is the over-all purpose and meaning of all life in its *every* sphere. Christianity is not an escapist religion. All other religions are essentially escapist in their outlook, and it is the paganization of the church when its faith is reduced to escapism. Pagans come to religion, not to face life's problems better, but to escape them, to evade the struggle. The task of the church must be to challenge every sphere of life in the name of the sovereign God and the Lord Jesus Christ. The Great Commission requires that all nations be made disciples, and every sphere of life be brought under the dominion of Christ the King, made to hear Christ the Prophet, and find its redemption and intercession in Christ the Priest. Anything less than this is a deformation of the Gospel.

Vv. 1-5.   We are given, first of all, a picture of the true kingdom under the authority of "the Lamb" (not "a Lamb," as in the King James Version), even Jesus Christ. The people of God are ever triumphant, and their song, their victory chant, is impossible for the world to learn. The world cannot understand the triumph that the true church always experiences. For the world, all things do not work together for good (Rom. 8:28), and therefore the church's "new song" (i.e., a song of thanksgiving) is to the world incredible and impossible.

The members of Christ are described as "virgins" who "were not defiled," in the sense of II Corinthians 11:2, "I have espoused you to one husband, that I may present you as a chaste virgin to Christ." (The word *virgin* in Greek is masculine in form even when used to refer to both sexes.) The phrase has no reference to sacerdotal celibacy: the reference is very clearly to the entire church, and the 144,000 is identical with the "huge multitude which no one was able to count" out of "every race," pictured in 7:9.

This virginity is clearly characterized as consisting of four things: (1) purity, (2) implicit obedience, (3) separation, and (4) utter truthfulness. The description concludes by declaring that they are "without blemish" (RV) or "blameless" in the sight of God. The "women" or whores who defile them are the nations, depicted soon as Babylon, which leads men and nations astray with its dream of a human paradise apart from God. Thus the virginity of the true church consists in its faithfulness to a God-centered faith as against the seductions of man-centered theology, and the virginity of the kingdom is its resistance to the concepts of a humanistic paradise apart from God.

Vv. 6-20.   Now, through the media of the seven angels, the full task of the believers is announced. The people of God cannot be mere by-standers or passive sufferers. Their task is a redemptive mission, a prophetic task, a governmental duty, to correspond with the threefold function of Christ as priest, prophet, and king.

I. vv. 6, 7. The first angel proclaims the everlasting gospel. This is the first and foremost task of the people of God, to declare the grace of God unto salvation through Jesus Christ. "The sound has gone out unto all lands." According to Carpenter, "The whole cycle of the gospel preaching is included in the vision."[3] Here is described not only the responsibility of the church but its work historically as it functions in every age, from the beginning to the end. The church has the duty to make known to every creature this gospel.

II. v. 8. The second angel proclaims the doom of the world-city, the capital of the world-power, Babylon. What does Babylon stand for? Babylon has a key significance in Scripture's typology. It represents all attempts by man, since the Tower of Babel, to erect a world paradise without God, to establish human unity on the principle of revolt against God by men who try to be as God. Babylon is man's attempt to give to himself everything which God plans to give the redeemed man, but to deny God in the process and revoke His sovereignty. Man declares, "I am the master of my fate: I am the captain of my soul." Thus the program of Babylon mimics the program of God: it points towards a good life, peace, unity, and the fulfilment of all man's potentialities, but all this apart from God. Thus, Babylon is constantly being confounded and plunged into confusion by God, constantly scattered in its attempts to gather. Babylon is forever doomed, and in every generation the true church must proclaim emphatically, "Babylon is fallen, is fallen."

Babylon is with us in every age. The sin of the nations is that without exceptions "all nations drink of the wine of the wrath of her fornication." Even as the true church is made up of those who do not defile themselves with women, i.e., the nations, so the nations are precisely those who become whores, who become part of Babylon, who commit fornication in Babylon and drink of the wine of her cup. Thus Babylon must be seen not only on the Thames, the Seine, the Rhine, the Volga, and the Bosphorus and the Nile, but also on the Potomac. All nations drink of her wine, and, unless they are brought to repentence, they must perish with her (cf. Ps. 11:6; 75:8; Isa. 51:17; Jer. 25:15).

[3] Carpenter in Ellicott: *op. cit.,* VIII, p. 602.

Thus the true church in every age has a mission to the state, to proclaim the fall of Babylon, to declare to the state that civil government can endure only under God and in obedience to His word, that every attempt of civil government to become as god, to be the purveyor of grace and of paradise, is damned and doomed. The cleansing of civil government and the indictment of it by the word must be the task of the church in every age.

III.   vv. 9-12. The third angel declares the third task of the true church, namely, warning men in every age that they must not fall victims to the lure of Babylon, to the dream of the world-state, the humanistic hope of paradise even when given the trappings and decorations of religion. To receive the mark of the beast means to place one's hope in this world and in the powers of this world rather than in God Almighty; it means to accept the controls of the state as salvation rather than slavery. The warning to men is a clear assertion that men are responsible and will be judged accordingly by God. Men in every age try to evade responsibility: they compromise constantly by insisting that compromise is the only possible course. Against all this, the true church must insist on full responsibility and allow no man to evade or escape this sin or the fact of his compromise. Those who bear the mark of the beast have "no rest day nor night."

IV.   v. 13. Here we have a mighty beatitude: the church gains its patience, not in passive endurance, but in fulfilment of its commission as declared in this chapter, by proclaiming the gospel, declaring the fall of Babylon, and pointing men to their responsibility. Patience is the fruit of faithfulness. Moffatt's translation of 14:13 reads, "This is what shows the patience of the saints—those who keep God's commandments and the faith of Jesus."

The fourth angel proclaims the comfort of the faith, therefore. The reference of our faith is ultimately to eternity, and the gospel proclaims the joy and victory which is ours in Christ. We have eternal life with the Lord, and receive a reward for our faithfulness. The church sins not only when she limits the gospel to eternity, but also by speaking too little about heaven.

V.   vv. 14-16. Here the church is reminded that judgment is not merely reserved to the end time but is an ever-present fact in every age, that Christ (v. 14) is constantly reaping a harvest and separating the tares and the wheat. Therefore the fact of judgment must be constantly proclaimed. Men must either meet Christ as their Saviour or meet Him as their Judge. To soft-pedal this fact and preach "peace," "sweetness and light" and dispense sweet music is the mark of a sinning and apostate church.

VI.   vv. 17-20. The treading of the winepress was a symbol of vengeance, and it is clearly so depicted: "the great winepress of the wrath of God." Winepresses usually stood outside the city: even so, those who refuse to find sanctuary in the City of God are cast into the winepress of the vengeance of God. Jesus once went outside the gates of earthly Jerusalem, sentenced to death by the City of Man. Now the condemned nations go outside the gates of the true Jerusalem, to be destroyed in the winepress of the vengeance of God. The earth is the Lord's: the ungodly will be cast out and destroyed. Thus, the church must declare that God is a God of vengeance: that every sin is directly an affront to God, a denial of Him, and an attempt to supplant Him. Man himself cannot take on the task of vengeance: it belongs to God, who in His absolute justice brings it to pass. The vengeance of God upon unatoned and unforgiven sin must be proclaimed. And the vengeance of God is to be executed through the God-ordained channels of its execution, in church, state, home, school, and all of life, and they shall be executed also by God in the providential government of history.

VII.   The last angel depicted is the angel of fire (v. 18), who rises from the altar, beneath which the murdered saints had cried, "How long, O Lord, how long?" The prayer of the saints is answered: fire is cast upon the earth in the form of judgment. Thus the church is pointed to its responsibility to pray. To be prayerless is to sin. The church is required to be in unceasing prayer concerning every aspect of her commission. Thus the church cannot be passive, nor can she be content with merely suffering. Her task is to establish the supremacy of Christ in every domain as Priest, Prophet, and King.

Verse 20 speaks of 1600 stadii being covered with the blood of vengeance. This is a symbol for fulness of judgment, i.e., world-wide in extent, at all times in history. Nothing escapes the vengeance of God which goes without atonement and without forgiveness. The distance is 1600 stadii, 4x4x100, i.e., the four corners of the world multiplied by itself and then multiplied by the fulness of 10, i.e., 100, a symbol of fulness itself. Thus the world as a whole is covered by the vengeance of God wherever it is uncovered by the atoning blood of Christ.

REVELATION 15: THE SONG OF MOSES

As noted earlier, the Book of Revelation echoes the framework of the Feast of Tabernacles and the Feast of Pentecost. The Feast of Tabernacles was a harvest festival celebrating Israel's sojourn in the wilderness and its entrance into the Promised Land. It was a celebration for Israelite and Gentile, a type of the ingathering of the peoples into the kingdom of God, reminding all that they were pilgrims and strangers on earth. Man's wilderness journey is his struggle from a fallen world into the new creation, and man's wilderness journey is his pilgrimage out of a fallen world into the kingdom of God re-established. Man's destination and citizenship is the kingdom of God, in heaven and on earth. Throughout Revelation, the ingathering is heralded, as well as the judgment on those who oppose the saints' entrance into the Promised Land.

Pentecost celebrated the giving of the law to Moses, and the Christian Pentecost celebrates the writing of the law on the tables of our hearts by the indwelling Spirit. The first Pentecost at Sinai was heralded by trumpets, the shaking of the earth, lightning, and storm, as the Lord and His hosts drew near to the sinful earth. Throughout Revelation, we see the same trumpet blasts of judgment, the shaking of the earth, the storm, and thunder as God approaches man and nothing stands between God and man except the judgment of the law.

Revelation 15 gives us two visions. Again, these visions are not to be understood chronologically, but as true for all time between the first and the second coming, and at every time.

I. vv. 2-4. The first vision is of the "glassy" or, better, transparent, sea, with the saints standing on the shore thereof singing "the song of Moses the servant of God, and the song of the Lamb." The Song of Moses was composed and sung when Israel was delivered from Egypt, taken through the Red Sea, and then privileged to witness its enemies overwhelmed by the returning waters of the Red Sea. Ahead of Israel lay the wilderness journey before they could enter the Promised Land. Before them also were enemies challenging their passage. But the great reality was deliverance from bondage, from slavery, and equipment with the glorious liberty of the sons of God. They were now a holy nation and a royal priesthood in God, whose presence marched with them and who made His royal tent in the center of the camp. Every line of this song echoes the psalms and the prophets. The deliverance foreshadowed in the Exodus, in every deliverance of Israel, in the return from the Babylonian Captivity, all these and more were fulfilled at Calvary in the great deliverance Christ wrought for His Church in overthrowing the bondage of sin and death. This is the joyful song of the redeemed of every age, and the joyful anticipation of full and final victory: "all nations shall come and worship before thee; for thy judgments are made manifest." Christ is King of the nations. This is the Christian expectation and must be the Christian program for action: the sovereignty of Christ over all things and all nations. The song of deliverance, in Moses' day and now, is the Song of the Lamb.

The sea has been seen elsewhere as dark and troubled, spewing forth the beast and storming against the Church. Now, viewed from the throne of God again, we see it as transparent, clear as crystal. Again, this witnesses to the glorious fact that there are no dark corners in God's universe, no brute facts in creation. Every fact is a created fact and has meaning only in the light of the creative purpose of God. Therefore, *no* facts are a hindrance to the saints, because all facts are God-given facts and are to be interpreted in terms of the glory of God and our glory in Him. We therefore know that all things indeed do work together for good to them that love God, to them who are the called according to His purpose (Rom. 8:28).

Verse 1 speaks of "another sign," so called because of the two "signs" which have preceded it (Rev. 12:1, 3). The first sign was the woman, or the true Church of God. The second, the dragon, or Satan, and his two beasts. The third sign is a vision of the fulness of judgment in the hands of God's messengers, and the vision of the transparent sea, the cosmos as completely transparent and subject to the triune God. The sea is mingled with fire, or judgment.

II. vv. 5-8. The second vision is of the tabernacle in heaven. The true sanctuary is unveiled or opened. This opening of the sanctuary was accomplished by the incarnation, atonement, and resurrection: "The only begotten Son, which is in the bosom of the Father, he hath declared him" (John 1:18). The Light shines forth, the glory of the Presence, into the entire world, making transparent the sea or world and laying bare the sins of the nations. Seven angels, representing the fulness of judgment, go forth with "seven golden vials (or bowls) full of the wrath of God." These angels are "clothed in pure and white linen, and having their breasts girded with golden girdles." This description suggests that of Christ himself (1:13). The angels are clothed with royal authority as they represent Christ the King inflicting justice on those who rebel against His authority and sovereignty, but they also discharge His priestly office. Intercession with God the Father results in God's judgment in history.

There is no entrance into the Temple without judgment. Judgment is always the necessary aspect of salvation. To expect God to by-pass judgment and institute a salvation bereft of it is to think in pagan terms.

REVELATION 16: THE GREAT SHAKING

Revelation gives us a contrast between two women and two cities, the Radiant Woman, and the Scarlet Woman, the Jerusalem which is above, and the Jerusalem which is below, the City of God and the City of Man. Between these two forces there is unremitting warfare.

The wrath of God is poured out upon the Scarlet Woman, the Jerusalem which is below, called also Babylon the Great, representing the pride and pretension of all nations as they claim to represent the true kingdom and the true paradise. In the ranks of Babylon we find those churches which serve the dragon, which feel that the kingdom is the result of man's effort and attainable by means of social action rather than regeneration, who identify the kingdom of God with a human   social order or predict, as did Richard Rothe, that "in the future the Church would be dissolved in the State."[1] For such men, paradise means the sovereignty of man. For the saints, it means the sovereignty of God and man's subjection to it and fulfilment within it.

The continual judgment on the world's attempt to create paradise is given to us in the vision of the seven vials or bowls of judgment. This chapter, as well as those succeeding it, suggests echoes of Ezekiel 14, the judgment upon Tyre. It also suggests Isaiah 14, wherein the king of Babylon, called Lucifer, is portrayed in his demonic pride, exalting himself against God, believing history to be fulfilled in his works rather than in the purpose and work of God. For the citizens of the earthly Jerusalem, of Babylon the Great, history leads to the fulfilment of man. Israel saw the kingdom of God as a Jewish kingdom, as the exaltation of the Jew. Jewish national pride led to the crucifixion of Jesus Christ because He came to inaugurate the kingdom of God rather than the kingdom of Israel. According to the Talmud, "Each Israelite is worth more before God

---

[1] Adolph Keller: *Religion and Revolution.* New York: Revell, 1934, p. 36.

than all the people who have been or shall be."[2] For the Judeans, the worst son of Abraham was better than the best Gentile. Israel at the time of Christ was a part of Babylon the Great; hence its opposition to and hatred of the kingdom of God. But this sin was not exclusive to Israel or to the Jew. All nations who seek through their programs of security and national development to fulfil man's hope, serve Babylon rather than the kingdom of God. And their excuse, after the testimony of Christ and the completed Word, the Bible, and the witness of history, is even less than that of Israel.

Two paradises are offered to man, one by Babylon and one by God. Babylon seeks constantly to destroy the paradise of God, but God destroys instead the paradise of man.

These seven bowls are similar to the seven trumpets of Revelation 8 and 9. Like them, they are God's dispossession notice and action against the world. The sealed roll, with its seven seals, is man's inheritance, made available by Jesus Christ. The inheritance is victory over sin and death, and the restoration of man's forfeited inheritance, paradise. But the sons of Adam, of the line of Cain, seek to establish a counterfeit paradise, an unblessed unity, in their towers of Babel. In the name of Babylon, they claim God's world. The judgments of the trumpets and bowls are God's eviction notice.

The Song of Moses, the song of salvation, precedes the plagues and judgments in Revelation. Salvation separates men, and the judgment which follows is salvation in action, to effect restoration and restitution.

1. *The first bowl*, 16:2. This plague recalls the sixth of the Egyptian plagues, the plague of boils (Ex. 9:8-12; Deut. 28:27). Egypt was a type of the world-power, and the plagues here are also to be understood typically. Spiritual and mental sores destroy the peace and self-complacency of the worshipers of the world power, the devotees of the paradise without God. There is no rest, saith my God, to the wicked.

2. *The second bowl*, 16:3. Cf. the first Egyptian plague (Ex. 7:17f.) and the second trumpet (Rev. 8:8). Here it is portrayed as more extensive and as total. Even as the Nile is the source of

<hr />

[2] Powell: *The Trial of Jesus Christ*, p. 24.

Egypt's natural advantage and strength and the life-blood of the nation economically, even so God's judgment on the Nile was the death-stroke against the nation. Their advantage became their disadvantage, and their strength, their destruction. So God uses the very advantages and the strength of the nations to destroy them. Every advantage of the nations must be used to the glory of God or will serve to the damnation of the nations.

3. *The third bowl,* 16:4-7. This suggests the third Egyptian plague, and the third trumpet (Rev. 8:10, 11). The altar concurs in this judgment; cf. 6:10; 14:15-18. "The streams and rivers feed the sea; they are the powers and influences which go to the making up of the great popular sentiment; these are smitten by the same corruption. The streams of life grow putrid, the fresh and bright gifts of God are polluted, when the ocean of public thought is unwholesome."[3]

4. *The fourth bowl,* 16:8, 9. Cf. the fourth trumpet, 8:12. The sun, the source of light and life and all blessing, becomes instead a destructive and blasting power, cursing instead of blessing. "The things full of beneficence are turned into powers of sorrow to those who follow evil."[4]

5. *The fifth bowl,* 16:10, 11. Cf. Exodus 10:21, and the fourth trumpet, 8:12. Darkness covers the antichristian world empire and throne. The throne is now attacked. First, the individuals or citizens of Babylon are struck with mental and emotional distress. Then the advantages of Babylon become disadvantages. The pollution spreads to every aspect of Babylon, and the things of blessing become instruments of curses. The coherence and organization of this great Babylon are undermined from within by the judgments of God. The very center of authority in Babylon is now affected. "The kingdom which boasted itself as full of light becomes darkened."[5]

6. *The sixth bowl,* 16:12-16. Cf. the sixth trumpet, 9:13f. The Euphrates represents the boundary between the promised land, the people of God, and their great enemies. The destruction of the

[3] W. Boyd Carpenter, in Ellicott: *op. cit.,* VIII, 607.
[4] *Ibid.*
[5] *Ibid.*

boundary is the end and objective of Babylon, the obliteration of all the standards and protections of the kingdom of God against the kingdom of man. The barrier is historically the great impediment to war. As long as the barrier is respected, peace remains. But Babylon constantly seeks to destroy the barrier, to erase the line of division, to obliterate Christ's kingdom and people. When the barrier is erased in the public mind, and all faiths are as one, then Babylon marches in to possess the kingdom of God as its own. The two forces meet at Armageddon, or Megiddo, a symbol of every battle in which the Lord delivers His people, even as He delivered Barak and Gideon at Megiddo. In both instances, the Lord's people were, humanly speaking, helpless and certain of defeat, but the Lord revealed His power to defeat the enemy. The "kings of the east" or, "from the sunrising" (RV) come in over the dry Euphrates to destroy Babylon itself (17:17) as well as to make war with the Lamb (17:14). Thus the forces of Satan destroy the kingdom of Satan. The conquest of the historical Babylon by the drying up of the Euphrates is also echoed here. The drying of the Euphrates forces the issue, and the forcing of the issue destroys Babylon, not the kingdom of God. The obliteration of God's law and order destroys the humanistic state, not the people of God. It should be noted that Harmageddon means the mountains of Megiddo. But there are no mountains of Megiddo, only the Plains of Megiddo. There is a deliberate destruction of the vision of any literal reference to the place; the reference is to the meaning of past events.

7. *The seventh bowl,* 16:17-21. The earthquake (cf. Heb. 12:26-29) is the shaking of the nations, so that only the unshakeable might remain. It is the fulness of all the preceding judgments. It is the continual destruction by God of man's every attempt to achieve security and permanence apart from God. The kingdom of evil seeks to concentrate itself against the kingdom of God, but God destroys its very coherency, so that it falls into "three parts" and destroys itself. The only unity which the kingdom of man truly holds is in the hatred of God and His kingdom. Each citizen of Babylon is ruled by his nature, by the old Adam in him, and seeks to be his own god and law. He unites only in his hatred of God, and this fails

to hold him long. Ultimately, his hatred expresses itself against his very allies. The destruction is a full devastation of his kingdom. Every island fled: the earthquake tests every spot and leaves only the kingdom of God unshaken (Dan. 2:44; 6:26; Heb. 10:28). What the earthquake does not destroy the great hail does. The hail is of undreamed force, each hailstone being between 60 and 100 pounds, and the result is the pulverizing of Babylon. This recalls the Egyptian plagues again, and also the defeat of Israel's enemies at Beth-horon (Josh. 10:1-11), when "the Lord cast down great stones from heaven."

The kingdoms of this world pass away, with all their pretensions and claims, in the great shaking which governs history, but the kingdom of our Lord Jesus Christ grows in power and demonstrates its full and total sovereignty over all nations, peoples, tongues, and tribes. As King of the universe, Christ commands the very stars in their course in the war against Sisera, and against the Siseras of every generation, and the firmament proclaims His glory and His majesty.

Armageddon is a symbol of God's victory, a reminder that the battle and the victory are the Lord's. At Megiddo, Josiah sinned by going to war; he had no business there, since God had made clear that He would deliver. The victory of Jehoshaphat is the victory of the saints.

REVELATION 17: THE WHORE OF BABYLON

Since Revelation gives us so vivid a picture of the man-centered state in revolt against God, it is important for us to understand by way of contrast the biblical doctrine of the kingdom of God and its government in order that we might both recognize Babylon in our midst and also work for the true kingdom.

Before the fall, man was created by God to live in paradise, in community, and to realize in that estate the kingdom of God, the perfect government. Eden was thus the locale of the kingdom of God on earth. The function of government in that original society was, *first,* to exercise dominion under God and in the name of God. As the psalmist declared (8:6), "Thou madest him to have dominion over the works of thy hands; thou has put all things under his feet." This dominion the first Adam forfeited by his sin; having lost dominion over himself, he lost it over creation. As a result, instead of exercising dominion, fallen man works out the implications of the fall. The death and havoc sin works in man's soul, man works out in the world around him. Fallen man is a destroyer; he brings, not dominion but destruction, to the world around him. The destined dominion of man over the earth the last Adam, Jesus Christ, possesses, as I Corinthians 15:22 and Ephesians 1:22 make clear, in view of His perfect obedience and representative work as head of the new humanity and re-creator of paradise. The command to exercise dominion meant to extend the ministerial authority of man into every area of life—in science, art, music, agriculture, and all things else. This was man's cultural task, the creation of a culture and civilization in terms of the sovereignty of God, recognized by man and exercised under God's jurisdiction.

Second, man was created in the image of God, in knowledge, righteousness, holiness, and dominion (Westminster Shorter Catechism, Q. 10; Gen. 1:27; Col. 3:10; Eph. 4:24; Gen. 1:28). Man has therefore the obligation to work out the implications of the image of God in him, in its meaning for his personal life, his life as a member of a family and of society, and in his relationship to the world of nature. He has a calling to knowledge, to know the world in terms of God and God's creative purpose; as a result, in every area, he must extend the boundaries of knowledge under God. He has a calling to righteousness, to know the law of God and to apply it in every sphere. Man is called to holiness, to separate himself and his activities to God and to His glory.

Third, man was created with the declaration that it was not good for him to live alone, and marriage and the family were divinely established in Eden. The primary function of marriage and the family is thus not children, for they are an added blessing rather than the purpose of marriage, but fellowship, community, and communion. To develop the life in community and communion, with the family as the basic institution, was thus a part of man's task in establishing the kingdom of God, the perfect government.

Fourth, man was required to live in obedience to God and to recognize His absolute sovereignty even when the reason for the commandment was not apparent to man. Adam and Eve were barred from the tree of the knowledge of good and evil (Gen. 2:17), and although they were warned from eating of it by a declaration of the consequences, the full significance of the violation and of the act were beyond their understanding. What was within their understanding was that it meant either believing God, walking by faith and in obedience, or doubting God and establishing their own norm of what constituted good and evil. *Faith* was therefore required of them in the kingdom of God. Adam and Eve were required to walk by faith rather than by sight, i.e., by actual experimentation, by a work which tested the commandment of God. The essence of faith and worship is obedience and submission, and this man was required to render unto God in paradise.

The basic reference of government as established in paradise was thus to God, not to man or the state. Government involved man's self-government, but basic to that self-government was the act of faith, covenant-keeping with God.

But, instead of walking by faith, man revolted against God and submitted to the temptation to be as God and to know for himself, that is, to determine for himself, what is right and wrong, good and evil (Gen. 3:5). The result was the fall of man and the entrance of sin and death. Man and his institutions are thus sin-ridden, and no single order of life today can claim to be the locale of the kingdom of God on earth. Rather, the cultural task of man is entrusted to the various spheres of life and reserved to them, and the basic fact of God's purpose for the human scene is a scattering of powers.

The kingdom of God is now to be achieved through Jesus Christ and its realization is reserved to Him. The kingdom is approximated by man as man serves Christ faithfully in the various spheres of life—in church, state, school, calling, family, and all things else.

The state has a duty to serve God, to be Christian, to be a part of God's kingdom, or else it shall be judged by Him. The state is declared in Romans 13 to be a ministry, the ministry of justice and social order. The church is the ministry of grace, of the word and the sacraments, and the discipline of the household of faith. Because God has since the fall, and dramatically at Babel, dispersed man in his attempt to centralize powers and authority, to order society totally, every area of life is strictly limited in its scope by the word of God. The state as civil government is strictly limited in that, *first,* it is under God and must administer justice in faithfulness to His word. *Second,* the state cannot assume as its own those areas which are properly the spheres of the home, school, church, art, economics, or anything else. *Third,* the state cannot limit the individual's freedom to work out the divine mandate for man as God's image-bearer. *Fourth,* the authority of the state is at all times ministerial, or delegated from God, not creative or independent. When the state becomes messianic in its claims and tries to usher in paradise, it has done so by declaring itself to be god and by making itself the source of law and authority. Babylon tries to create paradise without God by side-stepping the whole issue of sin and man's revolt against God. It is man's attempt to be God and to create his own new world.

Turning now to Revelation 17, specifically Babylon is not government itself but the ideal and dream of humanistic states, the human lust for a paradise without God and in contempt of God. The civil governments of this world, in their antichristian character, are depicted as the beast, and it is the beast on whom the woman, the Whore of Babylon, rides (v. 3), i.e., she is dependent upon the beast. It is the civil governments that carry this dream and give it strength and support. In turn, Babylon, the great whore, holds the governments with her fornication and her cup of drunkenness. Revelation identifies the whore with ancient Babylon, with Rome (the seven-hilled city), with Jerusalem, with Tyre (echoing Ezekiel), and with every nation and empire in their dreams of dominion apart from God and of self-realization without God. The name Babylon, however, is especially apt. Babylon was the great city of Nebuchadnezzar, who exalted himself. The prophets saw Babylon, in all her power, vice, and seeming omnipotence, as "the glory of the kingdoms . . . the golden city . . . who exalted her throne above the stars of God . . . who sat as a lady given to pleasures, and flattering herself that she would see no sorrow . . . the hammer of the whole earth . . . the golden cup that made all the earth drunken . . . a golden cup in the hand of the Lord." It was to Babylon that Judah was captive for 70 years, and Babylon that seemingly destroyed the kingdom of God by destroying Jerusalem and reducing the promised land to a sparsely inhabited wilderness. Babylon is a fitting symbol, having its roots in the old dream of Nimrod, of Cain, and of Babel, representing a counterfeit paradise, and an attempt to establish a one-world order without God.

Because Babylon does present an ideal of human unity, peace, and brotherhood which mimics the kingdom of God, it therefore tempts man and is properly called a whore. Because its temptation is the key temptation, declaring that man is his own god and can create his own paradise, therefore Babylon is called the great whore and the mother of harlots and abominations of the earth. She destroys the church's work too often and is "drunken with the blood of the saints."

The purpose of chapters 17 and 18 is to show us "the judgment of the great whore that sitteth upon many waters." In verse 15 we have an interpretation of these waters: the world of men. "The waters which thou sawest, where the whore sitteth, are peoples, and multitudes, and nations and tongues." The beast and the whore draw their power from the people and from the lust of the people for a paradise without God in which the central joy is to be freed from the law of God. Wherever people seek to "find God" by side-stepping the fact of man's sin, they are trying to escape the righteousness of God, His law, and are feeding the beast and the whore.

Attention is then turned to the beast. The beast "was, and is not." He was destroyed by Christ's coming, which inflicted a death-blow on the beast. The kingdom of man was shown to be futile, and Christ ushered in the kingdom of God. The crucifixion and resurrection inflicted the death-blow. But the beast still continues. John is told that "he is going to come up out of the abyss, but he is going to be destroyed" (Williams translation). In other words, the beast comes back into power through the powers of hell, but he shall be destroyed finally.

The beast has seven heads; there are seven hills on which the woman is seated, and Rome and all states and empires are typified here. The seven heads are the fulness of all antichristian states. They are also called seven kings: "five have fallen, one is on the throne." Thus the Old Testament era saw the destruction of five of the seven powers. It is not necessary to identify these five kingdoms. Seven is the number of fulness, and the seven typify all the antichristian governments of history. The sixth now is: in John's day, this was Rome in part, but it also included not only the provinces of the empire, including Judea, but also all the empires of the day beyond the frontiers of Rome. The seventh power was still to come: this was to be all the antichristian states after Rome's day, and the seventh head is portrayed as having ten horns, again a symbol of totality; but these ten horns have not yet become kings (v. 12). Their day was beyond John's time. The wild beast (v. 11) is in a sense the eighth, and yet is one of the seven, as a continuing reality and ideal; the kingdom of man has almost a separate existence from any actual states, but is yet one with them. However, of all them it is said, "They have one common policy. They give their power and authority to the wild beast" (v. 13, Williams trans.). But the Lamb will conquer them, "because He is Lord of lords and King of kings."

The whore sits upon the waters, i.e., the peoples, but her place of residence is the wilderness or desert (v. 3). The wilderness represents the world after the fall. Adam was established in paradise, but by his sin he turned the world into a wilderness. Christ, the second Adam, was tempted in the wilderness, but, by His victory, began the restoration of paradise, and, at the conclusion of His temptation, he "was with the wild beasts" (Mark 1:13), even as Adam in paradise. This was a token of the fact that by His victorious life and death, Jesus Christ restored man to paradise. The restoration is present and future: the image of God in man is restored, but man's sanctification is not complete. The work of restoration is begun, but it will be fully completed only at the end of the world. But every step of that restoration is glorious, and the extent of the restoration in this age must not be underestimated or diminished. Even as the first Adam destroyed paradise by his sin, the second Adam destroys the counterfeit paradise by His righteousness.

REVELATION 18: THE FALL OF BABYLON

The grand design of man is to create a paradise without God, a perfect world in terms of total self-affirmation. To this purpose, the politics of man are bent, and to this goal he bends every effort. The consequences of this grand design are described by Revelation 18.

This chapter echoes the Old Testament proclamations of doom on the nations. The prophets saw the nations at war, not merely against Israel or Judah, who received the just recompense of their sins, but against the LORD of hosts. God had raised up the nations as His scourge and instrument, but they had made self-deification and self-glorification their end. This, their pride, was the source of their corruption, their declaration of independence from God and man, their vicious profligacy with human life and the world, and their stubborn blindness in the face of judgment. Revelation 18 echoes and sums up the whole prophetic judgment of God upon the dream of the nations: it is the divine judgment upon the revived dream of Babel, one world apart from God, the counterfeit paradise of Cain and Nimrod. Isaiah's prophecies against Babylon (chapts. 13, 21, 47) are echoed, and also Jeremiah's (chapts. 50, 51), and Ezekiel's judgment on Tyre (chapts. 26, 27).

The first step in this judgment is the exposure, announced in verse 1. According to Lord, "The *Angel* of verse 1 symbolizes a body of men who shall with resistless light unveil the Apostate character of Babylon."[1] The angel or messenger represents the divinely given wisdom to expose the perversity, futility, and doom of Babylon. Under the light of Scripture, Babylon is shown to be worthless and corrupt. In advance of the fall of Babylon, the proclamation is made. "Babylon the great is fallen, is fallen, and is become the habitation of devils, and the hold of every foul spirit, and a cage of every unclean

[1] Cited by John Peter Lange: *Commentary on the Holy Scriptures, Revelation*. Grand Rapids: Zondervan, reprint of original trans. of 1871 German edition, with additions, p. 324.

and hateful bird" (v. 2). Even as the prophets announced the fall of the Babylonian Empire in advance, and God in faithfulness to His word brought it to pass exactly as He had declared, so the Christian is required to witness in the same spirit. Babylon, the dream of a paradise without God, the cradle-to-grave security by man's own act, is doomed and finished. The call to separation is part of the announcement (v. 4). Men must separate themselves from this dream of Babylon, and from everything connected with it, lest they share its doom.

The sins of Babylon (1. 5) are pictured as a huge mountain, another tower of Babel, reaching up to heaven in their pretensions and audacity. They have not been forgotten by God, but "God hath remembered her iniquities" and waited, for it is the longsuffering of the Lord which is our salvation (II Peter 3:8-15). The patience of God extends to the sinner an opportunity for repentance, and to the redeemed an opportunity to work out the meaning of his salvation. But, finally, judgment comes: because her sins were double, her punishment will be in strict justice double.

Babylon had been confident of her omnipotence and her permanence (v. 7). Now judgment descends upon her: "Her plagues are four-fold, as though from every quarter her trouble came: death for her scorn of the prospect of widowhood; mourning, for her inordinate revelling; famine, for her abundance; and fire, the punishment for her fornication."[2] She has been an enemy to mankind in seducing nations, kings, and merchants to a false evaluation of their function, their nature, and destiny, Now she perishes, totally, even as a great millstone (of the variety turned by animals) disappears when cast into the sea (v. 21).

The result of her collapse is the mourning of the merchants and the shipmasters (v. 11ff., 17ff.), in other words, the world of commerce and of business. They lose their markets for

1. treasures (gold, silver, etc.)
2. the luxuries of clothing
3. luxury items of housing
4. aromatics

[2] Boyd Carpenter in Ellicott: *op. cit.*, VIII, p. 615.

5. articles of food
6. means of transportation
7. the traffic or market in human beings.

The significance of this is clear-cut. The collapse of the dream of Babylon, of a human paradise without God, is precipitated by a great economic disillusionment or collapse. The situation can be described as economic chaos: the very means which should lead to the human paradise precipitate the collapse of the hope. All the normal trade channels break down and grind to a halt.

We have seen previously that the nations and powers who destroy Babylon are the very ones who mourn over her, being her followers. This is a significant aspect of the nature of sin. When Oscar Wilde wrote that "Each man kills the thing he loves," he described forcefully, not the Christian man, but the sinner moving relentlessly down the path of his own perversity. As Lenski commented on the fall of Babylon, "There *is* no reason in the unreason of antichristianity, least of all when its seduction works itself out to completion. The lover of a whore strangles her and then weeps like a fool."[3] Today we see the state destroying the foundations of the state, business destroying the foundations of business, labor destroying the nature and fabric of labor, and farming destroying the very soil that feeds it. In their greed they create conditions destined to bring their own collapse. This leads to the elimination of the very thing they desire, to the death of the Babylon they try to create, to the undermining of the tower of Babel they try to build. As Lenski rendered verse 14, "And the flush season of the lust of thy life went away from thee; and all the fat things and brilliant things perish from thee, and no longer them shall they find."[4]

In the face of all this, one clear duty is presented to the saints of God: to rejoice. It must be presented to them, because it will be their temptation to share in the grief of their generation, and to bewail the just recompense of sin. But the plain commandment is (v. 20), "Rejoice over her . . . for God hath avenged you on her." Whatever else may be said about the collapse of human hope, this must be

[3] R. C. H. Lenski: *Interpretation of St. John's Revelation*, p. 522.
[4] *Ibid.*, p. 524.

remembered (v. 24): the implications of the dream meant death, in every age, for the Lord's people. Not only the death of the prophets and saints is the responsibility of this paradise without God, but the blood "of all that were slain upon the earth," i.e., the war, tyranny, and horror of the ages have been due to man's rebellion against God, his desire to be his own god, and his attempt to reshape heaven and earth after the fashion of his own sinful nature. As James said, wars arise from the nature of men, as do all human conflicts (Jas. 4:1ff.). And the nature of man the sinner is to be his own god and to create his own heaven in defiance of God. From this urge flows the blood of the saints, and "of all that were slain upon the earth."

Rist has called attention to the fact that verse 21 is "obviously patterned after the symbolic act related in the oracle against Babylon," taken from Jeremiah 50, 51. Jeremiah, after prophesying against Babylon, sent Seraiah, who was travelling to Babylon, with a scroll of the prophecy, to be read there on his arrival and then, weighted with a stone, to be thrown into the river Euphrates. "As it sinks into the water he is to prophesy that Babylon herself will sink in a similar way as a result of God's judgment and will never rise up (Jer. 51:59-64)."[5]

Even as Babylon was declared to be finished in history, destined to vanish totally, so Babylon the great is destined to vanish and become no more than an ugly memory.

The judgment of Babylon described in this chapter reflects several historical events, past and future:

1. The Tower of Babel, and its fall, are clearly echoed.
2. The Babylon of the Old Testament, its rise and fall, are obviously in mind.
3. The Roman Empire and other empires and states of St. John's day are in mind.
4. Future attempts of men to build an antichristian order are condemned in advance.
5. The final grand attempt to build such an order culminates in a final disaster of world-wide dimensions.

[5] Martin Rist: *Interpreters Bible,* vol. 12, p. 503f.

REVELATION 18:4: THE CALL TO SEPARATION

Because the subject of separation is either neglected or over-stressed, a note on the matter is of importance. A brief summary analysis of key New Testament passages is thus in order.

First, Revelation 18:4 clearly calls for a separation from Babylon, from the dream of a one-world order without God. This is clearly a call to *political separation*: it requires the believer to divorce himself from liberalism and from socialism, and, ultimately, it clearly requires a Christian political order. This means a Christian party as a means to a Christian state. Since the dream of non-Christian politics is to create a working and finally perfect social order without God, and since the Christian must hold that such an order is futile and judgment-bound, Christian separation and action are necessary.

Second, in II John 10, 11, *ecclesiastical separation* is required. A true church cannot receive false teachers or ministers without becoming partaker to their "evil deeds." Since church services were in the New Testament era and later held in homes, the prohibition against receiving apostate religious leaders meant either as speakers or leaders, or as guests, since hospitality was then provided by believers. This did not prohibit true ministers of Christ from speaking in synagogues, as Acts clearly evidences; it did prohibit receiving false teaching.

Ecclesiastical separation has as its necessary implication the severance of religious association with heretics. St. Paul declared, "Mark them which cause divisions and offenses contrary to the doctrine which ye have learned; and avoid them" (Rom. 16:17). Paul also wrote to Titus, "A man that is a heretick after the first and second admonition reject" (Titus 3:10). Even more bluntly, Paul declared "let him be accursed" who brings another gospel (Gal. 1:8, 9). Jesus Christ himself spoke even more forcefully concerning false religious leaders, calling the Pharisees "children of hell" (Matt. 23: 15), "hypocrites" (Matt. 23:13, 15, 23, 25, 27, 29), "fools and blind

. . . full of extortion and excess . . . serpents . . . generation of vipers . . . blind guides . . . children of them which killeth the prophets" (Matt. 23:19, 25, 33, 24, 31), and much more. His attitude was not that of cooperative evangelism" or promiscuous love.[1]

The entire significance of the church is nullified if the church becomes itself an area of compromise and coexistence with unbelief, heresy, and hypocrisy. The church is called to be a holy, i.e., a separated congregation, a people set apart in terms of faith. Without separation, the church is not a church.

Third, the Old Testament forbad mixed marriages. The church now faced a different situation from that facing a covenant people. In Israel, the believer could not marry an unbeliever. But now, converts numbered men and women who were converted after their marriage, and their partners remained unconverted. The question raised then was simply this: should such marriages be rendered null and void, or else subject the person to excommunication, as Nehemiah did with the mixed marriages of his day? (Neh. 13:23ff.). St. Paul's answer was that, the cases being different, such marriages should be maintained. But, if the unbelieving partner departed or broke up the marriage, *then* the believer was free. The marriage was then null and void (I Cor. 7:10ff.).

Fourth, the great general statement on separation is II Corinthians 6:14-18: "Be ye not unequally yoked together. . . ." The Greek word translated as *yoked* is *eterozugeo,* to be yoked with one of another kind, to come under a different or unequal yoke, to have fellowship with one who is *not* an equal.

Several things are clearly apparent in this passage, which is general in reference, so that *first,* it applies to marriage, business, education, worship, and all things. Unequal yoking in any area is thus contrary to God's general purpose for His people. And the *yoking* of believer with unbeliever in any capacity is unequal yoking. The question is this: is the relationship a yoke? *Second,* it *must* be a *yoke,* a voluntary submission or union which involves a contradiction of faith. *Third,* unequal yoking prevents separation or holiness, and

---

[1] See Gary G. Cohen: *Biblical Separation Defended.* Philadelphia: Presbyterian and Reformed Publishing Co., 1966.

is therefore forbidden. *Fourth,* unequal yoking involves the equality of belief and unbelief; it assumes that there is no difference between the believer and unbeliever, and this we are not permitted to do. *Fifth,* the yoking is comparable to marriage: it is a close and binding union.

A fifth passage is important also in relationship to separation, I Corinthians 5:9, 10, which forbad the congenial or religious association with sinners, but also made clear that general business and polite associations were not meant: "for then must ye needs go out of the world." No yoking or submission is involved in such associations.

Beyond the plain letter of Scripture, there is Christian liberty, so that variations of practice are possible. But none can make private concepts of separation a law of God. The call to separation is real and specific. To over-extend its meaning is as clearly wrong as to deny its meaning.

REVELATION 19: THE TWO BANQUETS

In Revelation 19, the situation of two earlier chapters is recalled in order to reveal to us now the fulness of their meaning. In verse 11, Revelation 4:1 and 6:2 are brought into full focus. We see again "heaven opened," that is, creation and all its events and factuality viewed from the perspective of the triune God and His purpose. Again we see the Lord riding on "a white horse . . . and in righteousness he doth judge and make war." It is the Kinsman-Redeemer, going forth to redeem His own and to dispossess the enemy who holds the forfeited inheritance of man. To dispossess the enemy, the Lord sends forth His sevenfold judgment, which includes religious persecution, economic hardship, and death. These judgments both separate the believer from too ready an inclination to make common cause with the world, and at the same time to destroy the false dream of Babylon. When men find the recurring fact of economic hardship, corruption in high places, disillusion and death in history, they face the judgment of the Lord upon Babylon: it is His war upon the false paradise and its pretensions. Fallen man is cut off from the Garden of Eden, and the flaming sword keeps the way to the tree of life to prevent man in his sin from finding peace and security apart from God.

This battle is portrayed at the beginning and throughout the book, and it is again depicted for us now. The tribulation of the saints is an age-old and recurring fact, the battle of Armageddon is also an age-long struggle designed to destroy the dream of Babylon, culminating finally in the total destruction of that dream. Christ is now more clearly revealed as KING OF KINGS, LORD OF LORDS. As the absolute sovereign of all creation, He is here revealed in all His universal authority and irresistible power. But, more than battle, Armageddon signalizes the victory of the Lord, the defeat of the dream of Babylon.

In 19:1-10, the saints sing the great Hallelujah chorus, rejoicing in the Lord's victory. This is the rejoicing required of them in 18: 20, 24. It echoes the Hebrew Hallel, Psalms 113-118, which began with "Praise the Lord" or "alleluia" and proclaimed God's salvation of His people. A beatitude (v. 9) is proclaimed for those who are bidden to the marriage supper of the Lamb.

God is then revealed as proclaiming two great banquets, one, for His own people, the marriage supper of the Lamb, and the other, the banquet of wrath for the workers of iniquity. The goal of history is communion and community. Apostate, covenant-breaking man dreams of a communion on his own terms, all men as their own gods, determining good and evil for themselves and creating a perfect and happy world order in terms of man's autonomy from God. The purpose as stated at Babel is to build a "city," i.e., a community, to establish a communion in terms of a common cause and faith. Now the result of that dream is revealed: it disintegrates under the wrath of God. It becomes the table of vultures.

The goal of covenant-keeping man is community under God and communion in the Kinsman-Redeemer, the covenant-keeping federal representative of the new humanity, the last Adam, Jesus Christ. The goal is again or originally the city, the community, and the garden of Eden was intended to be and was in origin a city, a community, in that the basic communion, with God, was the foundation of man's communion with his helpmeet and with nature.

Now, in Revelation, the Church, or Bride of Christ, is clothed in the righteousness of Christ, and the banquet is the symbol of restored fellowship between God and man. To eat salt with a man, i.e., to sit at table with him, is a long-standing symbol of brotherhood and communion. God walked with man in paradise, and had communion with him. This communion was broken by man's sin and is now restored by God's grace. All believers enter into this communion at regeneration, partake of it in increasing measure as they participate in true Christian fellowship within the family of the Church, grow in it as they establish a Christian society, and enter into its fulness at the great resurrection.

The banquet of the sons of Babylon is the feast of vultures on the field of battle. It typifies the utter ruin of human society and fellowship, its devastation in war and death. The consequences of man's rebellion against God and his attempt to create his own paradise end in war and death, and the feast of the vultures. The scene is depicted in words echoing Ezekiel 39:4, 17-20. This banquet of the vultures is an old story in history, and a new one daily. Man's wars to make the world safe for democracy end up by creating a funeral for peace and freedom. Man's attempts to create a just and peaceful social order result in the most flagrant of social evils and social warfare, and provide more carnage for vulture feasts. The result is that finally the dream of Babylon is destroyed by the very attempts to realize it.

Not only is the dream of Babylon destroyed, the whore of Babylon eliminated, but the beast and the false prophet also (i.e., the two beasts, civil governments in their attempt to fulfil the dream of Babylon, and the false religions, both ostensibly Christian and pagan, which seek to give support to the beast and to Babylon). The messianic pretensions of states are destroyed, and the faiths which give support to these pretensions are destroyed with them.

This destruction is depicted in terms recalling the overthrow of Sodom and Gomorrah. Even as God wiped from the face of the earth the cities of the plain, with all their vaunted culture and contempt of God's law, so God shall destroy the beast and the false prophet. Man's vaunted strength, pride, and beauty, all his systems of power and authority, are swept aside by God and consumed by fire. The old Adam in man is confounded in all his pretensions and hope, and his every attempt to give form to his nature through civil government or religion is persistently eliminated and finally utterly destroyed. That this involves tremendous convulsions of history is clearly indicated: that the saints have a duty to rejoice in the face of these things, and in the face of their own sufferings in the process, is also clearly indicated. The benediction (Rev. 22:18ff.) which the Book of Revelation pronounces is for those who accept this totality of God's purpose and of His word, adding and detracting nothing.

Three symbols are used in this vision for communion. *First,* there is the symbol of the *city.* For modern man, the city scarcely represents communion, but the ancient concept of the city is of a communion, a community established on a common faith. In the ancient city, citizenship rested on religion, on communion in faith. From the biblical perspective, it can be said that the first city was in the garden of Eden. Adam and Eve were created to live in community, the essence of which was communion with God and community under God. Cain and Nimrod, as well as the builders of Babel, strove to establish another concept of the city, communion in man without God. The humanistic concept of the city, the City of Man, has been steadily productive of increasing anarchy and atomization. Its major accomplishment has been hostility against the City of God and the destruction of the people of God. But the destiny of the City of Man is the feast of vultures.

The *second* symbol is marriage. The wedding feast of Christ and the Church typifies fulness of communion and community. The ground of this community is Christ's atoning sacrifice *and* perfect obedience to the law as man's federal head. The wedding represents, as a symbol, the consummation of love and the beginning of life in community.

The *third* symbol is the "supper," eating, or banqueting. Combining a wedding with a supper heightens the sense of joy in community. Eating together is an ancient symbol, as has been noted, of brotherhood and communion, and, in the context of the true City, the Jerusalem from above, on the occasion of the great wedding it represents communion, peace, and community to the highest degree.

REVELATION 20: RESURRECTION

When our Lord began His ministry, Israel was expecting the millennium to begin. According to the Jewish expectation, a great Messianic age would be ushered in on the year 5000 and would last 1,000 years. This would be an era of Jewish supremacy and supernatural power and abundance. According to the Apocalypse of Baruch:

> The earth will bring forth fruit, one producing 10,000; in the vine there will be a thousand branches, in every branch a thousand clusters, in every cluster a thousand berries, and every berry will yield a cor [36 gals.] of wine.

According to the Book of Enoch:

> In those days will the whole earth be tilled in righteousness . . . and vines will be planted on it. The vine which is planted thereon will yield wine in abundance, and of all seed which is sown thereon will each measure bear 10,000.[1]

The 1,000 years were derived from a scheme whereby each day of creation was equal to 100 years in the sight of the Lord. According to Jewish scholars of that time, 5,000 years had passed and the millennium was about to begin. Since the first 1,000 began with the year 1, continuing to 999, the second 1,000 was 1,000-1,999, and so on, so that the year 5000 marked the beginning of the sixth millennium, comparable to the sixth day of creation. The millennium in this thinking was the age of man, and the concept was humanistic to the core.

Because of this expectation, there were many false messiahs ready to take advantage of the feverish expectancy. Hence also the high excitement when John the Baptist began his ministry, and the tremendous popular enthusiasm for Jesus. Our Lord made no public and

[1] Albertus Pieters: *Studies in the Revelation of St. John.* Grand Rapids, Mich.: Eerdmans, 1950, p. 283f.

open statement of His Messianic kingship in order to avoid a false conclusion on the part of the populace: He spent much time redefining the meaning of the kingdom of God, not in terms of the Jewish millennial hope, but in terms of His gospel and its fulfilling of the Old Testament prophecies. He refused the offered crown after the first feeding of the multitude. In every way, He rejected the millennial Messianic hope in favor of the biblical faith, of which He was the fulfilment.

All present-day millennial thinking is a revival of the Jewish hope, which has never been accepted by the church or approved by a single one of the great confessions and creeds of the church. In the early church, some millennial thinking was present as a result of the Judaizing influences. With the Reformation, as many of the Protestant clergy went to rabbis to learn Hebrew, they were taught the millennial hope in the course of their studies, and, for a time, such thinking flourished. Its modern revival is due to Darby, and to Scofield, whose Bible notes go so far as to assert that Jesus' primary work was to establish the Jewish kingdom, and, failing that, the atonement on the cross became a second-best plan of salvation.[2] Ultimately, according to Scofield, the Jewish plan will be restored to its primacy, with the temple and sacrifice re-established. Such a system is a practical denial of the Christian faith, a revival of the Phariseeism which crucified Christ, and an offense to the Saviour who came, not to establish a Jewish kingdom, but as the Lamb slain from the foundation of the world, come to give His life a ransom for many. The Jews continued, even after the fall of Jerusalem, to hope for their millennium. Josephus gives us a history of the Jewish nation for 5,000 years, thereby echoing this hope.

In one sense only, the Jews were right. The time was at hand. "Now after that John was put in prison, Jesus came into Galilee, preaching the gospel of the kingdom of God, And saying, The time is fulfilled, and the kingdom of God is at hand: repent ye, and believe the gospel" (Mark 1:4, 15). That kingdom was established and came by the death and resurrection of our Lord, whereby the power

[2] For a critique of Scofield's interpretation, see O. T. Allis: *Prophecy and the Church*. Philadelphia: Presbyterian and Reformed Publishing Co.

of Satan was broken, and His kingdom ushered in with power over sin and death, His church established so that the gates of hell cannot prevail against her. Jesus clearly said, "Verily I say unto you, That there be some of them that stand here, which shall not taste of death, till they have seen the kingdom of God come with power" (Mark 9:1; Matt. 16:28; Luke 9:27). Because the disciples persistently believed in the Jewish hope, they could not associate this coming kingdom with the crucifixion and were dumbfounded by both His words and the course of events. But, either Jesus was hopelessly wrong, since all of His disciples are now dead and the Jewish hope not yet realized, or the kingdom is not what men say it is, but rather exactly that which our Lord proclaimed, His kingdom, established by His victory over sin and death and extending that victory by grace unto all who by faith come unto Him. Any other kingdom hope is the dream of Babylon. It was sin and death which invaded the kingdom at the beginning, and it was sin and death which Christ destroyed by His work in order to re-establish His kingdom in His power and His righteousness.

The book of Revelation presents the kingdom age, not as a millennial pipe dream, but as a period of struggle, wherein Christ's Church victoriously marches against the enemy, its Redeemer dispossessing the powers of darkness in order to reclaim and repossess the lost inheritance, creation in its original state. Two aspects of this restoration must be distinguished. *First,* repossession, which Christ through His Church victoriously establishes during the gospel or kingdom age; this is the true millennium, the true reign of Christ and His saints, as they bring men and nations under the dominion of Christ. *Second,* re-creation, whereby the repossessed heaven and earth—the false prophet, beast, and dragon (or Satan) being destroyed and cast into hell—are now made anew, in order to become the eternal heaven and earth which is the habitation of the Lord and His people throughout eternity. The power of sin was broken on the cross, and death overcome in the resurrection. This victory is manifested throughout the gospel age, and its fulness manifested in the eternal kingdom of God, the new creation. The new creation is both the final act, and the process before that act. The new creation begins

with the first resurrection, i.e., the salvation of each sinner, and it
continues with his sanctification. The new creation involves bringing
every thought, realm, nation, and art into captivity to Christ and it
means the restoration of sovereignty to the rightful Lord, Jesus
Christ. It culminates in the great act, the creation of a new heaven
and earth.

Thus Revelation 20 is in a sense a recapitulation of the entire book.
In verses 1-6, the binding of Satan is proclaimed. This is referred
to in Scripture as accomplished in the atonement and resurrection:
John 16:11; Luke 10:18; John 12:31; Genesis 3:15; Hebrews 2:14;
Isaiah 53:12; Colossians 2:15; see also Luke 11:21, 22; I John 3:8.
The purpose of our Lord's coming was to destroy the work of the
devil and to reclaim man's forfeited inheritance, to save him from
the power of sin and death, and to re-create him in the image of
God. In Luke 11:21, 22, Jesus, answering the charge of being in
league with Satan, answered that instead "the kingdom of God is
come upon you" (11:20), because the "strong man" Satan, who had
ruled from Adam on, was now cast out by "a stronger" who not only
overcomes him but "taketh from him all his armour wherein he
trusted, and divideth his spoils." He declared, moreover, "Now is
the judgment of this world: now shall the prince of this world be
cast out" (John 12:31). Paul said that Christ, "having spoiled the
principalities and powers, he made a shew of them openly, triumphing over them in it" (Col. 2:15). The casting out and binding up of
Satan is the work of our Lord's first coming, and Satan is now
bound in "that he should deceive the nations no more." The gospel
works in power throughout the world, until its commission is fulfilled, "and after that he must be loosed a little season." In this
gospel era, the time of the first resurrection,[3] the souls of the faithful
are reigning with Christ. This first resurrection means our salvation
in all that it involves. It means our resurrection from the old humanity of Adam, the lost and dead humanity of men in revolt
against God and under condemnation of eternal death. This resurrection is spoken of throughout Scripture as a true rebirth, as a rising

[3] See J. Marcellus Kik: *Revelation Twenty*. Philadelphia: Presbyterian and
Reformed Publishing Co., 1955, p. 3ff.

from the dead (John 3:1ff.; Rom. 6:1ff; Eph. 2:1ff.). It is our salvation here and now, and also beyond the grave and for all eternity. The first resurrection is our spiritual regeneration for time and eternity. The New Jerusalem, the new creation, is our home from the time of our regeneration, and that new creation began with Christ's resurrection. Christ is the first-fruits of them that slept and the great Redeemer of heaven and earth. "He must reign until he has put all his enemies under his feet" (I Cor. 15:25). That reign is characterized by Christ's repossession of creation that it might be totally re-created. Hebrews 12:22, 23 plainly tells believers that here and now "ye are come unto mount Sion, and unto the city of the living God, the heavenly Jerusalem." The fulness of this new community of the renewed humanity we have not seen: but when we enter into Christ, we are on the threshold of that city and citizens thereof. In brief, the kingdom has come and is to come.

In verses 7-10, we see the release of Satan, that he might be destroyed in all that he presumes to be. This means that the gospel age sees the false prophet and beast destroyed in their Babylonian dream in the explicit revolt of Satan against Christ's kingdom. The tares and the wheat each becomes manifest, in that the harvest time is nearing. There is an epistemological self-consciousness in evil as it makes the last stand against the Lord by attacking His Church. This attack is world-wide. Some see a defeat of the saints and a victory for Satan in the end times, but only by importing other Bible passages into this text, all with doubtful reference, since they can be referred more intelligently to the Jewish war or "the great Tribulation," is such an interpretation possible. We are here told only of an attempt, and the attempt is now described as Satan's attempt. No longer are other names used for him: he is too clearly identified. Gog and Magog, i.e., prince and people, unite in open and avowed hatred of God. It is no longer masked as Christianity, no longer offers a paradise on earth, no longer offers any pretension. In its final thrust, it is openly satanic and it is simply a naked hatred for God. It fails, and God destroys forever the power of Satan.

In verses 11-16, we see judgment proclaimed. Verse 11 echoes Psalm 114, which shows creation fleeing before the wrath and judgment of God when He delivered Israel from Egypt. Here we see the same imagery:

> This is obviously a picture of God's judgment on his first creation and all pertaining thereto—the whole stands condemned in his eyes and in the eyes of Christ's Church which can now view all creation and history as he views them. Judgment upon creation and history there must first be that there may be room for a new creation and a new history—those of God's eternal abode.[4]

The echo of Psalm 114 is significant: Psalm 114 is the first song in the Hallel, used at the Feast of Tabernacle, a holy feast typifying the ingathering of all peoples into the kingdom of God. The whole process of judgment in and through history, and the end time judgment, has this purpose, and in the face of all its difficulties at times for the saints, their cry must be "Praise ye the LORD!"

The judgment culminates in the destruction of man's first enemy, death (I Cor. 15:26, 55), and in the second resurrection, i.e., the resurrection of the body and our eternal reward. We are saved by faith and rewarded according to our works, and this reward we receive both here and now in our Christian walk, and in its fulness at the resurrection.

One very important point appears in this chapter. In Ezekiel 39, Gog is completely destroyed *before* the kingdom era. In Revelation, Gog is destroyed *after* the 1,000 years. Either Ezekiel's kingdom is not the same as the 1,000 years, *or* neither account gives us chronology but doctrine. And this raises a very pertinent point: for too many people, the purpose of any reading of Revelation is to enable them to walk by sight. They demand a chart telling them what to expect and how to walk in full and open sight. But the calling of the Christian is to walk by faith, and the purpose of Revelation is to strengthen us against the enemy, prepare us to do battle, and to walk in the faith that our Lord will triumph, that the great work He has begun, He will accomplish. As a book for sight, Revelation becomes a frustration; as a book for faith, it becomes a joy and a comfort.

---

[4] John Wick Bowman: *Drama of the Book of Revelation,* p. 143.

REVELATION 21:1-8: THE NEW CREATION

According to Hebrews 12:22-29, "We ARE come . . . unto. . . the heavenly Jerusalem." The New Jerusalem is a present reality as well as a future realization. M. S. Terry summarized the matter aptly, writing in 1890:

> The New Jerusalem, then, is the apocalyptic portraiture of the New Testament Church and Kingdom of God. Its symbolism exhibits the heavenly nature of the communion and fellowship of God and his people, which is entered here by faith, but which opens into unspeakable fulness of glory through ages of ages.[1]

The creation of a new heaven and a new earth began with the resurrection, with Christ the first-fruits of the new humanity and the new creation. The new creation involves the "shaking" and re-creating of the old world. The first "shaking" of the earth took place at Sinai, when the holiness of God in His law was death to the world's sin and rebellion. The second and last shaking began with the resurrection: "Yet once more, I shake not the earth only, but also heaven" (Heb. 12:26). The Puritan expositor, John Owen, writing on Hebrews 12:25-27, said:

> It is therefore the *heavens of Mosaical worship,* and the Judaical church-state, with the *earth of their political state* belonging thereunto, that are here intended.[2]

Again, Roderick Campbell has pointed out clearly:

> The making of all things new has reference to moral and spiritual regeneration, to redemption in time, to "the resurrection of all things," to "the time of reformation," to the formation of the "new creation," to the making and completion of "new heavens and a new earth," in other words to the restitution rendered

[1] Milton S. Terry: *Biblical Hermeneutics.* New York: Eaton & Mains, 1890, p. 382.
[2] John Owen: *An Exposition of Hebrews,* vol. IV. Evansville, Indiana: Sovereign Grace Publishers, 1960, p. 366.

necessary by the entrance of sin and the fall of man (cf. 2 Cor. 5:17; Col. 1:20).

Note carefully the phrase "all things" which is repeated no less than six times in Col. 1:15-20. Note particularly verses 19-20: "For it pleased the Father that in him should all fulness dwell; and, having made peace through the blood of his cross, by him to reconcile all things unto himself: by him, *I say,* whether they be things in earth, or things in heaven." It should also be noted that the "all things" of 2 Cor. 5:17 has reference mainly, if not exclusively, to objective reality—to things outside the believer, as they now appear to him. In both passages the transformation of the "all things" relates to external fact rather than to subjective experience.[3]

Campbell further states:

The New Earth is the lower or manward side of the new universe which came into being as a result of the redemptive work accomplished by Christ when on the Cross. He said, "It is finished," and then expired (John 19:30). The New Earth means the redemptive effects on earth which are spoken of in the New Testament as "the regeneration," the "time of reformation," and "the restitution of all things." In contrast with and in opposition to this New Earth stands the world which still lies in the evil one (Gal. 1:4; cf. John 5:4).

The word "heaven" in Scripture (as, for example, "the heavens do rule") does not necessarily mean the physical or astral heavens, but rather the Divine government of the world and man. "Earth" does not necessarily mean the material planet on which we live or any part of it such as cities or fields. The New Earth does not mean (as some think) our present physical planet purified from its moral and spiritual evil. It does not mean that this present physical world will be purified so as to be a fit place in which the saints will dwell when Christ returns, or after the last trumpet sounds. The New Earth means something wholly new—something which came into being with the inauguration of the age in which we now live. It means something which can be seen only by faith.[4]

[3] Roderick Campbell: *Israel and the New Covenant.* Philadelphia: Presbyterian and Reformed Publishing Co., 1954, p. 108.
[4] *Ibid.,* p. 113f.

Calvin's comment on Hebrews 2:5 helps clarify this point:

> To make the thing clearer, let us suppose two worlds,—the first the old, corrupted by Adam's sin; the other, later in time, as renewed by Christ. . . . It hence now appears that here the world to come is not that which we hope for after the resurrection, but that which began at the beginning of Christ's kingdom, but it will no doubt have its full accomplishment in our final redemption.[5]

This makes the issue clear-cut: there is no kingdom for us, if we are not in the kingdom now; there is no new creation we can look forward to in eternity, if we are outside the new creation now. The kingdom is and is to come; the new heavens and new earth are and are to come. The fulness is at the end of time, but it is here today in reality. This means that Christians are neglecting their inheritance and failing to make use of their power in Christ: they live in terms of victory tomorrow instead of victory today, in terms of joy tomorrow instead of joy today. How can we enjoy heaven if we cannot enjoy earth? How can we rejoice in the eternal order beyond time, when we cannot rejoice in the new creation today? Revelation was written to suffering and troubled Christians, and also to smug and self-satisfied Christians, who alike waited for the kingdom to come and felt that the world's problems presented a hindrance to Christ and His kingdom. But Revelation makes clear that the kingdom is now, and that, not by evading conflict, responsibility, and suffering, but by assuming it, do Christians and the Church gain their inheritance. Both compromise with the world and flight from it assume that Christ is impotent and that His kingdom is in the future and has no power today.

The good news is announced: "no more sea." The sea is the world, the apostate and unbelieving world. The nations establish themselves as the true kingdom, as man's true commonwealth, in opposition to the kingdom of God. They claim dominion, control, and power. But God declares, "no more sea." The nations, He told Isaiah, are as nothing before Him (Isa. 40:15ff.). Now, the new creation having been established and Christ's atoning work openly

---

[5] John Calvin: *Commentaries on the Epistle to the Hebrews,* John Owen translation. Grand Rapids, Mich.: Eerdmans, 1949, p. 58.

set forth, the Lord moves against the nations. There shall be no more sea, and the good news is announced in advance. The kingdoms of this world shall become the kingdoms of our Lord and of His Christ. The apostate nations shall be broken, and the way prepared for the servants of the Lord.

In verses 1-8, we have the new heavens and the new earth portrayed in their eternal splendor and present reality, and contrasted with the eternal death of the world of Babylon. In verse 1, as we have noted, we have the great declaration, "and there was no more sea." The turbulent and raging sea, from whence came the beast, and which typifies the nations which establish themselves as the true kingdom, man's true commonwealth, in opposition to the kingdom of God, is no more, from the perspective of the eternal order. Through Isaiah, God declared emphatically that His judgment was upon the nations. Moreover, by the coming of Immanuel, the virgin-born Son of God, the sovereignty of the nations was revealed to be less than nothing, totally non-existent, and the sovereignty of the Lord was fully revealed. The Christian today, as in John's day, too often is overwhelmed by the raging of the sea, and feels that God is remote, but the Lord declares through John, "there is no more sea." "The heathen rage" (Ps. 2), but all their plotting against the Lord's dominion is set at naught by the coming of Jesus Christ, who proceeds to "break them with a rod of iron" (Ps. 2:9). What we are witnessing is not the triumph of the nations but their shattering, and we must "Serve the LORD with fear, and rejoice with trembling" (Ps. 2:11) as we see these things.

The tabernacling presence of God is portrayed both in its fulness, as the glory of the eternal order, and as the reality of the true church's life. Death and the sorrow of life is abolished by the resurrection of Christ and we enter into that victory here and now, and into its fullness at the resurrection of the dead. Not by compromise nor by sitting o the sidelines in separation from the conflict, but by overcoming and by thirsting do we receive our inheritance and drink of the water of life (21:6, 7). And the Lord is the beginning and the end, the Alpha and the Omega, of all things, including our Christian life, our hunger and thirst, our struggling, and our overcoming.

Therefore, "Kiss the Son, lest he be angry, and ye perish from the way, when his wrath is kindled but a little while. Blessed are all they that put their trust in him" (Ps. 2:12).

The word "new" is repeatedly used to describe this creation. Two different Greek words are translated "new" in our English text, "neos," which relates to time, and "kainos," which relates to quality. The word "kainos" is used to describe the tomb of Jesus (Matt. 27: 60; John 19:41), and also the "wine-skins" or "bottles" for new wine, indicating in both instance not that the tomb or the wine-skins were newly made, but rather unused or fresh for the tomb, and fresh and elastic for the wine-skins. This same word, "kainos," is used here and throughout the Book of Revelation.

⁶ W. Boyd-Carpenter, in Ellicott: *op. cit.*, VIII, p. 627.

REVELATION 21:9 – 22:5: THE NEW JERUSALEM

In Revelation 21:9 – 22:5 we have a symbolic picture of the Bride of Christ, the New Jerusalem, the kingdom in its fulness in eternity, and yet a picture for the people of God today of what they are in Christ today and are called to be in the world. As we have seen, Terry pointed out that the New Jerusalem, the true Church and the true kingdom, "exhibits the heavenly nature of the communion and fellowship of God and his people, which is entered here by faith, but which opens into unspeakable fulness of glory through ages of ages."

The New Jerusalem is described therefore in terms which must be used as a yardstick with respect to church and state, with respect to the people of God in their every institution and calling. The description makes use of symbolic language of great importance:

1. *As a Bride.* A bride is faithful, loving, pure, obedient, radiant with joy and confident in her love. So shall the church be in eternity, and so must it be today. The bridal joy in possession and in being possessed must be the Christian joy.

2. *Having the glory of God.* The glory, once dwelling in the most holy place in tabernacle and temple, is now in the church as a corporate body, in the individual believer in his obedience to the indwelling Holy Ghost, and in every aspect of the kingdom insofar as they reveal the glory of God and serve Him. "The chief end of man is to glorify God and to enjoy Him forever."

3. *Measured,* that is, made, cut out, even as a carpenter measures out lumber and cuts it to size. In every age, God is measuring out His people through the processes of history. The symbolism of form here sets as the goal the perfect cube. The cube is the ancient symbol of perfection, and the destiny of Christ's kingdom is perfection, but the perfection is not of us but of Christ, not attained in this life, but in the life to come. Yet the process of sanctification is the striving after this goal through the Holy

Ghost working in us. The dimensions of the Holy of Holies constituted a perfect cube.

4. *Gates open,* v. 25. *No Night* in the kingdom. The gates are open, even as Christ's kingdom is always open to sinners. A hymn declares, "Whosoever will may come," and this expression is used to justify heretical opinions regarding free will, but it is not free will but free grace which Scripture proclaims. Every Scripture text from which this phrase is derived is set in the context of grace, not will.

Acts 2:21; Romans 10:13. "Whosoever shall call on the name of the Lord shall be saved."

Romans 10:11. "Whosoever believeth on him shall not be ashamed."

I John 5:1. "Whosoever believeth that Jesus is the Christ is born of God: and everyone that loveth him that begat loveth him also that is begotten of him."

Together with this great fact is the declaration that there is no night there. Zechariah 14:7 made this prophecy concerning the kingdom: "At eventide it shall be light." This is an affirmation of the same great reality as Romans 8:28 proclaims. The Christian, even amidst the worst trials and darkness, has the assurance that all things are in the hands of God, who doeth all things well, and makes all things work together for good to them that love Him, who are the called according to His purpose. Therefore, the Christian knows that even the night shall be light round about him.

5. *The foundation stones.* The stones are those which the high priest bore on his breast-plate when entering the Holy of Holies and representing the twelve tribes of Israel, the people of God, and they were called "the chosen." These stones, significantly, are the same as those used in paganism to represent the signs of the zodiac, but they are here given in exactly the reverse order. Thus, instead of presenting the course of the sun, from dawn to darkness, a fitting symbol of the pagan outlook, they set forth a picture of the life in Christ, from darkness, the fall, to eternal dawn, the New Jerusalem. The Christian is the "chosen" of God and

moves steadily into light as he grows in Christ and enters into his
inheritance. These foundation stones thus represent again the radically different philosophy of history in the Bible. For pagan thought,
history is cyclical; it rises and falls, because it is doomed to decay
and death, to an eternal recurrence. For biblical faith, history re-
verses the natural pattern, because it is not "nature" which governs
man, but God. The destiny of the Christian man is not death, but
rather regeneration and resurrection. Non-Christian philosophies
are inevitably pessimistic, in the long range, because man has only
a dark destiny in death. For the Christian, history moves towards
the final conquest of sin and death. The course of history is thus not
from dawn to darkness, but from darkness to dawn. But another
assumption is also apparent: because there is judgment, the zodiac
is a fitting symbol for the non-Christian world. Its course is clearly
one of decline, of a progression into darkness and death. Characteristic of apologists for various forms of statism is the assertion
that the growing "problems" of the world necessitate a curb on ancient liberties; frontiers and liberties once common to man are
now declared forever ended. The world is held to be in its
maturity, and youthful liberties are no longer possible, so that
man must reconcile himself to a lesser existence. No Christian
can hold to such an opinion: the foundation stones assert the
contrary.

6. *No temple.* The Lord is now the Temple. Temple literally means
"house of God," and pagan temples were houses of gods. Thus
Solomon, in dedicating the temple, recognized in his prayer that
no house made with hands could contain God, and that no human
habitation could house Him (II Chron. 6:18). The absence of
a temple means here the prevalence of the true Temple, Jesus
Christ. The goal of history, contrary to Scofield, is not a return
to Jewish rites, but a forward movement in terms of the world's
acceptance of the true Temple, Jesus Christ. Scofield's belief that
the Jewish temple would be rebuilt and animal sacrifices restored[1]
was a denial of Christ, despite His assertion that the renewed
sacrifices would only be a memorial. Why should history see an

---

[1] See *The Scofield Reference Bible,* p. 890, note to Ezekiel 43:19.

exaltation of a shadow when the reality has come? Why should God re-establish the temple He thoroughly dishonored and destroyed as forever finished, when the true Temple has come? There is no progression in Schofield's view, nor is it biblical.[2]

7. The nations *"do bring their glory and their honour into it"* (vv. 24-26). When even the wrath of man praises God, and the wealth of the rebellious nations, according to Haggai (2:6-9), their gold and silver, all goes into the Lord's treasury and kingdom, how much more does God by His grace use the service of His saints and the godly nations. There is no waste in God's planning: all that the world does, only serves the glory of God and praises Him. Therefore, our labor is not in vain in the Lord.

8. *The walls.* Walls are built to keep out enemies (v. 27), to keep out evil and sin. Here the walls (cf. v. 18) are compared to jasper, which is used in 4:3 to describe God, His purity and clarity. Thus God is portrayed as the wall around us, around His people, as a sure defense. This was prophesied by Zechariah 2:5, "For I, saith the LORD, will be unto her a wall of fire round about, and will be the glory in the midst of her." The Lord is our strength and refuge, a wall of fire round about us.

9. The *garden* is now in the *city*. Paradise is restored, but in community. Again we find the tree of life and the river of the water of life, freely given to all. Here also we find joyful service, but now without the prospect of falling away. The "tree" of life literally reads the "woods" of life, a term used in Scripture to designate the cross. It is the cross of Christ which is a tree of life to humanity, the source of eternal life and righteousness, and is for "the healing of the nations." "Garden" is a word which evokes the beauty and freedom of nature, and city means life in community. But the concept of the city, in the hands of unbelief, instead of meaning community, has come to mean warfare and isolation, insecurity, and terror. The advantages of both the true city and the true garden are united in the Christian goal for society.

10. *"His name shall be in their foreheads"* (22:4). Christ shines

---

[2] Krauss: *Dispensationalism in America,* notes that Scofield's view is one of cyclical history.

forth through His saints. This is the church and kingdom, in eternity and in time, to be the people of God, in whom Christ and His righteousness are revealed. Thus, the picture of the New Jerusalem stands on one reality, Christ and His cross. With His atoning work, humanity is recreated, and the New Jerusalem begins to reign. The fulness lies before us, but the reign is a present reality and the basic reality. To live and pray therefore in terms of the sovereignty of Babylon is a sin. Too many Christians pray in terms of human possibilities instead of the divine possibilities, and they thereby limit God in their imagination.

One significant fact remains concerning this description of the New Jerusalem. The ancient city of Babylon in many ways mimicked not only the kingdom of God, but the very symbols of the kingdom. Babylon was built four-square, asserting thereby finality and perfection. Babylon had her hanging gardens, re-creating a paradise within her walls, and Babylon also was a city and a land of many waters.

Two other symbols in this passage deserve especial attention. *First,* there is the river of the water of life. John 7:39 declares that when Christ spoke of rivers of living water He referred to the Spirit of God: "This spake He of the Spirit, which they that believed on Him were to receive." In time and in eternity, the Spirit of life is the spirit in all who live by faith. In this vision of the river flowing through and nourishing the city, we are told that the believer is the channel through which the Spirit shall nurture the nations. "There is a river, the streams whereof shall make glad the city of God, the holy place of the tabernacles of the Most High" (Ps. 46:4).

Second, the tree is especially rich in significance. It is shown in perpetual blooming and fruition simultaneously. This signifies that in Christ potentiality and actuality are one. As the believer grows in grace, his potentialities become actualities, and his self-realization increases, as Schilder saw. In eternity, the believer's potentiality and actuality are one. The fulness of self-realization is thus attained in Christ, and only in Christ.

REVELATION 22:6-21: THE MORNING STAR

In Revelation 22:6-21, John, having received the revelation, is again confronted by Christ, who appears as the true author and source of the revelation. The angel who gives the vision at the commandment of the Lord directs worship away from himself and to the Lord. The unbroken sanctity of the book is asserted, and tampering with it is forbidden. There is a closing prayer to the Lord, and a blessing on the readers. The book self-consciously echoes the Old Testament. Rist observed,

> It has been noted before that John not only wants his book to be considered a divinely revealed prophecy, but that he also would like it placed on a par with the books of the O.T. (cf. 1:3). Accordingly, the first and last of beatitudes are pronounced on those who consider it as such and who are controlled by its teachings (1:3; 22:7). If, in contrast to these, any one takes the prophecy lightly and *adds* anything to it, God himself will deprive him of *his share in the tree of life and in the holy city* as these have been depicted.[1]

In a very real sense, Revelation concludes Scripture. It speaks deliberately as a final word. Moses, in Deuteronomy 4:2, declared, "Ye shall not add unto the word which I command you, neither shall ye diminish ought from it. . . ." Words were to be added by others, but the revelation would be one unchanging word. Now, with the conclusion of Scripture, adding or removing the "words" of the book are forbidden; words no longer can be added. The self-conscious parallel and alteration are too obvious to be accidental. The last words have been given of the unchanging word.

Jesus, in speaking, places himself above and beyond the human expectations concerning the Davidic kingdom. "I am the root and the offspring of David." This is an assertion of both His divinity and His humanity. Again, as in 2:28, Jesus calls himself "the Morning Star," this time with emphasis, "the bright and morning star." As Rist noted, an important meaning of this symbol was the fact that it "was the

---

[1] Rist: *op. cit.*, p. 440.

symbol of world dominion."[2] Christ reminds all His people of the fact of His world dominion.

The tree of life is declared barred (21:27; 22:15), as at the fall of man, to sinners. The saints of God have access to it. The designations for sinners (22:15) are more than literal. A murderer on repentance can be received into the kingdom, as was the thief on the cross. The reference to murderers thus has more than the criminal in mind. The sons of Cain, who in their murder raise their hands primarily against God, and who live in life-long war against Him, these are here meant. Here are the sons of Babylon, murderers by nature.

But even more significant is the first and foremost term for sinners: "dogs." Dogs in the East were not pets but scavengers, which wandered about cities and fields devouring dead bodies and offal (I Kings 14:11; 16:4; 21:19; 22:38; II Kings 9:10, 36; Jer. 15:3; Ps. 59:6). Fierce and vicious enemies are called "dogs" in Psalm 22:16, 20. Dogs were unclean animals and outside the house and city normally. But the significant usage of the term "dogs" is, in both Old and New Testaments, its religious usage, its symbolic application. In Deuteronomy 23:18, it is a term applied to the male prostitutes who were important to pagan worship in Canaan. In Philippians 3:2, Paul applies this same term "dogs" to Judaizers in the church. Only by understanding, first, the Eastern contempt for the dog, and, second, that in Scripture it is used to designate male prostitutes, homosexuals, can we appreciate what Paul called the Judaizers. This same meaning is applied here. Salvation is not by man's righteousness or goodness, not by any legalistic plan of life, but by the free grace of God through Jesus Christ. Those who, like the Pharisees, hold to the Scriptures, having the keys but refusing to enter therein and keeping others from entering by their perversion of the word, are termed "dogs" and barred from the tree of life. This is a sharp condemnation which no man could dare to use on his own; here it is used by Paul and reported by John under the inspiration of the Holy Spirit. Nothing is more hateful to God than a perversion of His truth which claims to be a seeming defense of it. It was the Pharisees who drew the wrath of Jesus upon them-

[2] *Ibid.*, p. 390.

selves. False churchmen now are accorded a similar judgment.

Dogs and murderers are thus excluded from the kingdom, both the ungodly outside the church and those within the church and the sharper term is reserved for the *dogs*. *Murderers* are at least men.

The Book of Revelation, given to troubled and to compromising as well as suffering believers, summons them to enter into their inheritance and to recognize the cosmic character of the victory of which they have been made partakers. But Revelation, the summons to victory, has been wrongly used to justify living in expectation of tribulation and horror. But the message of Revelation is instead this: "And the Spirit and the bride say, Come. And let him that heareth say, come. And whosoever will, let him take the water of life freely" (22:17).

Victory is basic to the Christian faith; certainly tribulation is basic also, but the tribulation is never given primacy in the focus of faith. The very sharpness of the judgment on the "dogs" is a part of the assurance of victory and of separation. Moffatt's translation of the two verses with reference to "dogs" gives us the flavor of the Bible's sharp language: Phil. 3:2—"Beware of these dogs, these wicked workmen, the incision-party!" Revelation 22:15—"Begone, you dogs, you sorcerers, you vicious creatures, you murderers, you idolaters, you who love and practice falsehood, every one of you!" This certainty and sharpness of judgment expresses the certainty and inevitability of sovereignty and victory. The New Jerusalem is the heir of the kingdom, and Christ's saints shall inherit the earth.

> By calling the holy city Jerusalem he declares that all God's intentions and purposes, all His promises and plans which we discern in the Old and New Testaments, come at last to their perfect fulfilment.[3]

"The time is at hand," we are told. The fulfilment is not left to the future but begins in the present. The commandment therefore is not to seal up the sayings of the prophecy of this book. "They are of immediate relevance and therefore of the most urgent necessity."[4] Both the battle and the victory are now.

[3] Thomas F. Torrance: *The Apocalypse Today*. Grand Rapids, Mich.: Eerdmans, 1959, p. 14.
[4] *Ibid.*, p. 153.

THE KINGDOM OF GOD

In Ezekiel 40 – 47, the prophet speaks of the re-established temple. Since Ezekiel wrote in the last days of Jerusalem, in the shadow of the collapse and captivity of Judah, it has been sometimes assumed that the prophecy is an idealized picture of the second temple, or a vision of an actual temple destined to be rebuilt at the end of time. In either case, the interpretation has a literal temple in mind. But Ezekiel's vision is not of a literal temple, since no literal temple has the unusual features of this one, such as a stream issuing from under the threshold and growing miraculously in size. The temple is obviously typical and symbolic. The temple of Ezekiel's vision lacks the Ark of the testimony and the veil and is clearly not a literal temple.[1] The temple is clearly Christ's kingdom and realm, whose destiny it is to renew the world.

This victory was clearly basic to the apostolic hope and preaching. This is apparent in the reference to Edom. Edom, as a kindred people, had laid claim to being the true people of God while in actuality being in enmity to Israel and and the Lord. The Edomites could be forgiven and could enter the congregation by faith in the third generation (Deut. 23:8). The destiny of Edom, when Christ came, was to be a possession of Israel, i.e., the remnant would become converted (Amos 9:11, 12). This meant that the enemies of Christ who are nominally of the Lord but in reality against Him will, after being judged and laid low, come into the kingdom of God by faith. St. James, in Acts 15:17, cited the prophecy of Amos as evidence of "Christ's mediatorial kingship over the Gentile believers. . . . He [James] refers to the prophecy in Amos 9:11-12, concerning the Messiah's conquest of Edom,—'that they may possess the remnant of Edom.'" As Wyngaarden noted, "Possessing the remnant of Edom is then spiritually understood by James in that he sees illus-

[1] Martin J. Wyngaarden: *The Future of the Kingdom in Prophecy and Fulfillment*. Grand Rapids, Mich.: Baker Book House, 1955, p. 113ff.

trated, here, the purpose of God, 'that the residue of men may seek after the Lord' (Acts 15:17)."[2]

The Church in Scripture is the household of faith. It rests on the confession of faith in Jesus as the Christ, the Son of the living God. On this confession, on Himself as the Rock, Christ declared, "I will build my church, and the gates of hell shall not prevail against it" (Matt. 16:18). But most of Christ's preaching went beyond the elementary act of faith, the necessary foundation of conversion, and stressed the kingdom of God: "I must preach the kingdom of God to other cities also; for therefore am I sent" (Luke 4:43). "The word of the kingdom" (Matt. 13:19) was the forgivenes of sins (Mark 1:1-4, 14-15; Luke 3:3; Matt. 9:2, etc.). The kingdom is a broader term than church or state. It is the reign of God in every realm, the total sovereignty of God and His word for every sphere of life. It is Christ's reign in *judgment* over His enemies as well as His reign in *peace and prosperity* over His triumphant saints. The Church is the instrument, the teacher and preacher, the messenger, and its message is clearly declared by Jesus Christ:

> And this gospel of the kingdom shall be preached in all the world for a witness unto all nations (Matt. 24:14).

In other words, whereas regeneration is the beginning of the kingdom as well as of the believer's membership in the Church, the gospel is much broader: it is the whole counsel of God, the totality of His word for the kingdom.

Apart from this fact, we cannot understand Revelation. To interpret this book in terms of the saints and their personal destiny, to read it in terms of the Hebrew peoples and their re-establishment, or to see it as the rapture of the people of God from history, is to miss the point of Revelation.

Revelation 1–3 obviously speaks to the churches, to prepare them for their responsibilities to their Lord, to make their stand in the face of a hostile world. In chapters 4–11, it is revealed that man's destiny in Christ is to be an heir of the kingdom of God, and that Jesus Christ is both the testator and the executor of the estate. But

[2] *Ibid.,* p. 110.

the false heirs, the sons of Cain and people of Babylon, have seized the earth and declared themselves to be the true heirs. As a result, Jesus Christ institutes judgment against the false heirs, to dispossess them of the earth and to give His people their inheritance. These seven judgments are patterned after the seven plagues against Egypt. The culmination is victory for Christ's kingdom: "The kingdoms of this world are become the kingdoms of our Lord, and of his Christ; and he shall reign for ever and ever" (Rev. 11:15).

Then, in chapters 12–20, this same fact is viewed from the perspective of the basic issue, the war between Christ and Satan. Two kingdoms are at war, the kingdom of man, or Babylon the Great, and the kingdom of God, the New Jerusalem. The Kingdom of man, or Babylon, seeks to establish a one-world order and a one-world religion; it seeks to enthrone man as god, to establish a total humanism in every sphere. In the battle that ensues, Babylon moves towards near triumph, but God brings catastrophe on Babylon in the form of a total economic collapse. The culmination of the battle is in two great banquets or communion tables: the wedding supper of the Lamb, i.e., the triumph of God's kingdom, and the vulture's feast, the total destruction of Babylon.

In chapters 21 and 22, the splendors of the New Jerusalem, God's kingdom are described. The triumph is glorious in time, the totality of perfection and glory for all eternity. The church's cry, in St. John's mouth, is "Even so, come, *Lord* Jesus," and the conclusion declares, "The grace of our *Lord* Jesus Christ be with you all. Amen." Jesus is both Christ—Messiah—and Lord—God and governor. When St. John cries, "come, Lord Jesus," he calls for the God-King to come in judgment and in the prosperity of His restitution.

The social gospel preaches the gospel of socialism and statism; the pietistic and Arminian gospel preaches the gospel of withdrawal, retreat, and rapture. The gospel of Jesus Christ is the good news of the kingdom of God.

THE TREE OF LIFE

In Eden, the tree of life was an actual tree whose fruit actually had, by the creative purpose of God, the ability to give continuing life. When man fell, it became necessary to bar man from access to that tree (Gen. 3:22-24). With the tree of life, man could have had perpetual earthly life. This tree "was the symbolic representation of God opening his hand to give life unending, that is, perpetual earthly life, to Adam." Moreover, the tree "was an emblem, a sign, of God's covenant."[1]

Man by his sin became a covenant-breaker, and the communion with God was broken. Sin and death became the human condition because man rejected the divine condition for his life, the covenant with God.

The forbidden tree, the tree of the knowledge of good and evil, was also a real tree. There was no evil in the tree in itself, nor in its fruit. Hoeksema, in commenting on the name of this tree, has observed:

> That name implies, in the first place, in connection with the command of God attached to it, that it is not man's lot, but God's prerogative to determine what is good and what is evil. And it is man's calling simply to listen and obey. God, the Creator, is sovereign; and man, the creature, is servant. And God's alone is the sovereign prerogative to determine what His servant shall do and what he shall not do, what is good and what is evil. And thus, in the second place, the name of this tree denotes that by not eating, that is,—put positively,—by the way of obedience, man would truly know by experience, know as taught by God, know in the sense that he would actively assume the right attitude over against good and evil. In this sense the tree was the means whereby man would have an experimental knowledge of good and evil. If he obeyed God's commandment, he would so know good and evil that he loved the good and hated

[1] H. C. Hoeksema, "The Tree of Life," in *Paradise the First and the Forbidden Tree.* Grand Rapids, Mich.: Reformed Witness Hour, 1968, p. 8.

the evil, and thus experience the favor and fellowship of God that constitute the true knowledge of God. If he disobeyed that command, he would so know good and evil that he would love the evil and hate the good, and thus experience the very opposite of the blessedness of the true knowledge of God, namely, the abject misery and desolation of spiritual ignorance and darkness, the wretchedness of that experience that is denoted in the words, "To live apart from God is death!"[2]

Man's covenant in Eden was basically the same covenant re-established after the fall with covenant men and then the covenant people, Israel in the Old Testament era, and, since then, the people of Christ. Although at times "the covenant of works" is used to describe the covenant with Adam, the expression is misleading.[3] Any and every covenant God establishes with man has as its *first* and foremost aspect, *grace.* God is absolute lord and sovereign, and man cannot contract a covenant of works with God; man can receive a covenant standing by the grace of God. The covenant has in every age been primarily and essentially a *covenant of grace. Second, obedience or works* is a secondary aspect of the covenant. Man's response to the covenant of grace is *faith and obedience.* But because the covenant is a covenant of grace, it has inescapably a *law.* Without a law, there is no covenant. *The law of the covenant* in every era—in Eden, Israel, and in the Christian age—is God's requirement of covenant-keeping man. To keep the covenant means to keep the law of the covenant, i.e., the terms of the covenant. Adam was required to abide by the law of the covenant. This meant *obeying every word of God, eating of the tree of life, tilling the garden in obedience to God, naming or classifying the animals, living with Eve in terms of God's calling and requirements, and refusing to eat of the tree of the knowledge of good and evil.* In its secondary aspect, the covenant was a covenant of works precisely because it was a covenant of grace.

The covenant with Adam required obedience from him in terms

[2] H. C. Hoeksema, "The Forbidden Tree: Its Name and Purpose," in *ibid.*, p. 15.
[3] See Herman Hoeksema: *Reformed Dogmatics.* Grand Rapids, Mich.: Reformed Free Publishing Association, 1966, pp. 214-226.

of prescribed duties and a calling. The covenant with Noah required obedience also (Gen. 17:1). The covenant with Israel was
marked by an extensive law code. The covenant, as renewed by
Jesus Christ, was designed to restore obedience to the law (Matt.
5:17-20). Christ's persistent charge against the Pharisees, who
claimed to be covenant-keepers, was precisely that they were
covenant-breakers in spirit and in deed (Matt. 5:17-20; 6:5, 16-18;
7:15-21, etc.).

Jesus Christ, by His perfect righteousness, and by His atoning
death and resurrection, and as the last Adam, the federal head of
the new humanity, restored the redeemed man into communion with
God and became man's new tree of life. Man in Christ is dead to
the law as an indictment, as a sentence of death for transgressions,
but man is alive to the law as the covenant requirement, as the righteousness of God which man must assent to, obey, and live by.

Thus, the tree of life in Eden had its law, and Jesus Christ, the tree
of life in Revelation,[4] has His law, the same continuing law which
requires man to serve God as priest, prophet, and king in Christ,
to obey God's word in every realm, and to glorify God in his
obedience.

To deny law is to deny the covenant. To deny law is to deny the
grace which gives the law of the covenant. The extensive echoes
of Genesis and Exodus in Revelation are not incidental to the book.
The covenant churches are summoned to faith and obedience in
chapters 1 –3; those outside the faith and against the law, who will
not hear Him whose word is law, receive the plagues and judgments
which are meted out to covenant-breakers (Rev. 4 – 19), whereas
those who walk in faith and obedience, feast again on the tree of
life. The parallel is clear-cut. Disbelief in God's word and dis-
obedience thereof barred man from paradise. Faith in God's incarnate Son, and obedience to the law of the covenant, restore man to
paradise, a new life on earth, and the fulness of life in the eternal
kingdom. St. Paul spoke of himself as "being not without the law
to God, but under the law to Christ" (I Cor. 9:21). Richard Baxter

---

[4] The cross is called a tree by Peter (Acts 5:30; 10:39), and by Paul
(Gal. 3:13).

declared the "Divine Instrument" for man's duty "is called a Law in one respect, and a Covenant in another."[5] As Kevan has summarized it, "God's Grace cannot destroy God's Law."[6]

The glorious vision of grace which concludes Revelation rests firmly on the covenant and its law. God is never antinomian at any point in His word. There is law because there is a covenant of grace. The covenant life, and the life of the new creation, is obedience to the law of grace.

---

[5] Cited from *End of Doctrinal Controversies*, by Ernest F. Kevan: *The Grace of Law, A Study in Puritan Theology*. Grand Rapids, Mich.: Baker Book House, 1965, p. 112.
[6] *Ibid.*, p. 155.

Part Three

Dimensions of the Future

MATTHEW 24

To understand this chapter, let us examine its setting. Jesus had confounded the disciples in their Jewish expectation of a millennial Messianic kingdom. He had spoken of His coming death at Jerusalem, and His resurrection. He had described the kingdom in terms very different from everything Israel expected. The Gospel of Matthew especially gives great prominence to His teaching concerning the kingdom, and nothing in that teaching is conducive to the Jewish hope. Instead of confirming the Jewish hope, He wept over the ruin Jerusalem faced, and immediately prior to the discourse of this chapter, He had declared, *"Behold your house is left unto you desolate"* (Matt. 23:38). He had, in His teachings throughout His last week, emphasized this point in parable and proclamation, saying bluntly, "Therefore say I unto you, The kingdom of God shall be taken from you, and given to a nation bringing forth the fruits thereof" (Matt. 21:43). It was precisely because Jesus denied the kingdom to the Jews and reserved it to God, and gave a totally different interpretation thereof, that His condemnation by the Sanhedrin was made inevitable, "that the whole nation perish not" (John 11:50).

The disciples, troubled by these words, called the Lord's attention to the temple, not because the buildings (24:1) were unfamiliar to Him, but to remind Him that this was God's temple, and a guarantee, they assumed, of the permanency of Israel. "And Jesus said unto them, See ye not all these things? verily I say unto you, *There shall not be left here one stone upon another,* that shall not be thrown down." This was staggering to the disciples. They thereupon assumed that Jerusalem and the temple could fall only if the end of the world were at hand, and Jesus to be ushered in as King of the world, in a recreated order. Their question shows that this correlation was clearly made: "Tell us, when shall these things be? and what shall be the sign of thy coming, and of the end of the world?" (Matt. 24:3). Their question thus assumes three things to be identical in time of occurrence:

1. The fall of Jerusalem and the destruction of the temple, together with the devastation of the nation.
2. His coming in power as King.
3. The end of the world.

Jesus, in answering their question, distinguishes between these three events, and, in His picture of history, eliminates entirely any reference to a millennium in the Jewish or premillennial sense. It was difficult for the Jews to visualize the fall of the temple and of Israel except in terms of the end of the world: they were confident in their righteousness, sure of their superiority, and emphatic on their special privileges with God. But Jerusalem fell in the war of A.D. 66-70, and the few stones left standing upon another after that savage war and the destruction of Jerusalem by Titus, were taken down in the time of Emperor Julian.

The first major section, verses 4-28, deals with the fall of Jerusalem and the coming of Christ in judgment upon Israel in that destruction. The question had been raised by four disciples, Peter, James, John, and Andrew (Mark 13:3), who asked for "the sign" of His coming and of the end of the world.

Thus, our Lord first of all deals with the matter of "signs" in His answer. "Take heed that no man deceive you" (Matt. 24:4), that is, with regard to the matter of *signs*. He warns them against *false* signs, and specifies them.

1. *False messiahs* will arise, *promising the millennium* and the *overthrow of Rome, and thereby lead many Jews astray* (Matt. 24: 5, 11, 23, 24). Because of the Jewish expectation at this time, the false messiahs were numerous, and often successful, at times leading thousands in revolt against Rome. It was easy for them

to flourish, since *the year 5000* had come and the age of the kingdom of God was ostensibly to begin.

2. *"Wars and rumors of wars" constituted another false sign.* Rome had enjoyed a long era of peace, but trouble began to break out throughout the empire, and in the capital itself the long procession of emperors began their swift successions and deaths. Jews were persecuted and slain in many parts of the empire, by the tens of thousands. These "signs" (Matt. 24:6) seemed to portend the end of the world to many.

3. *The next false sign was "famines, and pestilences, and earthquakes, in diverse places"* (Matt. 24:7). These occurred in especial sharpness in the first century. There were serious earthquakes throughout the empire, and in Pompeii as well. A famine in the days of Claudius Caesar is mentioned in Acts 11:28.

4. *Persecutions constitute another false sign* (Matt. 24:9-13), but, like the others, *these things are only "the beginning of sorrows" or birthpains* (Lenski), (Matt. 24:8).

All these false signs particularly characterized the era prior to the fall of Jerusalem, but they have also characterized other periods of history as well, and for this reason constitute false signs. *They are recurrent aspects of history, characterizing a sin-filled and shaken world.* All these things, occurring in their day and constituting misleading signs of the END, are (v. 8), instead, *only signs of the BEGINNING of the "travail"* (RV) *or "birthpains"* (Lenski) *of the messianic age.* Thus these events constitute false signs of the end, and true signs of the beginning. They are elements in the second shaking of the earth (Heb. 12:23-27) so "that those things which cannot be shaken may remain." Not that these sorrows are the true signs of the end, but rather that "this gospel of the kingdom shall be preached in all the world for a witness unto all nations; *and then* shall the end come" (Matt. 24:14). The Great Commission our Lord gave the church on His ascension emphasized that "All power is given unto me in heaven and in earth," and this power must be made manifest unto all peoples. "Go ye, therefore, and teach all nations, baptizing them in the name of the Father, and of the Son, and of the Holy Ghost: teaching them to observe all things what-soever I have commanded you: and, lo, I am with you alway, even unto the end of the world. Amen" (Matt. 28:18-20). It is not the conversion of every creature which is the sign of the end, nor is it a world free of opposition or unbelief in the gospel, but rather a world which has been brought under the discipline of the gospel and evangelized in every area. And this is far from being a specific or easily identifiable sign of the end, nor is it given as such. Rather, it is a reminder of the great responsibility which rests upon the church in every generation. In Colossians 1:6, 23, we see the extent to which the early church witnessed to the civilized world of its day. Lenski translates the concluding phrase thus: "Not until then" shall the end come. The time is not set: the church can only say that its responsibility before the end is given.

In verses 15-28, our Lord then speaks of the fall of Jerusalem as His coming in judgment, dissociating this from the end. The Day of the Lord and the coming of the Lord, also His *coming on clouds,* are often spoken of in the OT as a very real coming, and as distinct from the end and yet a part of it and a forerunner of it. His coming is both judgment and mercy (Isa. 19:1).

The desecration and destruction of the temple is immediately brought to the Jewish mind by verse 15. The reference to Daniel does not mean that Daniel 9:27 and Daniel 12:11 are fulfilled in the fall of Jerusalem. Daniel's prophecy was fulfilled before the time of Christ, and is described in I Macc. 1:20-68. *This desolation is analogous to the earlier one.* In this instance, however, the desecra-tion, took place during the Jewish War, under the instance of the Zealots themselves, as Josephus makes clear. Thus, the desolation which preceded the fall of the temple (v. 2), was in this instance Jewish. The Jews, having crucified the Lord of Glory, thought noth-ing, finally, of defiling the temple in their self-defense. The desolation of the temple, made possible by *the Zealots who admitted the Idu-means into the sanctuary,* as a result of which 8,500 men were slain, took place BEFORE the *seige of Jerusalem by Titus.* Thus, Jesus gave this event as a sign to the Christians that the nation was finished, and they must flee. The advice of these verses, therefore, is for

believers, who, trusting their Lord, will flee when His prophecy comes
to pass. Although the temple was further defiled by the Romans after
their conquest of the city, it was the earlier defiling which constituted
the warning to Christians in sufficient time to give opportunity for
hasty flight. Luke 21:20 associates the desolation with the com-
passing of Jerusalem with armies. The Christians were saved from
the horrors of the Jewish War precisely because they took warning
from these words and fled. The words of our Lord gave great urgency
to the flight, in stressing the horror and giving no permission to
dawdling or delay. He also called it (v. 21) the greatest tribulation
of history, one which shall never be equalled to the end of the world.
Jerusalem was filled with Passover crowds of pilgrims. *Approxi-
mately one million died, many of them by crucifixion, and two million
were sold to die as slaves.* But the greatest horrors were within the
city prior to its end, as hunger and fear drove the self-styled elect to
*unspeakable horrors and cannibalism. The Romans systematically
destroyed the city, sowed it with salt after even plowing up the
ground where it had once stood.* "And except those days should be
shortened, there should no flesh be saved: but for the elect's sake
those days shall be shortened" (v. 22). The elect, whose blood
relatives were among those doomed to destruction, were spared a
longer agony, and the time of the siege was shortened by God. Even
Titus acknowledged this: "We have certainly had God for our as-
sistant in this war, and it was no other than God who ejected the Jews
out of these fortifications, for what could the hands of men, or any
machines, do toward overthrowing these towers?"[1]

Again, Jesus dealt with the premature hope of His coming. During
the siege, *false messiahs abounded,* and many followed them in hopes
of a miraculous deliverance. According to Josephus, many of these
were in the pay of Rome. He also records signs and wonders, in the
form of strange natural phenomena. Jesus (vv. 23-26) brands as
false all these hopes: "Behold, I have told you before." His coming
at the end will need no announcing by false prophets and fear-crazed
men. It will be immediate and obvious to all men throughout the

[1] Marcellus Kik: *Matthew XXIV.* Philadelphia: Presbyterian and Reformed
Publishing Co., 1948, p. 62.

world (v. 27). As lightning is seen by all, and is in the heavens, so
His coming will be seen by all and will be in the heavens and not
upon the earth. These false messiahs, and false prophets announcing
them, abounded in Judea for one reason only: it had become a
rotting carcass and thus attracted the vultures. *Carrion draws the
carrion eaters,* and an abundance of religious charlatans indicates the
presence of spiritually dead and rotting people who are ripe for
the picking (v. 28).

Matthew 24:29-35 forms a commonly misunderstood passage,
interpreted without reference to the OT symbolism and its biblical
meaning. Isaiah 13:10 and 34:4, 5 must be read in this connection,
as well as Ezekiel 32:7, 8. The prophets describe the downfall of
the OT empires by speaking of the *sun* being darkened, the *moon*
not shining, *the stars falling from heaven,* the *host of heaven being
dissolved and the heavens rolled together as a scroll.* These things
are definitely considered fulfilled in terms of the fall of the OT empires, thus making it obvious that we cannot understand them literally.
These same occurrences are predicted for the gospel age by Peter,
quoting Joel 2:28-32, in Acts 2:16-21, and as taking place "*BEFORE*
that great and notable day of the Lord come." Thus, they are not
end-time manifestations, but gospel-age events. In the OT, they
signify the rulers and powers of the nations, even as in Joseph's
dream, they symbolized authority. The prophets in so speaking
declared that the human authorities of their age would be shaken and
destroyed before the coming of the virgin-born Son. Now, Christ
declares, "immediately after the tribulation of those days" (v. 29),
i.e., after the fall of Jerusalem, the shaking of the world shall again
occur, and the gospel age will see all human authority shaken, confounded, and destroyed, and Christ established as the only true
sovereign of men, nations, and the universe.

If the events of these verses (29-35) are referred to the end of
the world, then Jesus has declared something obviously untrue and
impossible in saying, "Verily I say unto you, This generation shall
not pass, till all these things be fulfilled" (v. 34). The same
applies to Matthew 16:28: "Verily I say unto you, There be some
standing here, which shall not taste death, till they see the Son of

man coming in his kingdom." If these statements are true, then the language of this passage must necessarily be figurative, in the same sense as it is used in the OT. Roderick Campbell points us to the true meaning when he writes: "Where we read of Christ coming 'with clouds' we should look for events in history in which the eye of faith will find evidence of the fact that Christ is now guiding His church, ruling among the nations of earth, and carrying out, in judgment and in mercy, His purposes in the redemption of man. At His ascension 'a cloud received Him out of sight' (Acts 1:9). It concealed Him from the disciples' physical vision."[2]

The destruction of the Jewish state in fulfilment of Christ's prophecy is the "sign" that He rules "with power and great glory," and all peoples shall see in it a manifest token of His absolute sovereignty. That the nations refuse to recognize His sovereignty is no objection: all things, including the heart, mind, and conscience of the unbeliever, testify to the total and absolute sovereignty of God the Son.

As soon as the old covenant and its temple, people, and city are finally judged and removed from the scene, the full proclamation to the Gentiles begins. This is described in verse 31. The "great sound of a trump" is often assumed to apply only to the end of the world. *OT usage makes clear that the trump sounds to summon God's people to worship, to march to victory, to herald the new moon, and to proclaim the jubilee.* All these meanings are involved in verse 31. It is the proclamation of the gospel to all creation, looking forward to its great re-creation. It is the proclamation of the new "year" or era of history, the time of jubilee, the redemption of the enslaved. It is the summons to march to victory, and the call to worship God the Son. The trumpet appears in like meaning in Isaiah 27:13, and Isaiah 61:1 was used by our Lord (Luke 4:17-21) to declare the beginning of the great jubilee of the gospel age.

The parable of verse 32 is clearly explained by our Lord in verses 33-35. Its significance is clear: the fall of Jerusalem, all these signs he has spoken of thus far, are *not signs of the end but merely of the beginning.* When the fig tree buds, and begins to put forth leaves, *we know that summer is near, NOT WINTER.* In these words of

---

[2] Campbell: *Israel and the New Covenant*, p. 71.

J. M. Kik, "The destruction of Jerusalem was not a terrible sign; it was the beginning of summer. All the terrible events which Christ mentioned, instead of discouraging the disciples, would encourage them, for they would know it was the beginning, not of a winter time for this world, but of summer. It was to be a *beginning of a world-wide harvest.*" Thus, they must be encouraged by these things, and despite the immediate grief of the fall of their nation, trust absolutely in His word in all things, for "Heaven and earth shall pass away, but my words shall not pass away" (Matt. 24:35).

Thus Jesus definitely and very forcefully dissociated the fall of the temple and Jerusalem from the end of the world. He very definitely predicted the fall of Jerusalem, and gave explicit warning signs of its coming, in order to save His disciples and followers from being involved in its tragedy. *Now He makes equally clear that there is NO SIGN of the nearness of the end of the world.* The world-wide preaching of the gospel and the shattering of human authority are given, but neither is sufficiently specific to enable men to pin-point His return. "But of that day and hour knoweth no man, no, not the angels of heaven, but my Father only" (24:36). "Watch therefore; for ye know not what hour your Lord doth come" (24:42; see also v. 44). Even as the men of Noah's day had no more warning of the coming of the flood other than the call to repentance and the declaration of judgment, "so shall the coming of the Son of man be" (24:39). The Christians could be warned of the Lord's coming in judgment on Jerusalem, and so save themselves. But now there will be no opportunity for the sinner to flee or the Christian to make ready: he shall be "taken" before he is aware of the event. The saints shall be caught up and taken away at the very moment that the world is destroyed.

The parable of verse 43 is used to teach watchfulness and must not be pressed further to conclude that the Lord is compared to a thief. Earlier, in verses 12, 13, *endurance* is given as a sign of true faith. *This is again stated* in verses 45-51. The false servant loses faith in the Lord's government because of the "delay" and promptly establishes his own order, which is the manifestation of sin. When men feel that God is remote and His government absent, they cast off restraint and reveal their true nature. The testing of delay and patience is the testing of the saints. More specifically, the servant is the steward of the Lord, the minister, elder, Christian worker, and every Christian with responsibility who, feeling that the Lord is failing him and failing to govern anything, uses what he regards as God's impotence as his opportunity to indulge himself and to establish his own government. Instead of doing his work in faith and in patience, he uses his Christian privileges to establish himself in sin, in power, and in self-indulgence. The Lord at His coming casts out such men and appoints them a portion with the hypocrites, for such they are (v. 51), but the servant who is mindful that he is a servant, and faithfully waits on the Lord and trusts in His government, shall be greatly rewarded. Those things that he previously held under stewardship, he shall now hold as a king in Christ. "Blessed is that servant, whom the lord when he cometh shall find so doing. Verily I say unto you, That he shall make him ruler over all his goods." *The kingdom shall be given to the saints as their inheritance in Christ.* The parables of chapter 25 are thus spoken to the church to urge her to faithfulness and endurance. They emphasize the fact of the long delay (from the human point of view) in the second coming: "the bridegroom tarried" (25:5; Lenski "the bridegroom delaying"); in 29:19, the words "after a long time the lord of those servants cometh" again emphasize the necessity for patience, and the feeling of delay from the human point of view.

Thus, our Lord warns us against trying to establish dates, seeking signs, and fretting at His delay. He offers the fall of Jerusalem as a token of His absolute government and sovereignty, a sign to make the nations mourn but the saints to rejoice. The same absolute sovereignty that He manifested in prophesying the fall of Jerusalem and ordaining it, he manifests today as the sole and absolute Lord of history. The "tribes of the earth" have very great reason for mourning, but we must rejoice, having entered into the jubilee and being commissioned to summon others into that life of victory, known here in very real power, and in its fulness in the age to come.

I AND II THESSALONIANS ON THE SECOND COMING

I Thessalonians 4:13 – 5:11

Paul, in writing to the Thessalonians, faced a situation not too unlike our modern one, in that the people of the church were divided into two camps, those who doubted the resurrection, and those given to extravagant beliefs concerning it. Paul writes so that they might avoid the pagan sorrow, "even as others which have no hope" (4:13). To believe that Jesus died and rose again (4:14) means also to believe in our own resurrection from the dead. Christ is the representative man, and all who are members of His new humanity share in His life and its resurrection. Therefore, those who die before His return will not live a lesser life, as some of the Thessalonians believed. For the pagans, there was a pallid and undesirable immortality of the soul, conceived of as a thin material substance, and the life of the soul was hardly an attractive one, but wan, meaningless, and sorrowful. The "shades" of the departed is a significant expression pointing to the pagan regard for the after life; it is a gray and shadowy existence. Paul assures the Thessalonians that no such meaningless life is in store for the dead. Their present life in Christ, as souls, is a glorious one, and, at the second coming, they shall arise in their resurrection bodies, and, together with those who are alive, "be caught up together with them in the clouds, to meet the Lord in the air: and so shall we ever be with the Lord" (4:17). In verse 16, Hendriksen translates "with a shouted command," i.e., as of a conqueror.[1]

In 5:11, Paul warns the believers to be prepared at all times. Men will have no warning of His coming. They will rejoice, saying, "Peace and safety" (5:3), when sudden destruction shall overwhelm them. Even as a thief comes unexpectedly so shall the Lord come unexpectedly and find unbelievers unprepared.

[1] William Hendriksen: *I and II Thessalonians.* Grand Rapids, Mich.: Baker Book House, 1955, p. 115.

In the face of this, He issues a warning to Christians. He urges them to avoid sleep and to be watchful (5:6-8). According to Hendriksen:

> *To sleep* (cf. Mark 13:36; Eph. 5:14) means to live as if there will never be a judgment-day. Spiritual and moral laxity is indicated. Luke 12:45 pictures this condition vividly. . . .
>
> *To be watchful* means to live a sanctified life, in the consciousness of the coming judgment-day. Spiritual and moral alertness is indicated. . . .
>
> *To be sober* means to be filled with spiritual and moral earnestness, being neither overly excited on the one hand, nor indifferent on the other, but calm, steady, and sane (cf. I Peter 4:7), doing one's duty and fulfilling one's ministry (II Tim. 4:5). The sober person lives deeply.[2]

In 5:3 Paul declares that the day is entirely in the Lord's hands, both with regard to the coming and the knowledge thereof. There is no escaping or preventing it. Even as a woman with child cannot, at the time of travail, prevent its coming, so men are helpless to prevent the coming of the Great Day of the Lord.

Both this passage and Romans 13:11-14 give us another important image, as Vos points out: history, Paul declares, is at present in a great world-night.[3] But, with the coming of Christ, it could be said that "the night is far spent" and the day is now at hand. The great world-night is being scattered by the Lord through His gospel, and the great Day will dawn at His coming. Believers are thus called upon to put on the "armor of light" and prepare. For the unbelievers, however, the Day of the Lord is darkness and not light (Amos 5:18). Moreover, the birth-pains described in 5:3 belong to the whole of creation, groaning and laboring to be delivered into the glorious liberty of the sons of God (Rom. 8:19-23).

II Thessalonians 2

In II Thessalonians 2, Paul again returns to the subject. In his previous letter (I Thess. 5:1), he had referred to his oral teaching

[2] *Ibid.*, p. 125.

[3] Geerhardus Vos: *The Pauline Eschatology*. Grand Rapids, Mich.: Eerdmans, 1953 (1930), p. 81.

on the "times" (stretches of time) and "seasons" (time marked by clear-cut trends and events) pertaining to the Lord's coming. He writes now to correct certain misimpressions. Wrong views of the second coming are prevalent, some expecting it immediately, and even apparently neglecting their work in this belief. Forged words, ostensibly from Paul, were being circulated to add to the confusion.

Paul deals with this issue by pointing out that certain things must transpire before the general resurrection occurs. These things are

1. the apostasy (2:3)
2. the revelation of the man of sin (2:3-6, 8-12)
3. the coming of the Lord (2:8)
4. the power that hinders or restrains evil for the time being is removed (5:6, 7).

At this point it is instructive to review some of the cardinal points of Revelation, as it views the future:

1. Humanism creates or seeks to create a world without God.
2. This order or dream is called Babylon the great.
3. There is a total collapse of this hope and its order.
4. The reign of the saints ensues.

It is necessary, moreover, to call attention to the fact that there is a common confusion of several terms. Antichrist, and that wicked one (or "lawless one") are made one figure, and the terms are made interchangeable. There is no valid ground for this.

First of all, antichrist is a name used only by St. John, in I John 2:18, 22; 4:3, and II John 7. The Greek reading makes clear the definition of antichrist, who is also described as already here, in John's day: "He is the antichrist, who denieth the Father and the Son." To read it as "*an* antichrist" is to mistranslate the Greek. There is no ground whatsoever for seeing antichrist as anything other than St. John declared him to be: any and every man, in or out of the church, who denies the Father and the Son. We have had antichrists with us since St. John's day.

Second, *the man of sin* brings out the real nature of sin, to be as God, to usurp His throne. Adam's sin is made the principle of religion for the man of sin, who, like Judas, is called "the son of perdition" (2:3), i.e., marked out like Judas as an apostate and a betrayer. He deifies himself, and he has "lying" power, signs, and wonders (in v. 9, "lying" modifies power, signs, and wonders, not wonders only). The Berkeley Version renders "mystery of iniquity" in 2:7 as "the hidden principle of lawlessness." Thus, either a movement, or a movement headed by a figure, embodies the principle of Satan and his temptation in a direct assault on God's order, in an attempt to substitute for God's order the order of man, the new god. This means, therefore, a total order in church, state, and all things else, in which the principle of anti-law, of anti-God, is incarnated. Church and state follow in the wake of this "working of Satan" (2:9).

Third, a God-ordained restraint, a power that hinders, will be removed. Lawlessness will thus govern, instead of being governed. Obviously, therefore, the principle of law in church, state, home, and everywhere, but especially in civil government, will be "taken out of the way," will be removed by the principle of lawlessness.

Fourth, Jesus Christ will destroy this lawlessness or the lawless one whom He "shall consume with the spirit of his mouth, and shall destroy with the brightness of his coming" (2:8). This is a process of destruction, first by the Word ("the spirit of his mouth"), and second, by His coming. A part of the process of destruction involves God's act whereby he sends "them strong delusion, that they should believe a lie: That they all might be damned who believe not the truth, but had pleasure in unrighteousness" (2:11, 12).

Fifth, Paul's purpose in this letter is not to satisfy men's curiosity concerning the things which are to come, but to prepare them for battle against the powers of darkness. Even as God became flesh, and the righteousness of God was made manifest in the person of Jesus Christ, so the anti-law shall be made manifest in the principle of lawlessness. Satan's temptation, instead of being man's shame, will be made man's pride and glory. But victory is assured in Jesus Christ, and the saints are called to battle to victory. Paul wrote to "comfort your hearts, and stablish you in every good word and work" (II Thess. 2:17).

PSALM 149: THE CALLING IS TO VICTORY

There was a time when Psalm 149 was greatly used by Christians in peril and in warfare. Granted that at times heretics like Thomas Munzer made use of it for evil, the fact remains that all who used it had at this point a more realistic awareness of Scripture's meaning than do Christians now. Psalm 149 and like texts of Scripture were used by orthodox and heretic alike because at this point both believed in Scripture's often repeated affirmation that God calls His people to victory in time and in eternity.

This is a Psalm of praise: it gives us aspects of the required and God-ordained praise of God.

There are *two ways* in which we are *called and required* to praise God. The Psalm begins and ends with a summons and a command: "Praise ye the LORD."

The *first* form of required praise is the praise of *exuberant worship, of joy and beauty* (vv. 1-4). The call is to sing "a new song," i.e., a song of thanksgiving for deliverance. The worship of God requires praise and thanksgiving (v. 1).

The people of God (Israel) must rejoice in their Maker; they must be joyful in Him who is their King. The fact of God's kingship follows from His creation of heaven and earth. As Maker of all things, God is the absolute law-giver, Lord and King over all.

The praise of God is one of exuberance, of joyful thanksgiving. They are to praise God (v. 3) with mind and body, with music and the dance (cf. Ex. 15:20; Judges 11:34; II Sam. 6:14; Jer. 31:4). The life of the believer is to be a joyful one in every respect. He is to be of a "sober" mind (I Thess. 5:6), i.e., to be steady, calm, avoiding either indifference or excitability. But a sober person can also be joyful and exuberant. Excitability, or emotional instability, and joyful exuberance are two different things.

The reason for this joy is in the fact that the Lord "taketh pleasure in his people." They are the "meek," here meaning "bowed down" with oppression, with suffering because of their stand for the faith. But the Lord "will beautify the meek with salvation" (v. 4). God's purpose, as Isaiah stated it, is "To appoint unto them that mourn in Zion, to give unto them beauty for ashes, the oil of joy for mourning, the garment of praise for the spirit of heaviness; that they might be called trees of righteousness, the planting of the LORD, that he might be glorified" (Isa. 61:3).

The *second* form of required praise is by means of battle *unto victory* (vv. 5-9).

The introduction to this is verse 5, which calls upon the saints to "be joyful in glory: let them sing aloud upon their beds." What verses 6-9 have in mind is actual battle and physical destruction of the enemies of God. These verses cannot be "spiritualized" away. They speak of the literal destruction of God's enemies as a means of praising God, a God-ordained means and a God-ordained victory. It is this trumph which causes them to sing aloud on their beds, unable to sleep for very joy. It is God's calling for His people.

This calling to victory involves *first,* the praise of God from the heart and mouth. *Second,* it requires warfare, total warfare, against the enemies of God, against evil. The people of God must be ready to war, "a twoedged sword in their hand" (v. 6). *Third,* God calls His people to exercise power in every area, in church and state, and to serve God by bringing justice to bear against evil-doers, "To execute vengeance upon the heathen, and punishments upon the people" (v. 7). *Fourth,* the nature of this vengeance is specified. Not all evil can be eliminated from the world. But godly law and order can "bind" down evil and impose "fetters of iron" and restraint upon all who violate the law. *Fifth,* "To execute upon them the judgment written" is not only the duty of the saints, but it is their "honour" or glory to do so. As Alexander wrote, "To act as God's instruments in this great judicial process, so far from being a disgrace or hardship, is an honour reserved for all the objects of his mercy and subjects of his grace."[1]

The misinterpretation of this psalm involves reading it as entirely

---

[1] Joseph Addison Alexander: *The Psalms.* Grand Rapids, Mich.: Zondervan, 1864, p. 563.

a document of the past, of Israel's history, and of no relevance to us. Granted that the psalm may have had reference, and probably did, to a specific historical incident, yet it is a perversion of history to limit a text to the past which is given without any such limitation. Was God for victory where Israel was concerned, and for defeat where Christian men and nations are concerned? Leupold reads this psalm in terms of the past, and defends it in those terms.[2] But such a defense is a sorry one, and regrettable in an able commentator. Was God's action moral then and immoral now?

The neglect of this psalm, and many similar passages, is because of the prevalent heresy of defeatism, a Manichaean belief that Satan will triumph in the material world, and only the second coming will over-rule this defeat.

This psalm speaks unconditionally, and it speaks of victory. Those who refuse to believe that history shall see the triumph of God's people, their vengeance on the enemies of God, and their rule in justice and truth, are denying to God the praise which is His due.

Psalm 149 is one of the psalms of "The Great Hallel" (Pss. 146-150). It is basic to the praise of God, of "praise expressed with power."[3]

One final point: the commentators who, treating this psalm as exclusively applicable to Israel's history, *then* and then only defend its morality, reveal their own immorality. To refer a justification of victory to long-past history only is appalling. Their God is dead: He functioned only in Israel's ancient past. Such men are guilty of blasphemy and deserve the vengeance of God, whether they be believers or not. The Lord is a God of battles, *and* of victory. There is no other God. The Scriptures know only one true God, and He does not change.

[2] H. C. Leupold: *Exposition of the Psalms.* Columbus, Ohio: Wartburg Press, 1959, pp. 1001-1005. In v. 3, Leupold insists on translating the simple word "dance" as "solemn dance"! If anything is clear in this psalm, it is that exuberant joy, *not* solemnity, is meant. A "solemn dance" *is* the kind of pretentious blasphemy staged by modernist churches. Leupold's assumption is that a religious dance is meant. From the standpoint of Scripture, *all* things are religious, but only acts of worship are associated with the sanctuary.

[3] Leslie S. M'Caw, "The Psalms," in F. Davidson, A. M. Stibbs, E. F. Kevan, editors: *The New Bible Commentary.* Grand Rapids, Mich.: Eerdmans, 1953, p. 513.

INDEX

CHALCEDON PUBLICATIONS

ORDER FROM: Fairfax Christian Book Store, 11121
   Pope's Head Road, Fairfax, Virginia 22030

By Rousas John Rushdoony:
Law and Liberty
Institutes of Biblical Law
Foundations of Social Order: Studies in the Creeds and
   Councils of the Early Church
Thy Kingdom Come: Studies in Daniel and Revelation
The One and the Many: Studies in the Philosophy
   of Order and Ultimacy
Politics of Guilt and Pity
Freud
Van Til
Revolt Against Maturity
The Messianic Character of American Education
Intellectual Schizophrenia: Culture, Crisis and Education
This Independent Republic
The Nature of the American System
The Biblical Philosophy of History
The Mythology of Science
Bread Upon the Waters
The Myth of Over-Population
By What Standard?
The Flight from Humanity
The Politics of Pornography
The Word of Flux
God's Plan for Victory

Books by Gary North
An Introduction to Christian Economics
None Dare Call It Witchcraft
Foundations of Christian Scholarship (editor)

The Journal of Christian Reconstruction
Vol. I, No. 1 Symposium on Creation
Vol. I, No. 2 Symposium on Satanism
Vol. II, No. 1 Symposium on Christian Economics
Vol. II, No. 2 Symposium on Biblical Law
Vol. III, No. 1 Symposium on Christianity and the
   American Revolution
Vol. III, No. 2 Symposium on The Millenium
Vol. IV, No. 1 Symposium on Education
Vol. IV, No. 2 Symposium on the Family
Vol. V, No. 1 Symposium on Politics
Vol. V, No. 2 Symposium on Puritanism